Woolf Studies Annual

Volume 18, 2012

Pace University Press • New York

41 Park Row, Rm. 1510
New York, NY 10038

ISSN 1080-9317
ISBN 978-1-935625-08-7 (pbk: alk.ppr.)

Member

Council of Editors of Learned Journals

Paper used in this publication meets the minimum requirements of
American National Standard for Information
Sciences–Permanence of Paper for Printed Library Materials,
ANSI Z39.48–1984

Many thanks to readers for volume 18 (in addition to the Editorial Board): Judith Allen (Writers House, U of Pennsylvania); Renee Dickinson (Radford U); David Eberly (Independent Scholar); Penny Farfan (U of Calgary); Christine Froula (Northwestern U); Elizabeth Willson Gordon (Simon Fraser U); Brenda Helt (Metropolitan SU); Erica Johnson (Wagner C); Phyllis Lassner (Northwestern U); Helane Levine-Keating (Pace U); Eleanor McNees (U of Denver); Jeanette McVicker (SUNY Fredonia); Natania Rosenfeld (Knox C); Roberta Rubenstein (American U); Tory Young (Anglia Ruskin U); Marilyn Zucker (Stony Brook U).

Woolf Studies Annual is indexed in *Humanities International Complete, ABELL* and the *MLA Bibliography.*

Call for submissions— a special issue of *Woolf Studies Annual* on Virginia Woolf and Jews/Jewishness

The 2013 volume of *Woolf Studies Annual* will be devoted to the topic of Jews and/or Jewishness in Woolf's writing. We are less interested in the question of whether or not Woolf herself was or was not antisemitic (except insofar as this can be articulated in readings of her texts) than in how the figure of the Jew operates within her work.

The special issue is not limited to work on Virginia Woolf herself, but also will welcome contributions on Leonard Woolf, and on the Bloomsbury milieu. In addition to full-length articles, we also envisage a forum of short commentary, and an annotated bibliography.

Forum
We invite brief commentary of up to 750 words on a relevant short passage from Woolf's writing: for example, from the "Present Day" chapter of *The Years*; "The Duchess and the Jeweller"; "Street Haunting"; *Three Guineas*; *Between the Acts*, and elsewhere—there is no limitation on what you might select.

Additionally, we welcome brief statements in response to the following broad questions:

- How do Woolf's representations of Jews compare with those of other modernist writers?
- How have treatments of Woolf's antisemitism/prejudice figured within Woolf scholarship?
- In treating this topic within Woolf's work, what are the salient issues?
- What is the relation between her fiction and the extensive biographical record of Woolf's comments/ruminations about Jews and Jewishness available in her letters, diaries, and memoirs?

A number of such brief commentaries and statements would then be shared for response, and the opportunity for dialogue enabled, with the resulting texts published as a forum on the topic.

Annotated Bibliography
Recommendations for previously published scholarship and sources on the topic are also welcome and will be included as an annotated bibliography in the special issue.

Deadlines

Forum commentaries/statements: June 30 2012
Full-length articles (8,000-10,000 words): August 30 2012—N.B. *WSA* submission guidelines apply (see http://www.pace.edu/press/journals/woolf-studies-annual)
Annotated Bibliography recommendations: November 15 2012

(General articles on any topic may continue to be submitted for consideration.)

PLEASE DIRECT ALL CORRESPONDENCE, INQUIRIES, SUBMISSIONS TO
woolfstudiesannual@gmail.com

Contents

*W*oolf *S*tudies *A*nnual

Volume 18, 2012

Abbreviations

AHH	*A Haunted House*
AROO	*A Room of One's Own*
BP	*Books and Portraits*
BTA	*Between the Acts*
CDB	*The Captain's Death Bed and Other Essays*
CE	*Collected Essays* (4 vols.)
CR1	*The Common Reader*
CR2	*The Common Reader, Second Series*
CSF	*The Complete Shorter Fiction*
D	*The Diary of Virginia Woolf* (5 vols.)
DM	*The Death of the Moth and Other Essays*
E	*The Essays of Virginia Woolf* (6 Vols.)
F	*Flush*
FR	*Freshwater*
GR	*Granite & Rainbow: Essays*
JR	*Jacob's Room*
L	*The Letters of Virginia Woolf* (6 Vols.)
M	*The Moment and Other Essays*
MEL	*Melymbrosia*
MOB	*Moments of Being*
MT	*Monday or Tuesday*
MD	*Mrs. Dalloway*
ND	*Night and Day*
O	*Orlando*
PA	*A Passionate Apprentice*
RF	*Roger Fry: A Biography*
TG	*Three Guineas*
TTL	*To the Lighthouse*
TW	*The Waves*
TY	*The Years*
VO	*The Voyage Out*

Phantoms, Fancy (And) Symptoms: Virginia Woolf and The Art Of Being Ill

Kimberly Engdahl Coates

Despite her own familiarity with the throes of illness, Virginia Woolf's important but frequently overlooked essay "On Being Ill" is far from just a meditation on sickness.[1] On the contrary, "On Being Ill" posits an aesthetic strategy, a strategy braided with the complexities of phantoms, fancies, and symptoms that speaks to Woolf's lifelong preoccupation with her mother as muse, nurse, Madonna, and the quintessential Angel in the House. To that end, as I will argue in this essay, "On Being Ill" functions as a response to Julia Stephen's *Notes from Sick Rooms*, first published in 1883.[2] When put into conversation with her mother's text, Woolf's essay fancifully rewrites illness as an aesthetic strategy that proves significant to her major fictions, from *The Voyage Out* to *The Years*. Illness allows Woolf to disavow and then reconfigure her own aesthetic heritage—most specifically the nineteenth-century novel—while simultaneously recuperating and revising a relationship that was central to it—that between mother and daughter.

I thus begin my essay with a discussion of "On Being Ill" as a text that deploys symptoms as a means of jettisoning the phantom who is mother and nurse. I then move to a consideration of illness as an aesthetic strategy, whereby symptoms

[1] As Jan Freeman has noted, before the 2002 publication of the Paris Press edition of "On Being Ill," Woolf's essay was relatively neglected (141). See Dubino, Coates, and Sorum for critical discussions of "On Being Ill." Providing a rare glimpse into the embodied and private experience that illness inevitably must be, Woolf's essay has also found an audience in a community of doctors and scholars interested in the field of medicine and the humanities and amongst writers and academics who themselves have experienced the psychological and physical disorientations associated with sudden, severe illness. See, for example, Lisa Kerr's review of the Paris Press edition in *The Yale Journal for Humanities in Medicine* (http://yjhm.yale.edu/reviews/rev-lkerr20080915.htm). Hermione Lee also notes the recognition the essay has received in literature of pathology (Introduction xxiii-xxiv). To her list of such literature, I would add Arthur Frank's *At the Will of the Body: Reflections on Illness* (1991), Susan Sontag's *Illness as Metaphor* (1978), Anatole Broyard's *Intoxicated By My Illness and Other Writings on Life and Death* (1992), and Kat Duff's *The Alchemy of Illness* (1993). Jan Freeman writes about her own two year experience with illness and her deep appreciation for Woolf's essay in "The Paris Publication of *On Being Ill*"; similarly, in "Being Ill/Being Well: Reflections on Illness," Susan Dick cites and echoes Woolf's essay as she writes movingly about her own ten-month hospitalization during which she was eventually diagnosed with a rare form of the neurological disorder Guillain-Barré syndrome.

[2] Smith, Elder, & Co., London, published this first edition of *Notes from Sick Rooms* and, with the exception of a letter to the *Pall Mall Gazette*, it constitutes Julia Stephen's only published work. See Hussey, *Virginia Woolf A to Z*, 192. Reference in this essay is to Gillespie and Steele's edition (Stephen 216-40).

and the visions and sensations associated therewith enable a return to the mother. Whereas in "On Being Ill" Woolf employs symptoms, which yield fancy, as a way of jettisoning the phantom who is both mother and nurse, *The Voyage Out* and *To the Lighthouse* call her back not as phantom but as symptom. Significantly, however, Woolf's return does not merely repeat the psychoanalytically predictable return to the maternal body, a return destined by the tenets of Freudian psychoanalysis to indicate only arrested development or regression to a pre-oedipal state. On the contrary, as Woolf fancies it in "On Being Ill," illness is never about fixation or a cessation of movement but instead invokes a mobile suspension, the corporeal dimensions of which, in novels such as *The Voyage Out* and *To the Lighthouse*, find expression in an art rooted in a maternal symbolic. If "On Being Ill" jettisons Julia Stephen as nurse, and *The Voyage Out* and *To the Lighthouse* call her back not as phantom but as symptom, not as maternity but as sensation, I close the essay by briefly suggesting the way in which *The Years* encapsulates Woolf's ongoing vacillation between these two positions without resolving either.

First published in 1926, "On Being Ill" should be read alongside other works Woolf was writing in the late twenties and thirties, works primarily concerned with defining the maternal phantom in concrete terms and with elaborating its negative professional and psychological effects on women's lives.[3] *A Room of One's Own*, published in 1929, is followed by Woolf's lecture "Professions for Women," delivered before the National Society for Women's Service in 1931. In 1932, Woolf begins *The Pargiters*, an effort that culminates in *The Years* (1937) and *Three Guineas* (1938). In each of these works, she is still engaged in what Gillian Beer refers to as the "protracted struggle" of "wrestling with the angel in the house," a struggle compounded by the fact that, for Woolf, this angel "is indoors, inside the self, a maternal figure whose worsting and expulsion might prove to have intolerable creative cost" (93). "On Being Ill" is no exception to this effort. Full of fanciful musings tempered by an astute understanding of how illness radically alters

[3] In 1926, "On Being Ill" first appeared in *The Criterion*. It was published again that same year in the American journal *Forum* under the title "Illness—An Unexploited Mine." In 1930, the Hogarth Press published the essay in its final version with the original title. See Hussey, *Virginia Woolf A to Z*, 195-96, and Lee, Introduction xi-xxxiv. Woolf's essay was likely a response to and a revision of an essay she had read by Henry David Sedgwick also entitled "On Being Ill." Sedgwick's essay appeared in a collection called *An Apology for Old Maids and Other Essays* and was first published in 1916. Woolf reviewed Sedgwick's collection in her essay "Melodious Meditations," which was published in the *Times Literary Supplement* on February 8, 1917 and is included in *E*2 80-82. Citing a passage from Sedgwick's "On Being Ill," Woolf proceeds to denounce it: "Almost any novel, certainly any book of facts, seems to us better reading than these melodious meditations" (80). Nevertheless, Sedgwick's emphasis on the perceptual distortions induced by illness—"in [health and sickness] man beholds two very different worlds" (82)—is echoed in Woolf's "undiscovered countries" as she writes her essay "On Being Ill" ten years later.

perception and the lived body, Woolf's essay directs its critique of the angel in the house primarily at Julia Stephen's nursing manual. Echoing Florence Nightingale's *Notes on Nursing* published in 1860, *Notes from Sick Rooms* similarly is a service manual for nurses in training that hails nursing as the most honorable profession for able young women and offers meticulous instructions on how nurses might provide the best care for those suffering illness and affliction.[4] While detailing how they are to rein in and control their patients' vivid imaginations, Julia Stephen also emphasizes that nurses must treat their patients as "cases" rather than individuals. Woolf's "On Being Ill," on the other hand, repudiates the "art of nursing" in favor of the "art of being ill," the latter phrase coined by Julia Stephen but carefully re-defined in the pages of her daughter's essay.

"The Art of Nursing"

Before she could define herself as an artist, Virginia Woolf had first to confront her Victorian legacy, a legacy in which invalids and the women who nursed them played primary roles. Jane Marcus has proposed that Woolf learned at a very young age that there were "two modes for a Victorian girl of her class, to nurse or be nursed, to care for invalids or be an invalid" (97).[5] Willingly submitting herself to what she liked to refer to as her "calling," Julia Stephen was, as Woolf represents her somewhat bitterly in her memoirs, the quintessential nurse.

The nurse, as depicted in *Notes from Sick Rooms*, must be a paragon of calmness and reason all the while working tirelessly to cultivate her "art": "A nurse's life is certainly not a dull one, and the more skilful the nurse the less dull she will be. The more she cultivates the *art* of nursing, the more enjoyment she will get,

[4] In this sense, Julia Stephen's work was very much in harmony with what Mary Poovey, in *Uneven Developments: The Ideological Work of Gender in Mid-Victorian England*, and Catherine Judd, in *Bedside Seductions: Nursing and the Victorian Imagination 1830-1880*, have discussed as Britain's effort at the turn of the century to promote nursing as a reputable profession for respectable middle-class women. Although Julia Stephen herself was never a professional nurse, *Notes from Sick Rooms* was well respected in the nursing community; the Julia Prinsep Stephen Nursing Association was still in existence when Woolf wrote her memoir "A Sketch of the Past" in 1939 (*MOB* 131).

[5] It is true that an obsession with describing, diagnosing, and attending to various symptoms was nothing less than a family tradition. Woolf's maternal grandfather, Dr. John Jackson, was a highly respected physician and medical consultant, who, during the twenty-five years he spent living in Calcutta, India, became the first professor of medicine at Calcutta Medical College. Her great-aunt Julia Margaret Cameron and her aunt Virginia Pattle were notorious for their obsequious interest in other people's health. Finally, there was Woolf's grandmother Maria Pattle Jackson, a full-time invalid, whom Julia Stephen began nursing at a very young age and continued to nurse throughout her adult life. See Reid (5); Gillespie, 4-5; Love, 50; Brian Hill,165.

and the same may be said of the patient. The art of being ill is no easy one to learn, but it is practised to perfection by many of the greatest sufferers" (217). This juxtaposition of the "art of nursing" with the "art of being ill" appears at the beginning of *Notes from Sick Rooms* and to some extent represents its overall structure. Elaborate details regarding the "art" of bathing, bedding, grooming, and preparing food for the patient are interwoven with attempts to explain and control what Julia Stephen refers to as the patients' tendency toward absurd fancies. "There is," she writes, "no limit to the sick person's imagination" (218). While acknowledging that there are certainly those patients whose delicate sensibilities enable them to detect a draught or a smell where even careful and discerning nurses can find neither, Julia Stephen generally denies the validity of the invalid's heightened perception and emphasizes that the nurse's "art" involves deterring the "nervous" dread provoked by such aggravated sensitivity.[6] No doubt equally disturbing for Woolf would have been her mother's insistence that the nurse treat her patient strictly as a "case": "The genuine love of her 'case' and not of the individual patient seems to me the sign of the true nursing instinct" (218). Although Stephen does emphasize illness's capacity to equalize human relationships—"the ordinary relations between the sick and the well are far easier and pleasanter than between the well and the well"—the flip side of this assertion is that an eradication of differences also suggests a relationship between the nurse and her patient that devolves into one between a subject—the nurse—and a recalcitrant object—the patient (217).

In fact, for Woolf, the nurse becomes a conspiratorial site for an ominous conflation between maternal and paternal authority and thus serves as a particularly dangerous agent bent on normalizing and policing the patient's desires and imagination.[7] Having little to do with art, the nurse, as described by Julia Stephen, represents an insipid and overbearing figure whose characteristics resemble those Woolf associates elsewhere with male doctors and psychoanalysts. Writing to Vanessa, for example, in reference to her brother Adrian, who was a practicing psychoanalyst, Woolf confesses: "I creep up and peer into the Stephen's dining room

[6] Nevertheless, Julia Stephen's imaginative attention to the sick room's details and the vivacity of her prose clearly anticipate her daughter's artistic energies and sensibility—echoes of Woolf's comic incisiveness can be heard, for example, in her mother's excoriation of a bed crumb as an evil tormentor that must "be stamped out of the sick bed as if it were the Colorado beetle in a potato field" (219).

[7] In this regard, Isota Tucker Epes's1990 painting of Woolf entitled "A Marriage of Opposites" is stunning. The painting depicts two reflected images of Woolf in profile—one looking up to the right and the other up and to the left. On the right side of the canvas, the viewer sees Woolf along with her Bloomsbury contemporaries. On the left, Woolf appears wearing the visage and in the shape of Edvard Munch's "The Scream." Directly behind her is a nurse, also screaming, with her hand firmly gripping Woolf's shoulder. I would like to thank Suzanne Bellamy for providing me with an image of Epes's painting.

Fig. 1."A Marriage of Opposites" oil, 30" x 36"
Reproduced with permission of the family of Isota Tucker Epes.

where any afternoon, in full daylight, is to be seen a woman in the last agony of despair, lying on a sofa, burying her face in the pillow, while Adrian broods over her like a vulture, analyzing her soul" (*L*3 381).[8] Here Woolf imagines her brother Adrian's patient as suffering quite painfully from the insertion of his will—his desire to know her and to translate her according to his newly acquired psychoanalytic principles. These principles, at least as Woolf understood them in the mid-twenties, reduced the aberrant and complex human spirit to a single determining narrative: "A patient who has never heard a canary sing without falling down in a fit can now walk through an avenue of cages without a twinge of emotion since he has faced the fact that his mother kissed him in his cradle" ("Freudian Fiction" 153). As an artist, Woolf objects to the psychoanalytic presumption that everything can be known about another human being. According to Woolf, Freudian psychoanalysis particularly becomes a "patent key that opens every door," a key that "simplifies rather than complicates, detracts rather than enriches" ("Freudian Fiction" 154). If we keep in mind Julia Stephen's requirement that the nurse discourage a patient's "fancies," and Woolf's own anxieties about the epistemological supremacy analysts

[8] Virginia Woolf's brother Adrian Stephen and his wife, Karin Stephen, were both professionally trained psychoanalysts. See Meisel and Kendrick.

and doctors tend to exert over their patients—one need only think of Dr. William Bradshaw wielding his doctrine of proportion over Septimus Smith in *Mrs. Dalloway*—it seems reasonable to assume that in Woolf's mind the nurse also came to represent a persecutory figure.

Woolf's ideas about the nurse and the nursing profession also reflect the fact that she had read Florence Nightingale's *Cassandra*, an impassioned piece of writing that laments the pathogenic condition forced on Victorian women. In *A Room of One's Own*, she refers to Nightingale's work as a "loud shriek of agony" (56). In addition, at about this same time, she had finished reading *Eminent Victorians*, in which Lytton Strachey demythologizes the image of Nightingale as the "Lady with the Lamp" by arguing that she was driven into nursing by her desire to be free of her family and by the ennui that accompanied the life of the Victorian lady (47). However, if Nightingale and Strachey present nursing as an escape from such ennui, Woolf, in "On Being Ill," sarcastically dismisses the so-called profession of nursing for having done nothing more than raise the angel in the house to the status of a national mother.

Indeed, as Woolf depicts her in "On Being Ill," the nurse represents the primary ambassador of that deplorable trait to be fostered by all Victorian women—sympathy: "Sympathy nowadays is dispensed chiefly by the laggards and the failures, women for the most part (in whom the obsolete exists so strangely side by side with anarchy and newness) who, having dropped out of the race, have time to spend upon fantastic and unprofitable excursions" (10). A woman who takes up nursing hardly escapes the staid life of a Victorian woman nor, as Woolf writes later in *Three Guineas*, do such philanthropic endeavors deserve the name of profession: "[W]hat are we to call the profession that consists in running a house, nursing an invalid, visiting the poor and sick, tending here an old father, there an old mother?—there is no name and there is no pay for that profession" (93).

Woolf's dismissal of nursing as a profession in *Three Guineas* should not be read as derogating working women but rather as reprimanding British society's refusal to value women's work as labor, labor deserving both the pay and the status of a profession. Nevertheless, in "On Being Ill," Woolf does mock women who, already relegated to the confines of the drawing room, voluntarily sink further into the folds of domesticity by occupying the gloom of the sickroom and therefore seeming oblivious to their own exploitation. Taking us from the cold, stale sickroom where C.L., "with touches both sober and imaginative," nurses her patient by telling stories, to the somewhat more comfortable confines ruled by the obsequious A.R. who would "ransack the markets of London" to fulfill her patient's most outrageous desires, and finally to the frivolous world of the rich where K.T., in spite of her nursing duties, remains "dressed in silks and feathers, powdered and painted as if for a banquet of Kings and Queens," Woolf satirizes, not without a touch of

Fig. 2. Julia Stephen at the Bear, Grindelwald, Switzerland, 1889, by Gabriel Loppé (1825-1913).
With kind permission of the Mortimer Rare Book Room, Smith College.

pathos, the relentless activity and often futile gaiety of the many women whose time and energy were given over to the thankless enterprise of incessantly caring for others (10). She finishes this comedy of manners by insisting that "such follies have had their day; civilisation points to a different goal" (11).

To signal that such "follies" have indeed "had their day" and to point her readers in the direction of different professional and aesthetic goals, Woolf closes "On Being Ill" with the summary of an obscure nineteenth-century novel written by Augustus Hare. Her rehearsal of this novel dramatizes the way in which pain, illness, and grief destabilize the domestic and the familiar to the extent that alternative narrative trajectories become visible. Taking readers into the enclosed space of the Victorian drawing room, Woolf proceeds to focus our attention on the familiar figure of the Victorian woman—in this instance, a Lady Waterford—embowered there. An artist, whom the "great Watts" declares to be "Titian's peer and Raphael's master," Lady Waterford finds her attentions entirely absorbed by shoring up her father's house, which is, as Woolf sardonically notes, nevertheless "forever falling into the sea" (22). When Lady Waterford's husband dies suddenly, she finds herself bereft and alone. Through the eyes of Sir John Leslie, we then see Lady Waterford standing at the drawing room window—an image reminiscent of an 1889 photograph of Julia Stephen taken in Switzerland, which catches her in a shaft of light while gazing out a window, looking very much like the other-worldly phantom who would haunt her daughter's imagination. However, rather than leaving readers to dwell on this iconic image, an image that for Woolf embodied the ontological, psychological, and epistemological tensions between two figures—mother and daughter, beatific handmaiden and female artist, nurse and patient—Woolf leaves her readers to brood instead upon Lady Waterford's anguish as marked by the imprint left on the velvet curtain she had been gripping so tightly in her hand: "[N]ever could Sir John Leslie forget, when he ran downstairs on the day of the burial, the beauty of the great lady standing to see the hearse depart, nor, when he came back, how the curtain, heavy, mid-Victorian, plush perhaps, was all crushed together where she had grasped it in her agony" (28). Evacuating Lady Waterford's figure, which can be, as Sir John Leslie's response indicates, all too easily framed and romanticized, Woolf moves us, in an essay on illness, to ponder pain and agony as potentially generative forces for this woman artist who finds herself on the cusp of the twentieth century without a master.

Thus, in the end it is sympathy—freighted with Victorian ideals of femininity—not symptoms that Woolf rejects in "On Being Ill." The "art of being ill," unlike her mother's "art of nursing," firmly entrenches itself in the notion that sympathy is an illusion: "Human beings do not go hand in hand the whole stretch of the way. There is a virgin forest in each; . . . Here we go alone, and like it better so. Always to have sympathy, always to be accompanied, always to be understood would be intolerable" (12). Dispensing with sympathy altogether, in its most familiar sense, Woolf claims an imaginative space swept clean by illness and its symptoms, a space that is uniquely "mine" and ripe to receive the "extravagant intensity of perceptions" generated by a highly sensate mind and body (*L4* 231).[9] Intolerable

[9] Here I am referencing Woolf's other title for the essay, "Illness—An Unexploited Mine," as it appeared in the American Journal *Forum*. Woolf plays with the words "mine" and "unexploited" in several different ways. "Mine," in its noun form, refers to a "large excavation made into the earth from which precious stones are taken or to a tunnel dug under

and presumptuous, sympathy reduces the "strange" experience that is illness to nothing more than a common language. Although Woolf does assert that illness is "common" in the sense that sooner or later everyone traverses the private world it generates, she nevertheless is adamant that the actual experience remains unique to the individual. In its conventional sense, sympathy, for Woolf, comes too close to a narcissistic identification on the part of the sympathizer with the ill subject's pain, an identification that only brings the divine relief of commiseration; it does not suggest that the sympathizer has accessed the profundity of the ill subject's vision and experience, a task best left, as Woolf's own work instructs us, to the artist.

If Julia Stephen deliberately emphasizes the "*art* of nursing" in *Notes from Sickrooms*, in "On Being Ill," Virginia Woolf offers up her own meditation on her mother's corresponding phrase, the "art of being ill" which, as presented in the nursing manual, intimates that illness is a performance perfected by the patient to great dramatic effect: "The art of being ill is no easy one to learn, but it is *practiced* to perfection by many of the greatest sufferers" (emphasis added, 217). However, in Woolf's essay illness is not, as her mother's words insinuate, an "art" to be learned and then "practiced" until it can be performed to perfection by the patient. On the contrary, illness generates a heightened state of awareness that cannot be learned, perfected, or replicated by another. Woolf's relationship to her body during an illness serves as a talisman for the relationship she feels she has as a writer with her surrounding world. "You know," she writes Vita Sackville-West, "how I like noticing physical symptoms. . . . These are the signs writers should watch for" (*L3* 570). If, as Woolf describes in "Professions for Women," thoughts about the female body stop cold the imagination, symptoms take the body as their analog without question—they confirm, rather than deny, the body as a source of experience. And these symptoms—"signs writers should watch for"—are what Woolf wants in turn to protect from her mother's "art of nursing."

"The Art of Being Ill"

But symptoms and sympathy are not entirely without affinity. As Woolf figures it in "On Being Ill," the ill subject's relationship to the world and others is fervently sympathetic: it is when we are ill that we find sympathy in its truest sense. Sympathy, however, as defined in the pages of Woolf's essay, refers to a sympathy born not of sameness or of one person's false identification with another's physical or

---

an enemy's trench or fort" (*Webster's New World Dictionary*). In addition, "mine" is a possessive pronoun: to be ill is to possess oneself in the fullest possible sense. The verb "exploit" means "to make unethical use of for one's own advantage or profit; to make profit from the labor of others without giving a just return" (*Webster's*), a word that may have come to mind given Woolf's personal experiences with Britain's medical establishment.

emotional state. Instead, Woolf articulates what I elsewhere refer to as a "physics" of sympathy.[10] The relationship that the ill subject has with self, world, and other is sympathetic in the sense that it is an intensely physiological affinity that does not refuse individuality but rather might be best described as a harmonious vibration. Images and words tremble, pulsate, waver and undulate for patients, as they cannot possibly for those who are healthy. While Woolf knew full well that she needed to be healthy and upright to work productively—returning health, as she writes, is "shown by the power to make images"—in "On Being Ill," she focuses on the sensual and perceptual changes that are a consequence of being ill, an attention she knows will render those images unique (*D*3 104).

Woolf reveals, for example, that while lying recumbent as ill subjects we have before us a "gigantic cinema" (14) an "extraordinary spectacle" (12) that when we are "upright" appears as a "mutilated" backdrop for life's events (13). Moreover, as illness removes us from life's obligatory performances in the "army of the upright" (12) and enables us to dwell in our body's sensations, it mobilizes the imagination. Woolf describes a gaze rendered cinematic as it zooms across the sky thrilling in the movement and incessant change it can capture but never contain: "This then has been going on all the time without our knowing it!—this incessant making up of shapes and casting them down . . . this incessant ringing up and down of curtains of light and shade, this interminable experiment with gold shafts and blue shadows" (13). As seen through the lens of an illness, it is this chaos, this endless activity and these momentary assemblies of "movements and colours, shapes and sounds" that "come together" and seem to be "wait[ing] for someone to seize them and convert their energy into art" ("The Cinema" *E*4 352).[11] If we might reasonably expect illness to shut down vision, to prohibit narrative, Woolf, on the contrary, presents it as energizing and mobilizing the creative imagination to the extent that new shapes and new narratives come into view. Leaving "nothing ready made," illness forsakes all that is familiar and allows us to "tak[e] [our] pain in one hand, and a lump of pure sound in the other . . . so to crush them together that a brand new word in the end [might] drop out" (7).

Further testimony to Woolf's privileging of illness as providing previously undiscovered vantage points from which to witness the world and its objects can be found in her letters to the dying painter Jacques Raverat, written during the

[10] See Coates 257

[11] In 1926, Woolf had also published her essay "The Cinema" (*E*4: 348-354). The ill gaze and the cinematic gaze are astonishingly similar in these essays. In "On Being Ill," for example, Woolf writes: "how the world has changed its shape; the tools of business grown remote . . . like the shore seen from a ship far out at sea" (8). And in "The Cinema": "The eye is in difficulties. The eye says to the brain, 'You are needed.' Together they look at the King, or the boat, the horse, and the brain sees at once that they have taken on a quality which does not belong to the simple photograph of real life" (349).

years 1922-1925, prior to the publication of "On Being Ill."[12] The correspondence between these two friends, each of whom knew illness intimately, was prompted by Jacques and his wife Gwen's move in 1922 across the Channel to southern France, for the sake of Jacques' health.[13] "Being ill," writes Woolf's friend, "is I sometimes think almost intolerable, but I rather despise the people who aren't—don't you? I'm sure we have a finer sensitiveness & keener appreciation of life" (75). While the exigencies of pain, and in Jacques' case the despair of immobility, are always near the surface, the tedium and horrors of living daily with illness do not overwhelm the letters. Taken in their entirety, they instead serve as a profound affirmation of life, spirit, and art. "I am at present very dependent on the letters of my friends," writes Jacques to Woolf, "[t]hey help to keep me human not a mere amorphous invalid" (Pryor 119). And Woolf, as she lay ill in bed, would find herself thinking of Jacques and communing with his horizontal world view: "I shall dwell upon you, as indeed I have been doing a great deal, lying here" (148).

Regarding Woolf's own aesthetic project, the letters she exchanged with Jacques Raverat indicate her efforts to write a new kind of narrative that might begin to represent her own slanted view of the world, a view which she knew her bedridden friend, as a fellow traveler in the "undiscovered countries" disclosed by illness, understood very well ("On Being Ill" 3). In a letter to Woolf, Jacques Raverat confesses that what he finds difficult about writing "is that it has to be essentially linear. I mean you can only write (or read) one thing at a time; & even memory doesn't alter this fact. Now that's not the way my mind works . . . . There are splashes in the outer air in every direction, & under the surface waves that follow one another into dark & forgotten corners of my past" (102). With painting, by contrast, he argues in the same letter, "you can see the whole of what you are doing at the same time. And the relations between sky & foreground, feet & hair, nose & navel, are there simultaneously" (102). Serious readers of Woolf's work know how very much she wanted to capture precisely this simultaneity—to bend the stubborn linearity of the written word towards the vicissitudes of her

[12] While several of Woolf's letters to Jacques Raverat can be found in the volumes of Woolf's *Letters* edited by Trautmann and Nicolson, the full extent of their correspondence was not made available until 2003 with the appearance of *Virginia Woolf & the Raverats: A Different Sort of Friendship*, edited by Jacques Raverat's grandson, William Pryor, and published by Clear Books. Pryor gathered the letters between Virginia, Jacques, and Gwen and then beautifully interspersed them with Jacques' paintings and Gwen's paintings and engravings, as well as Gwen's haunting pencil sketches of Jacques lying in bed. My page numbers here refer to this publication.

[13] In 1914, Jacques Raverat had been diagnosed with what was then referred to as "disseminated sclerosis," the disease we know today as multiple sclerosis. He died in 1925 after having been bedridden for quite some time. This correspondence between two artists, which also included Jacques' wife Gwen, Charles Darwin's granddaughter, was no doubt on Woolf's mind as she wrote "On Being Ill."

consciousness: "I want," she writes Jacques, "in my old age, to have done with all superfluities, & form words precisely on top of the waves of my own mind—a formidable undertaking" (110). In a move that was extremely rare for Woolf, she had sent Jacques and Gwen a copy of the proofs to *Mrs. Dalloway*. Her letter back from Jacques addressing the novel gave her, as she records in the *Diary*, "one of the happiest days of [her] life" (*D*3 7).[14]

After Jacques' death, his wife Gwen takes up the correspondence and writes in regard to *Mrs. Dalloway*: "the whole thing is alive and moving; it's like a ballet. That's what you meant, isn't it? All the movements in different directions both in time and space, going on at the same time" (Pryor 174). Had Jacques Raverat lived, he would no doubt have gone on praising Woolf's ability to shape narratives seamlessly around the waftings of her characters' consciousnesses just as she would go on, following his death, writing letters to him in her mind, where he remained an ever-present reminder of art's vitality and of "the trans-itoriness of existence, & the unreality of matter" (Pryor 63). In its vivid account of the visions afforded those who are ill, "On Being Ill" seems to cry "this is for Jacques" as Woolf tells Gwen so many things did following his death: "One thing that comes over & over is the strange wish I have to go on telling Jacques things. This is for Jacques, I say to myself" (Pryor 160).

In the final months of Jacques' illness, Woolf could be said to have served as a sort of "epistolary" nurse to her dying friend; however, as the letters reveal, their relationship was far from the conventional one touted by Julia Stephen's nursing manual.[15] Instead, Woolf's ministrations had everything to do with keeping Jacques' imagination and intellect alive to art, despite the steady and irrevocable deterioration of his body. Jacques Raverat's "splashes," akin to the darts and dashes of the imagination that Woolf describes in "Professions for Women," are precisely what Woolf wants to protect from her mother's "art of nursing," an art which, rather than facilitating flights of fancy, controls and manipulates perceptions. "Plants and flowers," Julia Stephen tells prospective nurses in *Notes from Sick Rooms*, "should be placed so as to show their best shape and colour to the invalid's eye, and in such a position as to be seen by her easily without any exertion" (231). If for the nurse, the sickroom is a space to be managed and the patient is a "case" whose symptoms and imagination must be closely monitored for signs of disturbance, for the

[14] Jacques Raverat's letter responding to *Mrs. Dalloway* read: "Almost it's enough to make me want to live a little longer, to continue to receive such letters and such books . . . I am flattered & you know how important an element that is to one's sensations, and proud & pleased" (*D*3 7 n.3)

[15] I would like to extend my appreciation to the anonymous reader who made the observation that Woolf might be considered an "epistolary" nurse to Jacques Raverat.

ill subject, the sickroom becomes a reprieve. Moreover, for the ill female subject who is also a writer, it may become the one place where she can allow body and imagination to encounter one another uninhibited.

How Do We Think Through Our Mothers? Well, or Ill?[16]

And yet, if the mother as legislator of the imagination must be jettisoned in order that the daughter as artist can emerge, Woolf imagines that this same mother also provides the physiological imperative for the making of art. Throughout "A Sketch of the Past," Woolf intercepts her impressions, "of the waves and the acorn on the blind; the feeling of lying in a grape and seeing through a film of semi-transparent yellow," with the sudden appearance of her mother: "But to fix my mind upon the nursery—it had a balcony. . . . My mother would come out on to her balcony in a white dressing gown. There were passion flowers growing on the wall; they were great starry blossoms, with purple streaks, and large green buds, part empty, part full" (*MOB* 65-66). Here is the Pre-Raphaelite Madonna not as the artist's nemesis but rather as her inspiration. The vision of "mother . . . in a white dressing gown" surrounded by "passion flowers" quickly becomes incorporated into Woolf's imaginative sense of herself as artist: "If I were a painter I should paint these first impressions in pale yellow, silver, and green. . . . Everything would be large and dim; and what was seen would at the same time be heard; sounds would come through this petal or leaf—sounds indistinguishable from sights" (66). As Woolf imagines her here, Julia Stephen funds the synaesthesia—"what was seen would at the same time be heard"—which she desires as a writer to paint with words on her own canvas, the blank page (66).

Woolf's desire to use her mother as the touchstone for an aesthetic response to the world corresponds to the psychoanalyst Melanie Klein's contemporaneous theorization of the same process. Born in Austria, Klein moved to England in 1926, coincidentally the same year "On Being Ill" was published, and radically altered the course of British psychoanalysis. As both Elizabeth Abel and Lyndsey Stonebridge have elaborated, the intellectual relationship between Klein's and Woolf's

[16] Hermione Lee, in *Virginia Woolf*, opens her chapter "Maternal" by asking the following questions: "Should we think through our mothers, or kill them? Must we kill the ghosts for whom we feel (and who feel for us) such a fatal attraction, who are always creeping back to life when we thought they were dead? *And does 'thinking through' mean well or ill?*" (emphasis added 79). It is the latter question that I find to be the most suggestive as it posits a link between maternal phantoms, illness, and the production of art, which, despite voluminous amounts of scholarship on the mother-daughter relationship in Woolf's work, has not explicitly been explored. It is also the question that I have been preoccupied with attempting to answer in this essay. For previous scholarship exploring mother/daughter relations in Woolf's work, see Ellen Rosenman, Jane Marcus, and Marylu Hill, to name only a few.

work is less one of correspondence than confluence. Likewise, I am not suggesting that Klein's theories had any direct impact on Woolf's work, especially given that the texts I attend to here, with the exception of "Professions for Women" and *The Years*, were published either before or only shortly after Klein began her lectures in London. It is, however, the case that Klein's vivid account of the infant's highly ambivalent relationship to two internalized maternal imagos—one who is persecutory and the other who is sensual and loving—resonates with Woolf's account of the mother/daughter relation as both hostile and yet utterly essential to creativity and art.

As Klein theorizes them in the 1920s, the imagination and symbol formation are funded by and founded in a relationship to the mother, which is to say that the Symbolic and its linguistic and artistic expressions, rather than being informed by a strictly masculine logic as Sigmund Freud and his successor Jacques Lacan depict them, are maternal in origin.[17] Furthermore, rather than presenting art as a symptom of repression, which, in Bloomsbury intellectual and artistic circles Freud had already been criticized for doing, Klein asserts that art represents the symbolic outcome of the infant's reparative desire to ameliorate the anxiety associated with aggressive and sadistic phantasies previously directed toward the mother.[18] If for Klein's boy these anxieties have much to do with fears of dismemberment, for Klein's girl these anxieties are associated with an intense feeling of lack—a lack connoting creative impotence rather than sexual inferiority. The little girl's "earliest danger situation" is in fact, Klein argues, represented by the girl's fear of the mother's assault on her own body and her own creative potential, a fear that intensifies if the mother cannot be seen—if she is, for example, as she was for Woolf, only a phantom. Hence, the Kleinian infant's psychological dimensions and its imagination emanate from a sensuous but equally anxiety provoking first encounter with the maternal body, an encounter which, rather than being consigned to the past as Freud and later Lacan would have it, finds itself repeated over and over in the present moment.

[17] Klein addressed creativity and sublimation most specifically in her 1929 paper "Infantile Anxiety Situations Reflected in a Work of Art and in the Creative Impulse," delivered before the British Psychoanalytic Society. Generally speaking, Klein's theories regarding the infant's development and relationship to its mother are articulated in her work during the years 1921-1945 both before and after her arrival in England. See *Love, Guilt and Reparation and Other Works, 1921-1945*. She continued to hone these theories throughout the early sixties. These later papers have been collected in *Envy and Gratitude and Other Works, 1946-1963*. The Hogarth Press was the original publisher for both editions.

[18] Regarding Bloomsbury's refutation of Freud's notion of art as symptom see Roger Fry, "The Artist and Psychoanalysis," and Clive Bell, "Dr. Freud on Art." Although he was not affiliated with the Bloomsbury Group, see also Aldous Huxley's "Our Contemporary Hocus-Pocus."

For Woolf as well, the encounter with the world is initially of a physical nature. Symptoms, as they are figured in "On Being Ill" and elsewhere in Woolf's fiction, do not imply a return of the repressed; instead, symptoms signify a way of registering a deeply felt engagement with the world and its objects. If, as I argue to be the case for Woolf, this engagement remains haunted by and anchored within an original relationship to the mother, then keeping Klein's theoretical imaginings in mind as referenced above helps us to see that the consequences of this maternal relationship are, for Woolf, also never regression and fixation but rather the various forms and characters she creates to embody her ever-evolving aesthetic vision. Furthermore, Klein's distinction between the girl's fears regarding creative impotence and the boy's castration anxiety resonates provocatively with Woolf's need to solve two aesthetic problems as she presents them in her 1931 lecture "Professions for Women": "The first—killing the angel in the house—I think I solved. She died. But the second, telling the truth about my own experiences as a body, I do not think I solved" (282). It is Woolf's desire to solve these problems—to find an aesthetic that repudiates the mother as angel/nurse and yet also communicates the affect associated with the mother's presence as it is indelibly connected to her own "experiences as a body"—that I am suggesting leads her to explore the "unexploited mine" that is illness in her major fictions.

Prior to the essay "On Being Ill," Virginia Woolf's first novel had already deployed illness as an aesthetic strategy capable of facilitating a voyage away from the Victorian novel and away from the role of Victorian daughter. *The Voyage Out* tells the story of one young woman's somatic symptoms and illness as they are deeply imbricated with the loss of her mother and the desire to express herself as an artist. The novel's maternal phantoms manifest as symptoms, and the yearning for an irretrievable intimacy mitigates the hostility Woolf would express later in "On Being Ill" toward the mother/nurse figure and revisit yet again in *The Years*. With the exception of the fact that its female heroine dies before she can be married, *The Voyage Out* appears to follow the conventions of the Victorian novel: It is stylistically conservative, and it charts a young woman's coming of age and betrothal. However, by frequently focalizing the narrative through Rachel Vinrace's feverish consciousness, Woolf indicates that her own aesthetic vision for the novel will be quite different from that of a Jane Austen or a Henry Fielding.

While Rachel does not officially fall ill until the novel's end, it is clear from the beginning that her way of being in and seeing the world contrast starkly with that of the other characters: "To feel anything strongly was to create an abyss between oneself and others who feel strongly but perhaps differently" (36). Brought up "with excessive care, which as a child was for her health" (34) and lacking the definitive beauty possessed by her mother—"[h]er face was weak rather than decided, saved from insipidity by the large enquiring eyes; denied beauty, now that she was sheltered indoors, by the lack of colour and definite outline"—Rachel Vinrace nevertheless possesses precisely the qualities that make her suitable as Woolf's protagonist (20). She is, to borrow a phrase used by T.E. Hulme, Woolf's ideal "aesthetic ego," which is to say that her intensely subjective way of viewing the world radically challenges the more conventional modes of representation she is forced to inhabit.[19]

As Patricia Moran points out, Rachel's relationship to her body is the novel's primary dilemma and that relationship "revolves around a central paradox: she is nothing but a body; she [has] been brought up to act as if her body does not exist" (147). Trained to subjugate her body to the demands of nineteenth-century domesticity, Rachel paradoxically discovers that she is all body—a physical object vulnerable to the manipulations and interrogations of others. Although she feels keenly that her own body is "the source of all life in the world" and nostalgically links this feeling to her dead mother, she comes to realize that in an undeniably patriarchal culture her body will never be her own (*VO* 258). As she confronts the literal representations of maternity the novel places before her, all of which threaten to cut off her own life force—"the hot current of feeling that ran down beneath" (58)—Rachel's yearning for her mother evolves into a fear and even a horror that she may be in danger of becoming her mother, a fear Patricia Moran labels "matrophobia" (154).

The novel, as Woolf finally imagines it, spins around a choice between marriage to Terence Hewet or illness. If love threatens to "plunge" Rachel into darkness thereby "dull[ing] and crippl[ing]" her artistic sensibility, illness offers the possibility for what Woolf refers to in "On Being Ill" as a "new hierarchy of the passions" (7). Rather than reading illness as Rachel's final escape from the "hedged-in" life promised by her love for Terence, it is more compelling to consider illness as a deliberate aesthetic choice Woolf makes as a writer. Aesthetically speaking, illness proves to be far more interesting and liberating than love. As she becomes increasingly ill, Rachel sinks into a space where she, her body, and sensation are all that remain: "At last the faces went further away; she fell into a deep pool of sticky water, which eventually closed over her head" (341). If Rachel's submission to illness signifies a withdrawal into her own body and a "fantasmatic reunion" with the maternal body, Claire Kahane contends that it also "foregrounds the dynamics of metaphor" by taking "language back to its fantasmatic origin as thing" ("Great" 103).[20] Kahane defines metaphor as a "constant way of promoting the

[19] I have in mind here T. E. Hulme's notion of "aesthetic egoism" which referred to the intense sensations associated with subjectivity as a means of challenging more conventional modes of representation. See *Speculations: Essays on Humanism and the Philosophy of Art.*
[20] See Hill and Rosenman for arguments suggesting that Rachel's illness constitutes a withdrawal into the mother's womb.

idea of an unspeakable original elsewhere," which simultaneously materializes "symbolic discourse by keeping sentience and sense in the idea, keeping the body in language" (102). Defined as such, metaphor allows Woolf to gesture toward the "unsayable," an "unsayable" that is a maternally inflected presence (102). Thus, although Kahane figures Rachel's illness as a return to the mother's body, she also suggests the notion that illness facilitates metaphor and that metaphor, if defined as "promoting the idea of an unspeakable original elsewhere," manifests the maternal in an otherwise masculine symbolic (102). Kahane therefore prompts us to consider Woolf as opening up "that speaking silence, that resonance of language that she and other modernist writers would so successfully plumb" (126).

Throughout *The Voyage Out*, Woolf emphasizes Rachel's desire to speak that silence, to bridge the gap between self and other, and to reconstitute a lost plenitude by joining self perceptually with the objects she sees.[21] For Rachel, as shall also be true of the shell-shocked Septimus Smith in *Mrs. Dalloway*, the body resonates as a chord between internal and external realities. However, once Rachel falls ill there is no more between: "[E]very object in the room, and the bed itself, and her own body with its various limbs and their different sensations were more and more important each day. She was completely cut off, and unable to communicate with the rest of the world, isolated and alone with her body" (330). Whereas earlier moments of association—with, for example, trees—suggest an extension of self, an attempt to render self like the object that it sees, once Rachel falls ill her body quite simply becomes the object.[22] Consciousness, for Rachel, becomes entirely a consciousness of the body: "for long spaces of time she would merely lie conscious of her body floating on the top of the bed and her mind driven to some remote corner of her body, or escaped and gone flitting round the room" (347).

However, much to Rachel's dismay—"she wished to be alone. She wished for nothing else in the world"—this bodily-based consciousness, conducive as it is to making metaphors, finds itself too frequently interrupted by none other than the nurse— Nurse McInnis (347). "Fastening the links on her cuffs, in preparation for the night's watch," Nurse McInnis lords over the sickroom with an ominous efficiency (343). McInnis resembles Woolf's account of the nurse as depicted by her mother in *Notes from Sickrooms*—an ominous figure bent on thwarting her

[21] Likewise, Claire Kahane argues that Woolf's notion that the "thing seen" and "the seer" are "inextricably mixed" suggests "that the self is dependent upon the thing seen, that perceptual objects themselves help to define the self" ("Nuptials" 72).

[22] Paul Ricoeur reminds us that the phrase "figure of speech" suggests that metaphor alludes to the presence of the body: "the very term figure of speech implies that in metaphor as in other tropes or turns, discourse assumes the nature of the body by displaying forms and traits which usually characterize the human face, man's "figure"; it is as though the tropes gave to discourse a quasi-bodily externalization. By providing a kind of figurability to the message, the tropes make discourse appear" (142).

patient's fanciful imagination—as well as Klein's punitive maternal figure. Both Woolf's nurse and Klein's mother threaten to rob the emerging female artist of her creativity.[23] When Rachel's fiancé, Terence Hewet, asks Nurse McInnis if she considers Rachel to be seriously ill, she answers in a "curiously stealthy tone" that "[it] may be a fancy, but I don't like to see anybody fall ill in May. Things seem to go wrong in May. Perhaps it's the moon" (344). Thus, Woolf, even before "On Being Ill," represents the nurse as curtailing her patient's odd visions and fancies, visions that Nurse McInnis links cryptically to an unsound mind.[24]

If Nurse McInnis suggests that Rachel is of "unsound mind," Rachel decides that nurses are vapid, insensitive conformists. Earlier in the novel, while fixating her eyes on the face of a hospital nurse sitting nearby her in church, Rachel comes to the conclusion that the nurse is "slavishly acquiescent . . . [s]he was a limpet, with the sensitive side of her stuck to a rock, forever dead to the rush of fresh and beautiful things past her" (228-29). Although it is not clear whether the nurse she sees in church is in fact Nurse McInnis, Rachel nevertheless is left with "an impression of keen horror" that has everything to do with the threat the nurse represents to her own febrile way of seeing the world: "How, indeed, could [the nurse] conceive of anything far outside her own experience, a woman with a commonplace face like hers . . . upon which trivial duties and trivial spites had drawn lines, whose weak blue eyes saw without intensity or individuality" (228-229). In a world that includes Nurse McInnis, mind and body are doomed to remain diametrically opposed. However, irrevocably ill, Rachel remains poised on the threshold between sensation and intellect precisely where Woolf wants her artist to be.

Nevertheless, since *The Voyage Out* ends tragically with Rachel's death, it is still the case, as many scholars have pointed out, that Woolf's first attempt to actualize the woman artist ultimately fails.[25] Unable to imagine how Rachel can

[23] Nurse McInnis may also be based in part on Woolf's own Nurse Traill, who had attended Leslie Stephen in his final hours and who then, in 1904 after Woolf's second major breakdown, attended her while she convalesced at Violet Dickinson's house, Burnham Wood, near Welwyn. Woolf was under Nurse Traill's care for almost three months. Although her diary entries in 1905 indicate that the two became friends of a sort, she regularly complains about the woman interrupting her work: "Traill came & interrupted for 15 minutes, which is an interruption one has to suffer, though I grudge it" (*PA* 235); and again "Traill came in at 12 & sat & talked so my morning came to an end" (*PA* 252).

[24] It is crucial here to point out that Woolf's emphasis in "On Being Ill" is not on mental illness per se—she mentions only melancholia—but rather the physiological impact of illness on the mind and body. Although it is true that Woolf's own doctor, Dr. George Savage, was presenting and publishing lectures on "Post-Influenzal Neuroses and Psychoses" (1913), Woolf, as I have insisted elsewhere, does not present the body as an object to be diagnosed. She had no interest in interpreting the body's symptoms as signifying pathology or neurosis. See Coates 247-248.

[25] For accounts of *The Voyage Out* as a failed female Bildungsroman see Wollaeger; Froula;

survive as an artist and live a relationship to her own body that will prove anything other than destructive to both art and self, Woolf chooses from two familiar endings for female protagonists of the Victorian novel—marriage or death. If at the time she was writing *The Voyage Out*, Woolf could not see beyond the latter of these two options, Rachel's "large enquiring eyes" (*VO* 20) do reappear years later in "the little Chinese eyes" of Lily Briscoe (*TTL* 21). It is in *To the Lighthouse* that phantoms, symptoms, and fancy seem finally to transmute into art.

In 1926, once again the same year "On Being Ill" was first published, Woolf was hard at work writing *To the Lighthouse* and brooding upon how it is that thoughts might become art. This brooding begins, quite significantly, following a conversation with Thomas Hardy, who recalls how Virginia's mother used to "come in & out when [he] was talking to [her] father" (*D*3 99). What if we could "[c]atch [thoughts]," queries Woolf, "hot & sudden as they rise in the mind?" thereby implying that the sensations aroused by thought prior to being subjected to the "slow & deluding" process of language and to the "form of the sentence, soliciting one to fill it" might be akin to physical symptoms—"hot & sudden"—that one might "catch" (*D*3 102).[26] Hovering around this effort to "catch" those thoughts is yet again the phantom who is mother. Although Lily herself is never ill in *To the Lighthouse*, Mrs. Ramsay is both phantom and symptom for the artist. Similar to the apparitional mother Woolf struggles to substantiate in her memoirs, the mother who can only be expressed in gasps and fragmentary sense-impressions, Mrs. Ramsay unravels the mind and disables language. Lily's struggle to communicate Mrs. Ramsay's absence is difficult because, like a symptom, that absence is felt most profoundly in the body: "It was one's body feeling, not one's mind. The physical sensations that went with the bare look of the steps had become suddenly unpleasant. To want and not to have, sent all up her body a hardness, a hollowness, a strain" (181). It is not that Mrs. Ramsay as mother evades Lily's powers of representation. It is rather that the bodily sensation associated first with Mrs. Ramsay's presence and finally with her almost unbearable absence, a sensation that locates Lily somehow between the material world and those ephemeral "splashes" Jacques Raverat spoke of, resists the "catch" of her brush precisely because to represent means to render still: "What was the problem then? She must try to get hold of something that evaded her. It evaded her when she thought of Mrs. Ramsay; it evaded her now when she thought of her picture. Phrases came. Visions came. Beautiful pictures. Beautiful phrases. But what she wished to get hold of was that very jar on the nerves, the thing itself before it has been made anything" (*TTL* 196).

While there is no sympathetic nurse in *To the Lighthouse* to interrupt Lily's

---

and DuPlessis.

[26] I am indebted to Mark Hussey's "Introduction" (xlii) to the recent annotated edition of *To the Lighthouse* for calling my attention to this moment in the *Diary*.

efforts to shape her sensations into a vision that holds but does not immobilize her affinity for Mrs. Ramsay, sympathy nonetheless casts its shadow over her canvas. That shadow is cast most definitively by the overbearing form of Mr. Ramsay, but also by Charles Tansley, who declares "women can't paint, women can't write" (51), and by Mrs. Ramsay's maternal beauty, which threatens to overwhelm Lily with its deceptiveness, "so that all [her] perceptions, half-way to truth, were tangled in its golden mesh" (54). Her ability to mold the sensation that is Mrs. Ramsay into art finally depends on a condition that Woolf, in "On Being Ill" and *To the Lighthouse*, credits illness with inducing—distance. "So much depends," thinks Lily Briscoe, "on distance. . . . So coming back from a journey, or after an illness, before habits had spun themselves across the surface, one felt that same unreality, which was most startling; felt something emerge. Life was most vivid then" (194). The reference to illness woven into Lily's thoughts takes us back to the "undiscovered countries" that Woolf reminds us in "On Being Ill" are disclosed "when the lights of health go down . . . what wastes and deserts of the soul a slight attack of influenza brings to view" (3). Indeed, like an illness, Lily's grief throws her suddenly and unexpectedly into these "wastes and deserts of the soul": "Was she crying for Mrs. Ramsay, without being aware of any unhappiness? . . . Could things thrust their hands up and grip one; could the blade cut; the fist grasp? Was there no safety? No learning by heart of the ways of the world?" (183).

However, on the other side of this grief, Lily finds that her perception has been rendered keen—"she could not shake herself free from the sense that everything this morning was happening for the first time" (197)—and that the intensity of her emotional journey, having strengthened her sense of self as both woman and artist, leaves her free to return to the island no longer feeling the need to make a choice between two opposite forces: "Mr. Ramsay and the picture; which was necessary" (196). It is distance that enables Lily to find that "razor's edge" between sympathy—as demanded by the ever needy Mr. Ramsay—and her art. And so in a moment of clarity, which she now knows will pass, as will—despite Mr. Carmichael's ideas to the contrary—words and paintings, Lily fills the empty space of those steps and the empty space that has been her canvas: "Yes, she thought, laying down her brush in extreme fatigue, I have had my vision" (211).

"And now?"

Lily's proclamation—"I have had my vision"—and Woolf's declaration in "A Sketch of the Past" that after writing *To the Lighthouse* she had "ceased to be obsessed by [her] mother" and "no longer heard her voice; I do not see her," would seem to indicate completion: the phantoms put to rest and the empty space sufficiently filled (80). However, I agree with Hussey that despite Woolf's own words, her "subsequent references" in work to follow "somewhat belie" her claim to closure in the memoirs ("Introduction" l). The fact that Woolf would return again to mothers, daughters, phantoms, and nurses in her second-to-last novel, *The Years*, only affirms that a return to the mother was never a final regression for the writer but rather a move backwards so as to move forwards to yet another shape for her aesthetic vision; furthermore, it also affirms that the hostility and ambivalence she felt toward her mother and her mother's professional care-giving role never entirely abated but, quite to the contrary, continued to have incredible imaginative force.

The Years brings together the entire cast of characters discussed in this essay: Delia Pargiter, the angry daughter who vehemently rejects domesticity and only reluctantly steps in to nurse her dying mother; Eleanor Pargiter, the daughter who assumes the role of mother and, like Julia Stephen, endlessly sacrifices her self so as to care for others; Sara Pargiter, Delia and Eleanor's cousin, the novel's visionary and potential artist figure, who is significantly marked by a proclivity for illness and a slight deformity; and finally Peggy, Delia and Eleanor's niece, who would seem to signify new professional gains for women since she works as a paid physician and has more authority than her Victorian predecessor, the nurse. With the exception of Sara, however, all these women are haunted by the novel's refrain "where am I?" A question which, like Eleanor's final query "and now?" echoes the epistemological and ontological uncertainty left to women for whom, though the angel is dead, the phantom remains very much alive. It is the uncertainty at this question's core that shakes the foundations of what appears to be Woolf's return in *The Years* to a more traditional narrative form.

As the novel opens, Mrs. Rose Pargiter has lain ill in bed for months and, as her daughter Delia sees it, is refusing to die. The sickroom, at the top of Abercorn Terrace, represents a more extreme version of the entrapment Delia already feels within the confines of her childhood home and in the grips of what her brother Martin, later in the novel, thinks of as that "abominable system . . . family life; Abercorn Terrace. . . . there all those different people had lived, boxed up together, telling lies" (210). Bracing herself by fixating momentarily on the vast expanse of sky narrowly visible through a hall window, Delia crosses the threshold into the "private world of illness" where her mother continues to loom as "an obstacle, a prevention, an impediment to all life" (21). True to the instructions Julia Stephen provides in *Notes from Sick Rooms*, the objects in Rose Pargiter's sickroom have been choreographed so that the sky's light reflected in a mirror placed strategically near the bed strikes "silver bottles and . . . glass bottles, all set out in the perfect order of things that are not used . . . . The flowers, too, looked unreal. There was nothing to do but to look" (21).

However, what is there to look at taunts Delia with the orderly constraint and patterns of domesticity she longs to escape, just as her mother, "soft, decayed but everlasting, lying in the cleft of the pillows," seems to mock her by continuing to live: "'You don't want to die.' She longed for her to die" (21). Far removed from the frequently sentimental bedside scenes played out in Victorian fiction, the scene Woolf offers us here seethes with Delia's anger and resentment. Refusing to be captured by the controlled gaze and mindset of the sickroom—"What then should she think of? . . . The prayer-book? The lilies of the valley? Or the looking-glass?" (20)—Delia struggles to call up some affection for her mother but fails miserably and, in an effort to escape the "borderland between life and death" the sickroom represents, finally gives in to her own fantasies, which take her to a platform where she stands "all in white" speaking to the "cause of Liberty" with Charles Parnell standing proudly by her side (22).

Curiously, with the exception of a few scattered references, Delia completely disappears from the novel following her mother's funeral. The only news we hear of her before the novel's end comes through Eleanor, who desperately tries to locate her sister following Parnell's death. It is then that we learn Delia has moved out of Abercorn Terrace and is living in what her elder sister perceives to be a "foreign and sinister" neighborhood rife with poverty (108). The novel's final section features an older, more conventional Delia who, though she once left her family behind, now is surprisingly responsible for bringing them back together for a party. Weaving through her guests in a black dress with gold spangles, Delia as hostess still appears "astonishingly young, handsome, and defiant" as she proclaims loudly in front of her guests, much to the dismay of her brother Martin, that "Abercorn Terrace . . . was hell" (396). She lives up to her role as rebel again when she defies class divisions and marches the caretaker's children in to partake of rather large slices of party cake, which they consume tentatively under the patronizing eyes of the guests.

But Delia is also married with three children. Furthermore, her ardent sense of social justice finds itself disturbingly overshadowed by the caretaker's children's "shrill, discordant, and so meaningless" performance of a song Martin bids them to sing for a sixpence (408). While it is clearly Martin who prompts this awkward performance, Delia nevertheless is responsible for allowing her brother's condescension to play out and thus, however indirectly, also for subjecting the children to humiliation before her wealthier guests, who proceed to poke fun at the children's incoherent accent: "'Cockney accent, I suppose,' said Patrick. 'What they teach 'em at school, you know'" (408). Rather than celebrating Delia as signifying progress or self-awareness, Woolf presents her with some ambivalence as having betrayed her younger self's proclamation that "somewhere there's beauty, somewhere there's freedom" for the role of a flamboyant, but nevertheless conventional hostess and mother (11).

Eleanor seems equally to have lost her way, most especially following her mother's death: "Where am I? she asked herself, staring at a heavy frame. What is that? She seemed to be alone in the midst of nothingness; yet must descend, must carry her burden" (41). Reminiscent of Julia Stephen and her daughter Stella Duckworth, the latter having valiantly played the role of substitute wife and mother following Julia's death, Eleanor has spent much of her life living for others. Despite her recent travels and adventures, she is hit hard by this realization at Delia's party. When Sara, for instance, asks her about her life, Eleanor thinks: "I haven't got one . . . My life's been other people's lives . . . my father's; Morris's; my friends' lives . . ." (347-48). The only reprieve she finds from this painful realization is the "now": "I've only the present moment" (348). Finally, there is the younger generation represented by Peggy, who ostensibly appears to have found herself—at least professionally—for she is a successful physician. But she too is wracked by uncertainty and the role of doctor seems to offer no respite from endless caring for others. She arrives at the party worn out, jaded, and distinctly unhappy with the prospect of having to engage with her relatives, many of whom are also her patients: "'Poor old body,' he began. [Patrick] was off again. All her patients said that, she thought. Rest—rest—let me rest. How to deaden; how to cease to feel; that was the cry of the woman bearing children; to rest, to cease to be" (337). It also appears, given Peggy's malaise, to be the cry of the woman doctor who finds herself, despite the forward march of progress, nursing her relative's symptoms with a sympathy she no longer feels. The only difference being, unlike Julia Stephen or Mrs. Ramsay, she is paid for doing so.

Only Sara Pargiter, the novel's quixotic visionary who is prone to bouts of illness and given to outbursts of song, dance, and poetry appears in the end at all satisfied with her lot. Upon arriving at Delia's party, she almost immediately locates a chair and promptly sinks into a deep sleep in what seems a deliberate effort to avoid the family gathering her nephew, North, has dragged her to in hopes that she will provide a buffer for his own discomfort. Sara's contentment contrasted with the discontent of those around her appears to have much to do with the fact that unlike Eleanor or Peggy, she has failed to find what Eleanor refers to as a "groove"; she follows no pre-determined path, only the whimsical musings of her eccentric mind and body. Therein lies her liberation: "Where did thought begin? In the feet?" (125). Called back to her body on a regular basis, Sara Pargiter, like Rachel Vinrace, discovers metaphor: "It was impossible to act thought. She became something; a root; lying sunk in the earth; veins seemed to thread the cold mass; the tree put forth branches; the branches had leaves" (125). Enacting a physical extension of self across the surface of the world, the eccentric Sara disrupts an otherwise conventional narrative with her queer dance and song and thus joins Rachel Vinrace, Clarissa Dalloway, and Septimus Smith—all consciousnesses inflected by illness—in creating the syntax and the wildly varying forms that we recognize as belonging distinctively to Woolf. And it is through Sara's field of vision, which renders the remnants of Delia's party "strange" and unfamiliar—"they looked prosaic but unreal; cadaverous but brilliant"—that Woolf asks her readers again to see (410).

I have argued here that illness and its symptoms, metaphorically speaking, solve an aesthetic problem for Woolf. As defined in "Professions for Women," the angel as icon of the selfless Victorian woman dies much more easily than does her phantom, incorporated as she is into the woman writer's psyche and imagination. It is this internalized apparition and all she represents that makes it continually difficult for Woolf to "tell the truth about [her] own experiences as a body," a truth that if denied "dashes" the imagination and "destroys [the] artist's state of unconsciousness" (281).

"All creation," writes Melanie Klein's protégée Hanna Segal, "is really a re-creation of a once loved and once whole, but now lost and ruined object, a ruined internal world and self. It is when the world within us is destroyed . . . when our loved ones are in fragments, and we ourselves in helpless despair—it is then that we must re-create our world anew, reassemble the pieces, infuse life into dead fragments, re-create life" (209).[27] Woolf infused "life into dead fragments" and so "re-created life" again and again as she experimented with alternate forms and shapes that might bring her vision to a point. The clairvoyance and artistic sense she asks us to appreciate in "On Being Ill" as being associated uniquely with the gaze through an ill body had already appeared in *The Voyage Out* and would continue to make its presence known throughout her writing career in the shape of women, who are never beauties to be seen but instead visionaries who see beyond the frames they must occupy. Woolf's vision of her own aesthetic project, which she began articulating in her earliest diary entries, was to emanate "a different kind of beauty . . . a symmetry by means of infinite discords, showing all the traces of the mind's passage through the world; & achiev[ing] in the end, some kind of whole made of shivering fragments" (*PA* 393).

Distorted by agitation, sudden chills or fevers, and inexplicable alterations in pallor, Woolf's ill subject in "On Being Ill" offers us a lens through which we might come to see a "different kind of beauty" than the kind represented by Julia Stephen or her fictional counterpart Mrs. Ramsay, both of whom affirmed rather than challenged conventional modes of representation and who in turn bore the burden of expressing that most dreaded of Victorian sentiments—sympathy. And yet, Woolf's radical revision of illness as an aesthetic strategy also never leaves the phantom that was Julia Stephen or the mystery that became Mrs. Ramsay entirely behind; instead, it recuperates these maternal figures as the stimulus for Woolf's

[27] When she wrote this summary of Melanie Klein's theory of reparation, Hanna Segal had just finished quoting Proust at length—the writer who, according to Woolf, best communicated the "nerves of language" (*L2* 525).

"shivering fragments," leaving us to muse that perhaps, if phantoms cannot be killed, they are best lived as symptoms.

Works Cited

Abel, Elizabeth. *Virginia Woolf and the Fictions of Psychoanalysis.* Chicago and London: U of Chicago P, 1989. Print.

Beer, Gillian. "The Victorians in Virginia Woolf: 1832-1941." *Virginia Woolf and the Common Ground.* Ann Arbor: U of Michigan P, 1996. 92-111. Print.

Bell, Clive. "Dr. Freud on Art." *The Nation and The Athenaeum.* 6 Sept. (1924): 690-91.

Broyard, Anatole. *Intoxicated By My Illness And Other Writings on Life and Death.* Ed. Alexandra Broyard. New York: Fawcett Columbine, 1992. Print.

Coates, Kimberly Engdahl. "Exposing the 'Nerves of Language': Virginia Woolf, Charles Mauron, and the Affinity Between Aesthetics and Illness." *Literature and Medicine.* 21:2 (2002): 242-263. Print.

Dick, Susan. "Being Ill/Being Well: Reflections on Illness." *Illness in the Academy: A Collection of Pathographies by Academics.* Ed. Kimberly R. Myers. Indiana: Purdue UP, 2007. 421-435. Print.

Dubino, Jeanne. "On Illness as Carnival: The Body as Discovery in Virginia Woolf's 'On Being Ill' and Mikhail Bakhtin's *Rabelais and His World.*" *Virginia Woolf: Emerging Perspectives. Selected Papers from the Third Annual Conference on Virginia Woolf.* New York: Pace UP, 1994. 38-43. Print.

Duff, Kat. *The Alchemy of Illness.* New York: Bell Tower, 1993. 13. Print.

DuPlessis, Rachel Blau. "'Amor Vin': Modifications of Romance in Woolf," *Writing Beyond the Ending: Narrative Strategies of Twentieth-Century Women Writers.* Bloomington: Indiana UP, 1985. 47-65. Print.

Frank, Arthur W. *At the Will of the Body: Reflections on Illness.* Boston/New York: Houghton Mifflin Company, 1991. Print.

Freeman, Jan. "The Paris Publication of *On Being Ill.*" *Woolf in the Real World: Selected Papers from the Thirteenth International Conference on Virginia Woolf.* Ed. Karen V. Kukil. Massachusetts: Clemson UP, 2005. 141-146. Print.

Froula, Christine. "Out of the Chrysalis: Female Initiation and Female Authority in Virginia Woolf's *The Voyage Out,*" *Tulsa Studies in Women's Literature* 5.1 (1986): 63-90. Print.

Fry, Roger. "The Artist and Psychoanalysis." London: Hogarth Press, 1924. *A Roger Fry Reader*. Ed. Christopher Reed. Chicago: U of Chicago P, 1996. 351-56. Print.

Gillespie, Diane F. "The Elusive Julia Stephen." *Julia Duckworth Stephen: Stories for Children, Essays for Adults.* Eds. Diane F. Gillespie and Elizabeth Steele. New York: Syracuse UP, 1987. 1-27. Print.

Hill, Brian. *Julia Margaret Cameron: A Victorian Family Portrait*. New York: St. Martin's Press, 1973. Print.

Hill, Marylu. "The Mother Lost and Regained: *The Voyage Out* and *To the Lighthouse*." *Mothering Modernity: Feminism, Modernism, and the Maternal Muse*. New York: Garland Publishers, 1999. 169-88. Print.

Hulme, T.E. *Speculations: Essays on Humanism and the Philosophy of Art*. London: Routledge & Kegan Paul, 1924. Print.

Hussey, Mark. *Virginia Woolf A to Z: A Comprehensive Reference for Students, Teachers, and Common Readers to Her Life, Works, and Critical Reception*. New York: Facts on File, Inc. 1995. Print.

——. Introduction, *To the Lighthouse*, by Virginia Woolf. New York: Harcourt, 2005 xxxv-lxviii. Print.

Huxley, Aldous. "Our Contemporary Hocus-Pocus." *The Forum*. 13 (1925): 313-320. Print.

Judd, Catherine. *Bedside Seductions: Nursing and the Victorian Imagination, 1830-1880*. New York: St. Martin's Press, 1998. Print.

Kahane, Claire. "The Great Refusal: *The Voyage Out*." *Passions of the Voice: Hysteria, Narrative, and the Figure of the Speaking Woman, 1850-1915*. Baltimore and London: Johns Hopkins UP, 1995. 99-126. Print.

——."The Nuptials of Metaphor: Self and Other in Virginia Woolf." *Literature and Psychology* 30. (1980): 72-82. Print.

Klein, Melanie. *Envy and Gratitude and Other Works: 1946-1963*. New York: Delacorte Press, 1975. 247-269. Print.

——. "Infantile Anxiety Situations Reflected in a Work of Art and in the Creative Impulse" (1929). *The Selected Melanie Klein*. Ed. Juliet Mitchell. New York: The Free Press, 1986. 84-94. Print.

——. *Love, Guilt and Reparation and Other Works 1921-1945*. New York: The Free Press, 1975. Print.

Lee, Hermione. Introduction, *On Being Ill*, by Virginia Woolf. Ashfield, MA: Paris P, 2002: xi-xxxiv. Print.

——. *Virginia Woolf*. New York: Alfred A. Knopf, 1997. Print.

Love, Jean. *Virginia Woolf: Sources of Madness and Art*. Berkeley: U of California P, 1977. Print.

Marcus, Jane. "Virginia Woolf and Her Violin: Mothering, Madness, and Music." *Virginia Woolf and the Languages of Patriarchy*. Bloomington: Indiana UP, 1987. 96-114. Print.

Meisel, Perry and Walter Kendrick. Introduction. *Bloomsbury/Freud: The Letters of James and Alix Strachey, 1924-1925*. New York: Basic Books, Inc., 1985. 3-49. Print.

Moran, Patricia. "Epilogue: Electra's Complex." *Word of Mouth: Body Language in Katherine Mansfield & Virginia Woolf*. Charlottesville: UP of Virginia, 1996. 137-156. Print.

Poovey, Mary. *Uneven Developments: The Ideological Work of Gender in Mid-Victorian England*. Chicago: U of Chicago P, 1988. Print.

Pryor, William. Ed. *Virginia Woolf & the Raverats: A Different Sort of Friendship*. Bath: Clear Books, 2003. Print.

Reid, Panthea. *Art and Affection: A Life of Virginia Woolf*. New York and Oxford: Oxford UP, 1996. Print.

Ricoeur, Paul. "The Metaphorical Process as Cognition, Imagination, and Feeling." *On Metaphor*. Ed. Sheldon Sacks. Chicago: U of Chicago P, 1979. 141-157. Print.

Rosenman, Ellen. *The Invisible Presence: Virginia Woolf and the Mother-Daughter Relationship*. Baton Rouge: Louisiana State UP, 1986. Print.

Savage, George. "Post-Influenzal Neuroses and Psychoses." Clinical Lecture. London Post Graduate College. 19 Nov. 1913. *Medical Press and Circular*. 96 (1913): 578-81. Print.

Sedgwick, Henry David. "On Being Ill." *An Apology for Old Maids and Other Essays*. New York: Books for Libraries Press, 1916. 82-109. Print.

Segal, Hanna. "A Psychoanalytic Approach to Aesthetics." *Reading Melanie Klein*. Eds. John Phillips and Lyndsey Stonebridge. New York: Routledge, 1998. 203-22. Print.

Sontag, Susan. *Illness as Metaphor and Aids and Its Metaphors*. New York: Doubleday, 1989. Print.

Sorum, Eve. "Masochistic Modernisms: A Reading of Eliot and Woolf." *Journal of Modern Literature* 28.3 (2005): 25-43. Print.

Stephen, Julia. *Notes from Sick Rooms. Julia Duckworth Stephen: Stories for Children, Essays for Adults*. Eds. Diane F. Gillespie and Elizabeth Steele. New York: Syracuse UP, 1987. 216-240. Print.

Stonebridge, Lyndsey. *The Destructive Element: British Psychoanalysis and Modernism*. New York: Routledge, 1998. Print.

Strachey, Lytton. *Eminent Victorians*. Modern Library: New York, 1918. Print.

Wollaeger, Mark A. "The Woolfs in the Jungle: Intertexuality, Sexuality, and the Emergence of Female Modernism in *The Voyage Out*, *The Village in the Jungle*, and *Heart of Darkness*." *Modern Language Quarterly: A Journal of Literary History* 64.1 (2003): 33-69. Print.

Woolf, Virginia. "The Cinema." *The Essays of Virginia Woolf., Vol. 4, 1925-1928*. Ed. Andrew McNeillie. London: Hogarth, 1994. 348-354. Print.

——. *The Diary of Virginia Woolf.* Ed. Anne Olivier Bell. 5 vols. New York: Harcourt Brace Jovanovich, 1977-84. Print.

——. "Freudian Fiction." *Contemporary Writers*. London: Hogarth Press, 1965. 152-54. Print.

——. *The Letters of Virginia Woolf, 1912-1922*. Vol. 1. Eds. Nigel Nicolson and Joanne Trautmann. New York: Harcourt Brace, 1976. Print.

——. "Melodious Meditations." *The Essays of Virginia Woolf: 1912-1918*. Vol. 2. Ed. Andrew McNeillie. New York: Harcourt Brace Jovanovich, 1987. 80-82. 5 vols. Print.

——. "On Being Ill." Ashfield, MA: Paris Press, 2002. 3-28. Print.

——. *A Passionate Apprentice: The Early Journals, 1897-1909*. Ed. Mitchell A. Leaska. New York: Harcourt Brace Jovanovich, 1990. Print.

——. "Professions for Women." *The Virginia Woolf Reader*. Ed. Mitchell A. Leaska. New York: Harcourt Brace, 1984. 276-282. Print.

——. *A Room of One's Own*. New York: Harcourt Brace, 1981. Print.

——. "A Sketch of the Past." *Moments of Being*. Ed. Jeanne Schulkind. New York: Harcourt Brace Jovanovich, 1985. 64-159. Print.

——. *Three Guineas* (1938). Annotated and with an Introduction by Jane Marcus. Orlando: Harcourt, Inc. 2006. Print.

——. *To the Lighthouse* (1927). Annotated and with an Introduction by Mark Hussey. Orlando: Harcourt, Inc., 2005. Print.

——. *The Voyage Out* (1915). New York: Harcourt Brace, 1948. Print.

——. *The Years* (1939). Annotated and with an Introduction by Eleanor McNees. Orlando: Harcourt, Inc., 2008. Print.

A Balancing Act: Specialization in *Between the Acts*

Evelyn T. Chan

Virginia Woolf's last novel, *Between the Acts* (1941), is famously composed of scattered scraps of speech, thoughts, music, and past literary works, "often shorn of context or contextual urgency" (Beer, "Introduction" xix), making up an unprecedented broken form in her fiction. Isa Oliver, for instance, is able to quote from one of Percy Bysshe Shelley's poems at one moment, and switch to the more mundane topic of food the next: "'The moor is dark beneath the moon, rapid clouds have drunk the last pale beams of even ... I have ordered the fish,' she said aloud, turning, 'though whether it'll be fresh or not I can't promise'" (14). Words are frequently inaudible during the village pageant which Miss La Trobe directs, breaking up actors' speeches and performances. The gramophone player fails to work properly, coming on and off throughout the play.

Yet at the same time, unity is often presented alongside, or even created out of, fragmentation in the novel. The literary allusions throughout, although they crop up seemingly randomly, assume a shared literary history and tradition. Pieces of language and sound are constantly recycled and repeated in different contexts. Snatches of tunes and nursery rhymes create a sense of affinity, resulting in "[m]uscles loosened; ice cracked" (49). The gramophone sounds "chuff chuff chuff" throughout, "a noise a machine makes when something has gone wrong" (47-48), yet this apparent sign of chaos creates in its insistent repetition and regularity an order of its own, becoming, contrary to its original use, a marker of time: "Chuff, chuff, chuff went the machine in the bushes, accurately, insistently"; "Chuff, chuff, chuff went the machine. Time was passing" (90-91). The phrase "[d]ispersed are we" (117), played continuously in the intervals and at the end of the pageant, thematically signifies fragmentation, but formally creates the backbone of the pageant. The book seems to suggest the two are different sides of the same coin: after dispersal there can be assembly again, and after assembly, dispersal, which the structure of the pageant, with its many intervals, enacts.

This is what Patricia Laurence has called "[t]he structure of oppositions and the rhythm of alternation" in the book. It has often divided critical scholarship; Laurence points out that critics often focus either on the fragmentation or the unity of the novel, and fail to see that both are present and important (Laurence 245). Indeed, Woolf's vision of the novel was "a rambling capricious but somehow unified whole—the present state of my mind?" (*D5* 135). Many studies have attempted to provide accounts which consider both these forces in the novel. Michelle Pridmore-Brown, for instance, has cogently argued that interruptions by "static or noise" in the gramophone's sounds "serve to fight totalitarianism" through "short-circuiting the instantaneous connection among rhythm, emotion, and collective action" (411-12). Jane De Gay has similarly written that the novel's "fragmentation of the literary past" undermines "conventional understandings of tradition," which can be used to counter "the rise of Fascism" (210). Such views pose formal fragmentation as a tool used by Woolf to break apart methods of cohesiveness in the novel, be they those of an unthinking collectivism or of literary tradition. Yet Joshua Esty has also pointed out that such communalism in the novel can clearly be seen in both positive and negative light: he writes that, for instance, while "national tradition could easily sponsor stultifying ideologies and mob aesthetics," it also poses "a meaningful shared history against the social fragmentation of the metropolis" (107). Esty concludes that "the novel is designed precisely to express both antinationalist and nationalist sentiments, to reflect both authoritarian and antiauthoritarian possibilities in group ritual" (93). The challenge is thus to find a perspective which does not judge these varying forces as either damaging or beneficial: fragmentation and cohesiveness can be both dangerous and reassuring, both destructive and valuable. One example of an angle which is able to achieve this is that taken by Pridmore-Brown in the latter part of her article, who incorporates the concept of wave-particle duality in physics in her reading of the novel to describe a state in which meaningful connectedness and individuality can coexist (418-19). Another example is Christine Froula showing how the sounds, voices and music at the pageant, instead of settling for either unity or discord, "strain apart, crash, solve, unite," addressing and creating an inclusive and multivocal "we" who are "the people, the demos, the community" (312-21). Here, I wish to explore the influence of a different historical aspect to account for these seemingly contradictory forces in *Between the Acts*: Woolf's concern with specialization, a means to describe the progression of humankind throughout history and a concept which can harbor both cohesiveness and disparity. This article will show that ideas of specialization and the closely related themes of prehistory and money contribute to the aesthetics of concurrent cohesion and fragmentation in *Between the Acts*, through which the novel reflects on the state of human civilization at a time when the world seemed on the brink of destruction.

Just as Karl Marx argued in the nineteenth century that the division of labor had alienated workers from their work and its final product, so Aldous Huxley writes in *Beyond the Mexique Bay* (1934), which Woolf read in May 1934 (*L4* 306), that specialization had created incomplete people in modern society who were incapable of being fully alive:

> Man's biological success was due to the fact that he never specialized. Unfitted by his physique to do any one thing to perfection, he was forced to develop the means of doing everything reasonably well. *Civilization*

> *reverses the evolutionary process. Generalised by nature, we impose upon ourselves, artificially, the narrowest specializations.* Primitives are men who have never succumbed to the suicidal ambition to resemble ants. Generalisation—this is the great, the vitally important lesson they have to teach the specialists of the civilized world. The problem is to evolve a society that shall retain all or most of the material and intellectual advantages resulting from specialization, while allowing its members to lead to the full the life of generalized human beings. (260) [my italics]

Woolf subsequently invited Huxley to visit her, which he did in June (*D*4 222-23); at another dinner together in November 1935, she describes him as "g[etting] off on biology" (*D*4 351). Specialization, described as a process which "reverses the evolutionary process," seems unnatural, and human civilization has perhaps over-specialized, requiring reminders, such as those recurring in *Between the Acts*, of common origins in prehistory.

The first part of this article looks at the significance of prehistory as the time before specialization in the novel. Specialization has served as a cohesive force, helping to build and sustain communities, cultures and civilizations. The nursery rhyme "Tinker, tailor, soldier, sailor, apothecary, ploughboy" which recurs thrice, when Mrs. Manresa counts the stones from her cherry tart, when Bart follows suit, and when he murmurs the rhyme in his sleep towards the end of the book, playfully suggests the very foundation of society is made up of people dispersing into specific roles within particular occupations.[1] Yet now, it also seems to be threatening to break people apart, to pull asunder. A similar effect can be argued for money, the focus of the second part of the article, which will place this issue within the context of discussions on the economics of war in the 1930s. Money is a key tool which has facilitated specialization throughout human history and which highlights people's interdependence. But in the novel, money also becomes a focus of both the potentially destructive force of specialization, and of the unthinking mentality of the "mob" (Woolf, *Pointz Hall* 91), its accumulation an ultimate and common goal to strive for. To achieve the right amount of specialization and money is therefore crucial to thwarting the psychology of the herd, and to mending the excessive fragmentation of modernity, both of which were leading the world to war.

The question of specialization was particularly significant in the 1930s, when political and economic instability forced people to re-evaluate its benefits. John Maynard Keynes, arguing for some level of national protectionism in a decade when free trade seemed to have pushed the international specialization of indus-

[1] A review of *A Dictionary of Occupational Terms* (1927) in the *The New Statesman* entitled "Tinker, Tailor" uses it to refer to "[t]his immense diversity of modern industrialism," the results of the specialization process in the foregoing century ("Tinker, Tailor" 668).

tries and resources too far, wrote to Ramsay MacDonald, the Prime Minister, in 1930: "I am no longer a free trader...in the old sense of the term to the extent of believing in a very high degree of national specialisation and in abandoning any industry which is unable for the time being to hold its own" (*Collected Writings* 20: 379-80). Excessive national specialization put the industries in a country, and the wages of its workers, too much at the mercy of outside industry and market forces, when the world had not yet achieved an optimal international economic system in equilibrium. Keynes saw the need for national protectionism not as an end in itself, but rather as necessary in the 1930s, writing that "for the time at least and so long as the present transitional, experimental phase endures," it is best "to be our own masters, and to be as free as we can make ourselves from the interferences of the outside world," in order to transition more safely towards "an environment in which other ideals can be safely and conveniently pursued" (*Collected Writings* 21: 240). Keynes's views varied from Leonard Woolf's, who believed that because free trade, and the specialization it entailed, made nations highly interdependent, it could be used to thwart the dangers of national sovereignty, making "the economically autarkic sovereign independent state an anachronism and an impossibility"; such free trade would have to be co-operative, not competitive, as it had been in the nineteenth century ("De Profundis" 469). The resultant specialization could then serve as a cohesive force for world peace.

Between the Acts, I will show, although resonating with both Keynes's ideas of national protectionism and his criticism of overspecialization, and Leonard's "renunciation of sovereignty" ("Introduction" 17) and his approbation of maximum international specialization, finally refuses conclusion with either. The novel contains a regressive yearning for the prehistoric, and a protectionist nostalgia for past national culture and Englishness; but it also does not accept these as final states, and where they threaten to consolidate they are broken up by fragmentation. The novel accepts that "civilization" cannot be built without the modern discreteness of identity and individuals; but it also broods over the shattered state of modernity, in which discreteness has been taken too far without prior considerations of a greater whole. Woolf's own slightly modified vision, I argue, as expressed through the aesthetics of the novel, was of a balanced amount of specialization and money: enough to build the meaningful whole that is civilization, but not so much that the building materials could not fit together, or so little that there were not enough, propelling humanity towards primeval mess.

I

In a passage in the earlier typescript of *Between the Acts*,[2] written in September 1938, Woolf describes the villagers streaming onto the lawn to see the pageant:

> Many were old; others in the prime of life. Some were lame. Yet there was a certain air […]. [I]t was as though they were specialized. It was not a mob, a heterogeneous assembly, each clutching a shilling or a half crown, which would give them a right to enter. They were sure of places, even if they came late.
>
> Mr. J. F. Figgis, who had written the Guide Book in 1830, would have supplied the reason for that nameless common element; that dignity; that specialization. "The family of Dyce Odgers," he wrote, "whose present representative is Reginald Dyce Odgers of Dicker Hall, has been settled in the neighbourhood since the days of Henry the Eighth." […]
>
> It was true that these facts referred to the parents, grandparents, and in some cases to the great grandparents of those who were actually crossing the lawn […]. But roughly speaking, had Mr. Figgis suddenly come to life and called the roll call of those names and flocks, half the ladies and gentlemen present would have said, "Adsum" [...]. And the consciousness that they would thus have answered [...] gave their movements even now in 1938 [...] a different motion or air from that [...] in a London crowd [...] <herded> in Oxford Street under the ruby light, <a dignity, a specialty.> (*Pointz Hall* 91-92)

The nostalgic undertones in this passage would become part of what Alex Zwerdling describes as "an acute longing for an earlier, more civilized phase of English culture" in the face of "the barbaric present," one which is "rural rather than industrial, feudal rather than democratic, simple rather than complex, and above all, unified" (308-11). Here, the villagers' "specialized" state, derived from tradition and genealogy, creates both a degree of certainty of identity and an interconnectedness which Woolf thinks is lacking in a modern-day "London crowd." This is not because there is no specialization in the modern city, but rather because there is too much. Woolf tellingly imagines such a city "mob" as "hetero-

[2] Mitchell Leaska, who edited the typescripts of the novel, has named the three existing versions the earlier, later and final typescripts, the former two of which Woolf was working on from April 1938 to October (?) 1940, and to November 1940 respectively (Woolf, *Pointz Hall* 25-29).

geneous": people have become so isolated from each other that they have lost their places in a meaningful whole, and subsequently lost the fixed and various identities which the villagers seem to have.

Yet in the corresponding passage in the published version of the novel, the villagers are not as harmoniously integrated as the draft would suggest. The explicit reference to the villagers' meaningful "specialization" is removed, the past is made less unambiguously redemptive, and the possibility of fragmentation which modernity might bring more immediately pressing:

> Roughly speaking, however, had Figgis been there in person and called a roll call, half the ladies and gentlemen present would have said: "*Adsum*; I'm here, in place of my grandfather or great-grandfather," as the case might be. At this very moment, half-past three on a June day in 1939 they greeted each other, and as they took their seats, finding if possible a seat next one another, they said: "That hideous new house at Pyes Corner! What an eyesore! And those bungalows!—have you seen 'em?"
>
> Again, had Figgis called the names of the villagers, they too would have answered. [...] True, there were absentees when Mr. Streatfield called his roll call in the church. The motor bike, the motor bus, and the movies—when Mr. Streatfield called his roll call, he laid the blame on them. (*BTA* 47)

The reference to Figgis is not followed by the differentiation between the villagers and the "London crowd" as it is in the draft, but instead by markers of change and modernity: new houses, new forms of transport which close the protective distance between the countryside and the city, and new forms of entertainment. Although the places the villagers inhabit through their "specialization" may still give them "dignity," the countryside setting of the novel, and the characteristics it retains of older English community, now also seem threatened by the rupturing aspects of modernity.[3]

The implications of specializing differentiation in modern-day society have changed: where specialization has been vital to the building of communities, of "civilization," throughout human history, it has possibly been carried through to an excessive extent, with people in the present dispersed into shards with which it will be hard to build a lasting whole. The root of the word "special," from which "specialization" is derived, comes from the Latin word *species*, meaning "appearance, form" ("Special"). The theme of acting, of appearances, of superficial form, of pretence, by people living in ill-fitting, incomplete or deceitful roles in a society

[3] For a recent discussion of the relationship between modernity and fragmentation in the novel, see Maren Tova Linett, *Modernism, Feminism and Jewishness* (Cambridge: Cambridge UP, 2007) 84-97.

is present throughout the whole novel. The pageant itself, covering different periods in English history, and in which the village people take up different roles, significantly ends in the present day with the pageant actors holding mirrors which are directed at and reflect the audience, reminding them that they too are actors, who exist "only [...] in parts" (*BTA* 109). At this point, the anonymous voice addressing them asks: "*how's this wall, the great wall, which we call, perhaps miscall, civilization, to be built by [...] orts, scraps and fragments like ourselves?*" (111).

But the novel continuously reminds us that if we go back far enough, we share common origins, that people used to be made up of one whole. Latin's *species*, from which "specialization" is derived, became the English word "species," one of the meanings of which is "[a] group or class of animals or plants having certain common and permanent characteristics which clearly distinguish it from other groups" ("Species"). Charles Darwin's *On the Origin of Species* (1859) is perhaps the best known book which makes use of this sense of the word. It proposed that the differentiation of species was the result of the evolution of specialized functions in response to the demands of different environments. The significance of Darwin's work on the novel has been analyzed by Gillian Beer, who has related its emphasis on the continuity of prehistory into the present, and the prehistoric roots which bind life together, to Darwin's thinking ("Virginia Woolf and Prehistory"). Here, another significance of Woolf's use of prehistory will be explored: prehistory as the time before specialization.

If human history has been one of increasing specialization, perhaps only in prehistoric and primeval mess can complete unity be glimpsed. In *Between the Acts*, the prehistoric is more present than in any of Woolf's novels. The novel's frequent references to it create an undercurrent of peculiar nostalgia for it as the source of mankind's common origins, when specialization, as part of civilization, had not yet occurred. As Lucy Swithin thinks, this was "when the entire continent, not then, she understood, divided by a channel, was all one; populated, she understood, by elephant-bodied, seal-necked, heaving, surging, slowly writhing, and, she supposed, barking monsters; the iguanodon, the mammoth, and the mastodon; from whom presumably, she thought, jerking the window open, we descend" (8). Throughout the novel, the prehistoric can be glimpsed underneath the surface of the here and now: the bellowing of the cows is "the primeval voice sounding loud in the ear of the present moment" (85); "the great lady in the bath chair" (58), with her undefined age, is "the indigenous, the prehistoric" (121), so that "even her body, crippled by arthritis, resembled an uncouth, nocturnal animal, now nearly extinct" (58). Even the antics of the village "idiot" remind others of their origins, prompting Mrs. Parker to ask Giles: "Surely, Mr. Oliver, we're more civilized?" (68).

Although specialization has created welcome order out of the primeval soup, it has perhaps gone too far, and needs to be reset by reminders of bygone unity:

"*Dispersed are we; who have come together. But,* the gramophone asserted, *let us retain whatever made that harmony*" (116). The use of rhyme in the novel can be seen as an effort to provide the most basic connections again.[4] As Beer argues, the novel's "semantic cacophony of rhyme" finds similarity "in the sounds of the language, not in any reasoned relationships" ("The Island and the Aeroplane" 285). Rhyme, for example, binds separate conversations into one mass: "So abrupt. And corrupt. Such an outrage; such an insult; And not plain. Very up to date, all the same. What is her game?" (109). It seems a last attempt to find relations in a world split apart by overspecialization, invoking memories of a common tradition through identical sounds in a shared language. The loose connection of words with similar sounds, seen in such phrases as "[s]hall I [...] go or stay? Slip out some other way?" (59), "Hadn't she, for twenty-five minutes, made them see? A vision imparted was relief from agony" (60), and "[s]he looks such a dear. Someone I know said his hair ... "(64), also gives them a playfulness which is more commonly seen in language used in childhood, for example in nursery rhymes, which, as Beer writes, hint at the "primitive" in their association with our childhood past, when boundaries between individuals, objects and concepts are blurred, their roles not yet demarcated by clear semantic limits. The rhymes used here undo adult order by invoking the looser associations of childhood, as part of the return to the primitive in the whole novel ("Rhyming as Resurrection" 191). This is both attractive and threatening, a balancing act between the awareness, suffering and commitment which comes with knowledge, meaning and identity, and the escapism and potential nihilism of meaninglessness.

But although prehistory may be attractive for its vision of complete wholeness, in *Between the Acts*, Woolf does not seem to claim it as a state to aspire toward. As Huxley writes, although people should learn to be more generalist, the goal should not be to regress to the state of "[p]rimitives," but "to evolve a society that shall retain all or most of the material and intellectual advantages resulting from specialization, while allowing its members to lead to the full the life of generalized human beings" (260). The idea of the undifferentiated chaos of primeval mess rested uneasily with the prospect of the mess another world war was about to create. Moving toward this was for Woolf, as for many others, a horrifying thought, and the time when this novel was set, "on a June day in 1939" (47), when Britain was on the brink of the Second World War, linked it uneasily to the vivid memories of the First. Trudi Tate has pointed out the association made in the First World War between primeval mess and tanks in the devastated landscape in various media, from newspapers to literary works. She writes that "the most advanced weapon of

[4] Beer writes that "[r]hyme is one of the last things; it stays—a final skill—when other ordering principles have fled the mind," and that it "offers connection still, even when semantic clues may have been voided" ("Rhyming as Resurrection" 203).

1916 takes civilization into a new phase of modern technology at the same time as plunging it back into prehistory—an image both terrifying and pleasurable," and that *Between the Acts* includes this notion of simultaneous progress and regression (125). The military tank, a product of specialized technology and a potent reminder of it, does not appear in *Between the Acts*. Instead, we have machines of which Woolf had first-hand experience: "Twelve aeroplanes in perfect formation like a flight of wild duck came overhead" (114). They appear while Mr. Streatfield gives his speech at the end of the play, and become part of the play in the audience's mind: "The aeroplanes, I didn't like to say it, made one think ..."; "[t]hen when Mr. Streatfield said: One spirit animates the whole—the aeroplanes interrupted. That's the worst of playing out of doors ... Unless of course she meant that very thing ...." (118-19). If, as Huxley writes, "[c]ivilisation reverses the evolutionary process," the danger at the time was that civilization could ultimately, seemingly paradoxically, turn people back towards prehistory, towards the prehistoric mess of war.

Beer has pointed out the multiple significances of the aeroplane in Woolf's work, for instance as a symbol of new possibilities, as the disturber of geographical boundaries, and as a war machine ("The Island and the Aeroplane"). In *Between the Acts*, its ambiguity derives from its symbolic status as the product of technological advances made possible by specialization, its potential to bomb the land back into prehistoric chaos and reverse all progress, and the possibility it provides to escape the present mess altogether. After the play, one of the strands of conversation among the villagers is that "[i]f the worst should come—let's hope it won't—they'd hire an aeroplane, so they said ..." (117). And when Isa thinks of "the infinitely quick vibrations of the aeroplane propeller that she had seen once at dawn at Croydon," she imagines it going "[f]aster, faster, faster, it whizzed, whirred, buzzed, till all the flails became one flail and up soared the plane away and away." The place it goes to is "[w]here we know not, where we go not, neither know nor care" (12). Like the tank in the First World War, the imagery of the potency of the rotating propeller here is both exhilarating and terrifying. It suggests that the immense possibilities of the plane come hand in hand with enormous danger. Bomber planes could destroy landscapes and level homes in a matter of seconds, as Giles reflects on while looking at the view: "At any moment guns would rake that land into furrows; planes splinter Bolney Minster into smithereens and blast the Folly" (34). Perhaps only the primal imagery of prehistory was sufficient to evoke the dramatic scenes of destruction in war.[5]

[5] Interestingly, a more recent common expression for threatening to wage war against another country is "to bomb it back to the Stone Age," a widely reported example being when the then U.S. Deputy Secretary of State Richard Armitage purportedly used the words in 2006 to pressure Pakistan into joining the American fight against al-Qaeda.

Therefore, although imagining the primeval mud might be satisfying in certain ways, its absolute chaos threatens to replace the existing order with nothingness. Complete unity would mean no differentiation whatsoever would exist, rendering the world meaningless. Specialization creates communal identity by creating ways to distinguish oneself from the rest. In arguing this, I observe what Sam See has called the promise which Woolf saw in "the transformative possibilities inherent in the atavistic human" in the novel (643), without considering this reversion to prehistory as ultimately desirable, as something which must be taken to its extreme in order to bring about its regenerative possibilities. Woolf's more ambiguous application of the motif of prehistory differs slightly from Leonard Woolf's in his political writing. In *Quack, Quack!* (1937), Leonard calls the "instincts and emotions of barbarism" which allow "the politician who desires to [do so to] control large masses of men" (109) "prehistoric savagery and quackery" (40). These, Leonard argued throughout the 1930s, must be countered by an international organization like the League of Nations, which "regulat[es] the relations of states on a basis of compromise and co-operation" (*The War for Peace* 222). I will refer again to the League in the second section of this article when discussing how *Between the Acts* engages with the economics of war. The international community formed by the League would thwart not just the primal emotions which drive groups of humans, but also the ego of the single, charismatic politician who tried to take advantage of it. It would use, as he put it in *The War for Peace* (1940), "the power of the community" to "resist by communal force the use of force by an individual member of society," "the savage with a stone in his hand," so preventing "the anarchy of the man-ape" (105). In his book, "community" is the key concept which Leonard keeps returning to, one which encapsulates the meaningful balance between the extremes of formlessness and excessive egotism, both associated by him with the prehistoric. Though this is very similar to the vision underlying *Between the Acts*, in the novel, the prehistoric also becomes a powerful device for countering the overspecialization of the present. Isa says in the earlier typescript: "to build a wall, we must rebuild <recollect> ourselves. Out of fragments" (*Pointz Hall* 181). Here, besides the meaning of gathering ourselves from fragments, "recollect" perhaps also means to remember. Through recollecting, or remembering, our common origins in prehistory, we can recollect what has become overly fragmented, and build a lasting whole again.

The book ends with Lucy finishing "the end of the chapter": "'Prehistoric man,' she read, 'half-human, half-ape, roused himself from his semi-crouching position and raised great stones'" (129). This is the point at which mankind starts to build up civilization through specialization, when people must take up their different roles. Yet in the present, this has been taken so far that people are torn by "motives" which are "mixed" because they are always "after money" (*Pointz Hall*

401). That is why the anonymous voice in the pageant, after asking how civilization is to be built, ends by espousing things done for their own sake:

> *there's something to be said: for our kindness to the cat; note too in today's paper "Dearly loved by his wife"; and the impulse which leads us—mark you, when no one's looking—to the window at midnight to smell the bean. Or the resolute refusal of some pimpled dirty little scrub in sandals to sell his soul. There is such a thing—you can't deny it. What? You can't descry it? All you can see of yourselves is scraps, orts and fragments?* (*BTA* 111-12).

Specialization, which had the potential both to encourage cooperation and interdependence, and to cause disharmony and conflict, seemed poised to do the latter, with disastrous results. By starting and ending with references to prehistory, the novel has come full cycle: as the day draws to an end and will soon be renewed, the question is perhaps also whether civilization will be renewed from the metaphorical prehistory into which war was about to plunge Europe.

II

> [M]oney, like dynamite and other tools used by men, can very greatly damage, as well as very greatly service, his society.
>
> —Norman Angell, *The Story of Money*

In the later typescript, written in the fall of 1940,[6] Bart thinks, upon hearing that "[t]he profits [of the pageant] are to go towards the fund for installing electric light in the Church":

> All motives are mixed. Especially in England. Had it been so – say, in the middle ages? The monks – were they disinterested? He doubted it. Ourselves. The rise of the professional class. And so on. Aloud he said – he would have said, but was it worth it? – "The English, wherever you find them, <are> always <after money; always> say one thing, mean another. Villagers, gentry, clergy, all the same." (*Pointz Hall* 401) [my emphasis]

Woolf's phrase "[t]he rise of the professional class" shows her acutely aware of this social force in British society. Professionalization, the specialization of knowledge, is one particular and later manifestation of the general process of specialization, the

[6] Leaska estimates that Woolf started writing the later typescript in October 1940, finishing it the next month (*Pointz Hall* 29).

division of roles, throughout human history. Here, "[t]he rise of the professional class" is associated with mixed motives, which are caused by people being "always <after money>." This common true motive, however, splits people apart: it needs to be covered up with hypocrisy, so that people "say one thing, mean another." In the published version, Mrs. Manresa responds to Bart's cynicism:

> "What's the object," said Bartholomew, suddenly rousing himself, "of this entertainment?"
>
> "The profits," Isa read out from her blurred carbon copy, "are to go to a fund for installing electric light in the Church."
>
> "All our village festivals," Mr. Oliver snorted turning to Mrs. Manresa, "end with a demand for money."
>
> "Of course, of course," she murmured, deprecating his severity, and the coins in her bead bag jingled.
>
> "Nothing's done for nothing in England," the old man continued. Mrs. Manresa protested. It might be true, perhaps, of the Victorians; but surely not of ourselves? Did she really believe that we were disinterested? Mr. Oliver demanded.
>
> "Oh you don't know my husband!" the wild child exclaimed, striking an attitude (105).

Although in this village community, people can still assert "a right to enter" and be "sure of places, even if they came late" without having to pay "a shilling or a half crown" (*Pointz Hall* 91), the pageant necessarily "end[s] with a demand for money" (*BTA* 105). The irony in Mrs. Manresa's claim is that, as Maren Linett has shown, Ralph Manresa, the absent Jewish businessman, is problematically associated with such negative aspects of modernity as money interests which threaten to transform the community. Linett points out that at the end of the pageant in the earlier typescript, Woolf writes: "'Liars and thieves.' (Ralph Manresa. Manresa was here exposed to view.)." Ralph is thus used "to represent the general state of affairs Bart is deploring, that English culture is invariably interested, made up of 'liars and thieves'" (92).

Historically, specialization was greatly helped by money, which enabled people to buy necessary products and services outside their own area of work. In *The Story of Money* (1930), Norman Angell, with whom Woolf was acquainted,[7] and who was involved with Leonard Woolf on much political work on war and

[7] Woolf mentions seeing him in a letter to Julian Bell, in which she says that "Norman Angell was rather fun" (*L5* 33). They also both signed, together with others, a letter to the editor of *The Times* to highlight the plight of the Spanish government and people in the Spanish Civil War, which appeared in the newspaper on 19 Aug. 1936. Leonard Woolf also cooperated with Angell on such books as *The Intelligent Man's Way to Prevent War* (1933) and *Does Capitalism Cause War?* (1935).

peace, writes that "division of labour immediately sets up the need for a medium of exchange...If a man can in Robinson Crusoe fashion be entirely self-sufficient, producing all he needs, there is no reason for exchange" (22). Like specialization, money, as a symbolic form of common value which people can use to meet their diverse needs, can be used both to build a diverse yet integrated whole, or what Woolf calls "civilization" in the novel, and can fragment excessively: the drive for money can destroy, as Woolf had detailed in *Three Guineas* by describing financially successful professionals as "cripple[s] in a cave" (197), and as the international conflict caused by the pursuit of financial interests by different countries in the 1930s had shown. A reason for German aggression in the late 1920s and throughout the 1930s was precisely "the economic question," as Keynes had predicted in *The Economic Consequences of the Peace* (1919). Keynes had argued that the unrealistically harsh terms in the Treaty of Versailles, which demanded reparations which post-World War One Germany could not pay, would create international conflict (103-210). It became increasingly clear that his predictions were accurate. For example, from 1928 to 1930, a policy of deflation in Germany, enacted to ensure that the mark would retain a high value to enable Germany to pay off its war reparations and debts more efficiently, created massive unemployment and a plunge in wages (Skidelsky 336). Such economic instability contributed significantly to the rise of Nazism.[8]

Throughout history, the availability of money accelerated specialization until the goal for work often became money itself, alienating people from the greater purpose of their work. This is a problem which Woolf would have been aware of. Leonard Woolf calls this "[t]he curse of the capitalist system," which "produces states of mind in individuals and classes which contaminate society by inducing a profound, instinctive conviction that the object and justification of everyone's work, trade, profession, in fact of nine-tenths of a person's conscious existence ... are and should be money" (*Downhill* 88). The only type of society in which specialization could exist with a more secondary use for money was the cooperative society which he had advocated in *Co-operation and the Future of Industry* (1918), in which he describes an economy which would not be "geared to and judged by its ability to provide work, wages, and salaries," but instead "to produce what the community wants or needs to consume" (*Downhill* 86). His vision is of a "Co-operative Commonwealth" in which everyone contributes their part to the greater whole of the community, even if this means there should be a system of "conscription ... for industrial labour," where "[e]very consumer, male and female, should be required to perform an equal share of this labour." But this was not likely to be put into practice. It was such a radical departure from the way society had been run that it

[8] "The percentage of votes cast for the Nazis rose from 2.6 in 1928 to 18.3 in 1930" (Skidelsky 336).

would "seem ridiculous and impossible," and that "many readers on a first hearing will either smile or shudder" (*Co-operation* 126-27). Later, in his autobiography, Leonard would write that "the psychology of capitalism" was "so firmly established in modern society that to most people the idea that the object of industry should be consumption, not production or profit, seems Utopian and even immoral. I never imagined, therefore, that my argument in favour of socialism controlled by consumers would cut any ice in the Labour movement" (*Downhill* 88). There seemed to be few realizable ways of separating specialization and money.

Giles is the only major character in Woolf's novels who is a stockbroker, his profession the epitome of such a profit-driven, overspecialized society, in which money-making has become disconnected from physical objects in the real world. Stockbroking makes use of money not in its earlier sense, as "[a]ny generally accepted medium of exchange which enables a society to trade goods without the need for barter; any objects or tokens regarded as a store of value and used as a medium of exchange" ("Money"), but in its subsequent sense, when money went beyond being a mere tool of exchange, and became a precious commodity in itself, inflating its exchange value with additional symbolic worth and power. But while making use of the derivative value of money, and earning money out of managing money, Giles is also a conscious captive of money: "Given his choice, he would have chosen to farm. But he was not given his choice. So one thing led to another; and the conglomeration of things pressed you flat; held you fast, like a fish in water" (30-31). Because "he had no special gift, no capital, and had been furiously in love with his wife" (30), becoming a stockbroker had been his only option. This is the source of the antipathy which Giles feels towards his aunt. Where he has had to take up a City job, Lucy has been able to lead a free and quiet life in the countryside: "It was Aunt Lucy ... who made him change. He hung his grievances on her.... Aunt Lucy, foolish, free; always, since he had chosen, after leaving college, to take a job in the city, expressing her amazement, her amusement, at men who spent their lives, buying and selling—ploughs? glass beads was it? or stocks and shares?" (30).

The stigma attached to a profession which had its history in disrepute,[9] and which existed to allow people to make money out of money which was traded often in exchange for quick and large profits, had not disappeared. This was despite the fact that by the 1930s it had become a well-organized profession, with its own code of rules, an elected Committee, and strict membership requirements (Carr-Saunders and Wilson 273-74). Nicholas Davenport, in an article in *The New Statesman* in 1940, describes it thus: "I used to make some money on the Stock

[9] A. M. Carr-Saunders and P. A. Wilson write: "Stockbroking was first heard of towards the end of the seventeenth century, and several attempts were made to suppress the practice. In 1697 an Act was passed 'to restrain the Number and ill practice of Brokers and Stock Jobbers'" (273-74).

Exchange whenever it was possible to make it, which meant, of course, exploiting the follies of other investors more greedy than myself.... I do not know of any profession more soul-destroying than that of handling money for ungrateful and unimaginative capitalists" (Davenport 376). He quotes from *The World of William Clissold* (1926) by H. G. Wells, which Woolf read in August 1926 (*L*3 286), in which William, the protagonist, attacks the vacuousness of the City:

> Men follow science and art, pursue agriculture, organise manufactures ... because these things are profoundly and sustainingly interesting. But no one is in business in the City for the sake of business in the City. Men go there to come out of it again, successful ....
>
> The men who rush about [the City's] narrow ways do not know what they are up to .... [T]he sense of being a possible part of one complete organisation has not come to them....Their great enterprises, their debts, their loans, their technicalities and methods, are solemn vast puerilities; it does not make them any the less puerilities that all mankind suffers because of them. (220-22)

Giles's occupation seems to be symbolic of the wider fear in the 1930s that people and nations would develop into unthinking entities which pursued money for the sake of money without a consideration of a part to play in a greater whole, becoming, as noted above, "cripple[s] in a cave." In the novel, money, disconnected from its material foundation, gives characters a common goal, yet also creates splits between and within them:

> "When we wake" (some were thinking) "the day *breaks us* with its hard mallet blows." "The office" (some were thinking) "*compels disparity. Scattered, shattered,* hither thither summoned by the bell. 'Ping-ping-ping' that's the phone. 'Forward!' 'Serving!'—that's the shop." So we answer to the infernal, agelong and eternal order issued from on high. And obey. "Working, serving, pushing, striving, earning wages—to be spent—here? Oh dear no. Now? No, by and by. When ears are deaf and the heart is dry." (73) [my emphasis]

"[E]arning wages," the final and foregrounded item in the series of activities described, is part of the "eternal order issued from on high." Money, from being an instrument of exchange and interconnectedness, has become something which people must "obey." Not even spending, the reward of earning, can bring any subsequent pleasure: it is deferred until it can no longer bring enjoyment, when people's physical and mental states have been wrung dry by the common pursuit of money. Just as excessive specialization has left people with little sense of a greater belonging in modern society, so money, as a tool which developed alongside specialization, has become the master, and people its servants. With Britain poised on the brink of another world war, the fear underlying the novel is that specialization has disrupted beyond repair. The constant replaying of short phrases throughout the book, such as "dispersed are we," are like the constant "tick, tick, tick" and "chuff, chuff, chuff" of the haphazard gramophone, jaded and decrepit, and similar to the gramophone player in *Three Guineas* "whose needle has stuck," and whose "old tune" is "grinding out with such disastrous unanimity": "Here we go round the mulberry tree, the mulberry tree, the mulberry tree. Give it all to me, give it all to me, all to me. Three hundred millions spent upon war" (181).

On an international level, one perceived means to prevent this and create a meaningful global community was to encourage co-operation and interdependence through the specialization of resources, industries and businesses, which would also link countries' financial systems together. This would prevent what Leonard, in the introduction to *The Intelligent Man's Way to Prevent War* (1933), which he edited, called "economic imperialism," which could lead to the destructive ideals of "the self-sufficient state and economic nationalism" (16-17). In the final chapter in the book, Angell, quoting an academic at Leyden university, writes: "There was a time when man could live in a self-sufficient life, when the family, tribe or nation could live selfishly, with utter indifference as to the fate of other tribes or nations. … With the progress of science and of modern technique, with the advent of the machine or power age, all this changed" ("Educational and Psychological Factors" 488). For better or worse, in modern times, individuals and nations comprised a reciprocal system. The way to peace was to create the League of Nations, an international cooperative community which worked under "common rules of conduct and institutions," "apply[ing] to international relations the commonest, the most universal, the most conclusive human experience" ("Educational and Psychological Factors" 491). The idea behind this, as Angell puts it in the first chapter, is "to deprive the local states of their sovereignty for the benefit of society as a whole, without at the same time depriving them of their existence" ("The International Anarchy" 29) so that discreteness and unity can co-exist in a peaceful state.

Leonard did not relinquish the idea of the League of Nations and its having a crucial role in building an international community, not even after its failure to handle the Italian-Abyssinian crisis, which according to him effectively destroyed the League's credibility at the time (*Downhill* 241-43). In 1940, he writes that the League had failed because of "the psychology of conflicting interests and the organization of power politics," which needed to be replaced by "the psychology of common interests and the organization of international co-operation" ("Utopia and Reality" 181). His view, in *War for Peace*, is that since the nineteenth century, "the lives we lead have demanded more and more international co-operation and closer economic and political articulation of national communities." But because of "the lethal influence of nationalist psychology," countries have worked against, instead of with, this international system, so that there is "ever-increasing political and economic conflict" (238-39).

Therefore, in the same book, Leonard acknowledges the need to change the old League system, which assumed that nations were "completely undifferentiated," and so "impos[ed] upon all the same obligations in all cases and in all regions of the world" (238-39). The new League should at least for now be run on a "confederate" system instead of under one single federation: smaller groups of nations, which are economically and psychologically close, can cluster together into smaller federations, which could comprise a larger international confederation (202-09; 223). But a uniform "federate" system still seems Leonard's ultimate vision, one which would "imply a colossal leap forward both from the organization and the psychology of the national state as they exist today" (211), but "which is no doubt ultimately the most logical and desirable form of international government" (225). Therefore, although he acknowledges that current psychological conditions do not yet allow this, if people and nations could remove themselves from "the lethal influence of nationalist psychology" (238), maximum international specialization would ensure maximum cooperation under a uniform federate system.

The problem throughout the 1930s, however, was not only that there was no real sense of cooperation, but also that there was too much international specialization, which of itself seemed to hinder cooperation, making nations highly yet uncomfortably interdependent with each other. As a result, like the villagers in *Between the Acts*, they were " too close, yet not close enough" (41), too close even to temporarily retreat into themselves and escape from each other's influence, beneficial or detrimental, yet not close enough to create a comfortable whole. This, I suggest, is the basic question which *Between the Acts* tries to consider before Leonard's solutions, although the novel shares many of Leonard's ideas on the fundamental need for cooperation. International specialization in the novel seems immediately threatening. Giles describes "the whole of Europe" as unbearably close, with its "guns" and "planes" which could at any moment "rake that land into furrows" (34). It also meant that financial systems of different countries were closely linked together, and the two references at the beginning and at the end of the novel to the newspaper article on the pegging down of the franc which Bart reads (11; 128) highlight these links. One possible source for this is an article entitled "The Daladier Franc," which appeared in *The Times* in May 1938. It reported that Edouard Daladier, the Prime Minister of France, had announced the devaluation and stabilization of the franc to a level "on which it can be effectively defended," with the goal to peg it to the pound at a fixed exchange level, in response to attacks on the franc which had rendered the currency and the financial system in France unstable. This decision, Daladier stressed, was taken with "the agreement of the

British and American Governments," "within the framework of the Tripartite Agreement" (A16), which was necessary because the value of the franc had the potential to affect these countries' economies. Such interconnectedness meant that when things went wrong, not even being, as Bart is, in the countryside or on the other side of the Channel could protect people from the disastrous effects of policies made elsewhere. With Europe compared to a "hedgehog" by Giles, "bristling with guns, poised with planes," international cooperation and interdependence through specialization, which had often been regarded as the best guarantors of peace, seemed so no longer.

This idea had in fact been put forward by Keynes, who in "National Self-sufficiency" (1933) argues that "a greater measure of national self-sufficiency and economic isolation among countries than existed in 1914 may tend to serve the cause of peace, rather than otherwise." He sees the drives toward "the maximum of international specialization" and "the maximum geographical diffusion of capital wherever its seat of ownership" as resulting in "[t]he protection of a country's existing foreign interests, the capture of new markets, [and] the progress of economic imperialism." International specialization disconnects what should be intricately linked: it aggravates the "remoteness between ownership and operation," "an evil in the relations among men, likely or certain in the long run to set up strains and enmities," which offsets any financial benefits (*Collected Writings* 21: 236-37). Although Keynes admits that "[a] considerable degree of international specialization is necessary," he points out that it also leads to "the economic loss of national self-sufficiency," which disallows protection from turmoil in other countries. A balance is then needed between such specialization and national sovereignty, so that nations have the freedom to conduct "different types of experiment" suited to their "different national temperaments and historical environments" (238-39). "[A]bove all," Keynes says, "let finance be primarily national" (236).

Like excessive specialization in *Between the Acts*, excessive international specialization could then lead not to meaningful integration, but to destructive fragmentation. A high degree of interdependency before a cooperative mentality had been attained could backfire, provoking the worst in people and nations. Both Woolfs understood this problem. Leonard recognized that if interdependency did not lead to cooperation, it would result in war ("De Profundis" 469). Woolf herself had written in *A Room of One's Own* (1929) how "fear and bitterness" are removed from one when one can become financially independent from others, in this case through the narrator receiving an annual provision of five hundred pounds from the legacy of her deceased aunt, so that she can say that "I need not hate any man; he cannot hurt me. I need not flatter any man; he has nothing to give me" (34). But where Leonard, also identifying the lack of "common international interest in law, co-operation, and peace" (*The War for Peace* 202) as the cause of war, hoped ultimately that the "reason" and "common sense" which human beings were capable of would prevail (241-44), *Between the Acts* suggests the need for some regression from overspecialization, for the possibility of drawing back into oneself, allowing some degree of insularity as a measure of protection and privacy.

Of course, such ideas, if taken to their extreme, would be ruinous. In the specific case of Germany, the violent move towards autarkie, or complete self-sufficiency, began in the same year Keynes published "National Self-Sufficiency." *The New Statesman* at the time was filled with articles which discussed the economic rationale behind Germany's increasingly aggressive manoeuvres. One entitled "The High Road to Peace and Prosperity" in 1935 explains the close relationship between unbalanced specialization and war. It argues that in advanced industrial countries, the rate of increase in the powers of production had been much greater than that of internal domestic consumption within a country, and that this had necessitated the search for external markets which had hindered "a genuine political and economic co-operation that shall establish the two pacific conditions of a fair and equal access of members of all nations to the resources of the common world" (Hobson 67). Germany, which was "unfortunate, by comparison with the great imperial Powers, in that her industry has been developed out of all proportion to her territorial possessions, and cannot in the present condition of the world find an assured market," had instead resorted to "the economics of war" to establish the condition of autarkie. This included the policy of rationing certain types of imports, butter amongst them, in order to ensure that it had enough money to keep on making armaments. Such a policy was clearly unsustainable: "the belly of a nation will not for ever be satisfied with cannon instead of butter" ("Hunger Breeds War" 4). Although unaware at the time of writing his essay that Germany would fully embark on such a program, Keynes did caution about the possibility, saying that "[i]n those countries where the advocates of national self sufficiency have attained power, it appears to my judgment that, without exception, many foolish things are being done," and warning against implementing national self-sufficiency too hastily and irrationally (*Collected Writings* 21: 243).

Autarkie would do away with the idea of a "whole" which accommodates the balanced existence of discrete nations, and the vision of which I argue underlies *Between the Acts*, in pursuit of the almost impossible goal of becoming an entirely self-sustaining, homogeneous "whole" in oneself. The concept of complete self-sufficiency links the idea of autarkie and the "[p]rehistoric man, ... half-human, half-ape" (*BTA* 129) who, according to Huxley, survived through "[g]eneralization" (260). Advocating autarkie would be as destructive as advocating a return to the primeval. For Germany, this pursuit created an impossible financial predicament. The more Germany devoted its policies to its autarkie and armament programs, the more its financial reserves suffered, and the more compelling it became for it to use armed force. It was a vicious cycle. The economic root of Germany's aggression led to proposals in Britain to combat it with economic sanctions. Louis Fischer analyzes the dire situation in Germany in an article in *The New Statesman* in March 1936, in which he writes of the "economic impasse in Germany; capital is being frozen in armaments, in road building, in heavy Government subsidies, and in numerous other pursuits which bring no immediate financial return." Thus "if the League Powers desired, Hitler could be checked by a few well-aimed economic measures which would cost Europe much less than the billions it is spending on armaments and be at least as effective" (446-47). Ironically, it seemed that the most effective way to build up a whole would be first to break up the whole: war could be thwarted, this article suggests, with harsh economic measures such as threats of punitive trade sanctions, which capitalize on the impossibility of the German ideal of autarkie and the specialization in resources of the countries.

Between the Acts rethinks these debates on specialization and money in society, putting them into the context of an English country village. Money defines many characters' relations, connecting them together but also separating them. Isa, for instance, is unhappily stuck in her marriage with Giles, whose "little trick" is to assume "the pose of one who bears the burden of the world's woe, making money for her to spend," which is why "[i]t made no difference; his infidelity—but hers did" (68). The links between Giles's occupation as a stock broker, the setting for this occupation, and money, are even clearer in the earlier typescript: "Giles then did the usual trick; shut his lips; frowned; took up the pose of one who bears the burden. He had been in the City all week making money; on the Stock Exchange" (*Pointz Hall* 119). Isa's hopes for alternatives to her financial dependence on Giles mainly rest on Haines, who is "a gentleman farmer" (*BTA* 11).

Through Haines, Woolf depicts Isa's yearning for a pre-industrial society, before the excessive specialization which characterizes modernity. Unlike Leonard's description of modern society in which the sole purpose of work is money, Haines's occupation perhaps retains some of the last vestiges of what Angell described as "household" societies, in which money played a minimal role. In these societies in the Middle Ages, "the essence of the social arrangement did not depend upon an exchange, but upon everyone doing an assigned task and the product being divided by well-established custom or according to traditional hierarchical rights" (*The Story of Money* 22-24). That communities rooted in farming were less influenced by fluctuations in the value of money was attested to by recent events. As Angell writes, "a few years ago in Central Europe, when the device of money had utterly broken down in the midst of the most orderly civilization in the world, and men hurried to get rid of money for goods, since it had lost all stable value," people in the cities, "helpless without money," "starved and froze," whereas "the peasants on the farms and in the forests recked little of the lack of money" (21). The secondary role of money in farming may account for Isa's attraction to Haines as an alternative to her stockbroker husband. He represents an older, simpler world order, which holds more romance in Isa's eyes: "the ravaged, the silent, the romantic gentleman farmer" (11). However, although Woolf contrasts the village community in the novel with that of a "London mob," neither would it qualify as Angell's "'household' type of social organization"; Isa, for example, thinks that everyone here is guilty of the ulterior motive of money: "none speaks with a single voice. None with a voice free from the old vibrations. Always I hear corrupt murmurs; the chink of gold and metal" (94). She herself hides her private thoughts in an object linked to financial interest, writing her poems in a book "bound like an account book in case Giles suspected" (12).

Zwerdling has written that Woolf was "perfectly aware of how easy it is to ignore reality in fabricating" "an older English culture" (308-11). Indeed, the appeal of "gentleman" farming as a return to simpler forms of society was not without its ambiguities. By aligning herself with Haines, Isa would merely be substituting one way of dependence for another. The hierarchy of "gentleman" farming is also problematic. But Isa deliberately refrains from deeper examination, instead always keeping a safe distance from which she can admire and idealize Haines. Throughout the pageant, she keeps turning around to look for him, because he is always separated from her: "She half turned in her seat .... Who was she looking for? William, turning, following her eyes, saw only a man in grey" (51). Apart from his occupation, readers only know that Haines has a "ravaged face" (6) and is married. In his fragmentary representation he retains his "mystery" (6), which may be necessary to maintain Isa's fascination, enabling him to serve as her icon. But it also ensures that he is a distant dream rather than a realistic alternative. Haines is as enigmatic to Isa as the prehistoric imagery is to the characters in the novel, and although both provide some imaginative relief from the predicament which excessive specialization has led to, the narrative prevents the final vindication of either.

Between the Acts, therefore, shares to a certain extent Leonard's view that a wholly isolated, self-contained English culture and nationhood, suggestive of "the economically autarkic sovereign independent state," has in the present day been made an "anachronism and an impossibility" by the "large-scale industrialization of production" since the nineteenth century, which has made nations inextricably interdependent ("De Profundis" 468-69). It also acknowledges that specialization and money are necessary for building "civilization," or the "wall" (111) which the voice at the end of the pageant refers to, because, inevitably, "we are members one of another. Each is part of the whole" (114). They seem fundamental to Woolf's aesthetic vision for the attainment of a meaningful human community, whether on the scale of the village, the nation, or the world. But there are, as I have suggested throughout this article, slight but significant differences between Woolf's and Leonard's views. In *Between the Acts*, there is, to a carefully limited degree, some relief to be found in visions of prehistory and pre-industrial England. The overspecialized state of modernity, which has created ever higher levels of interdependency, and an ever larger role for money, would, it seems, benefit from some regression. Such a partial retreat from excessive interdependency could in fact aid, rather than hinder, the goal of more cooperation.

A balanced use of specialization and money can thus help reconcile the tension between discreteness and unity, so that people neither regress entirely to the undifferentiated mess of the primeval swamp, or become so specialized, without prior coordination and cooperation, that they are mere "orts, scraps and fragments," unable to fit together into a bigger whole. It is the hopeful message, always intermeshed with the darker sense of despair, in *Between the Acts*: "Dispersed are we; who have come together. But, the gramophone asserted, let us retain whatever made that harmony" (116). The aesthetics of simultaneous cohesion and fragmentation in the novel mirrors this precarious balance between the states of an absence of specialization and overspecialization, becoming a vehicle for averting the chaos of either extreme.

Works Cited

Angell, Norman. "Educational and Psychological Factors." *The Intelligent Man's Way to Prevent War*. Ed. Leonard Woolf. London: Victor Gollancz, 1933. 488; 491. Print.

——. "The International Anarchy." *The Intelligent Man's Way to Prevent War*. Ed. Leonard Woolf. London: Victor Gollancz, 1933. 29. Print.

——. *The Story of Money*. 21-24; 147. London: Cassell & Company, 1930. Print.

Beer, Gillian. "Introduction." *Between the Acts*. London: Penguin, 2000. Print.

——. "The Island and the Aeroplane: The Case of Virginia Woolf." *Nation and Narration*. Ed. Homi K. Bhabha. London: Routledge, 1990: 265-90. 265-90. Print.

——. "Rhyming as Resurrection." *Memory and Memorials, 1789-1914: Literary and Cultural Perspectives*. London: Routledge, 2000. 191. Print.

——. "Virginia Woolf and Prehistory." *Arguing with the Past*. London: Routledge, 1989. 159-182. Print.

Carr-Saunders, A. M., and P. A. Wilson. *The Professions*. Oxford: Clarendon Press, 1933. 273-74. Print.

"The Daladier Franc. Stabilization at New Level. 175 to the Pound. Britain and U.S. Agree. Dollar Unchanged." *The Times* 5 May. 1938: A16. *Times Online*. Web. 20 Jan. 2011.

Davenport, Nicholas. "State Capitalism—The Coming Money Revolution." *New Statesman and Nation.* 7 Dec. 1940: 376. Print.

De Gay, Jane. *Virginia Woolf's Novels and the Literary Past.* Edinburgh: Edinburgh UP, 2006. 210. Print.

Esty, Joshua. *A Shrinking Island: Modernism and National Culture in England.* Princeton, NJ: Princeton UP, 2004. 93-107. Print.

Fischer, Louis. "The Economic Crisis in Germany." *New Statesman and Nation.* 21 Mar. 1936: 446-47. Print.

Froula, Christine. *Virginia Woolf and the Bloomsbury Avant-Garde: War, Civilization, Modernity*. New York, NY: Columbia UP, 2005. 312-21. Print.

Hobson, J. A. "The High Road to Peace and Prosperity." *New Statesman and Nation.* 19 Jan. 1935: 67. Print.

"Hunger Breeds War." *New Statesman and Nation.* 2 Jan. 1937: 4. Print.

Huxley, Aldous. *Beyond the Mexique Bay*. London: Chatto and Windus, 1934. 260. Print.

Keynes, John Maynard. *The Collected Writings of John Maynard Keynes*. Ed. Donald Moggridge. 31 vols. Vol. 20-21. London: Macmillan Press, 1981-82. Print.

Keynes, John Maynard. *The Economic Consequences of the Peace*. 1919. London: Macmillan, 1924. 103-210. Print.

Laurence, Patricia. "The Facts and Fugue of War: From *Three Guineas* to *Between the Acts*." *Virginia Woolf and War: Fiction, Reality, and Myth.* Ed. Mark Hussey. Syracuse, NY: Syracuse UP, 1991. 245. Print.

Leaska, Mitchell A. "Dating the Manuscript." *Pointz Hall: The Earlier and Later Typescripts of* Between the Acts. New York: University Publications, 1983. 25-29. Print.

Linett, Maren Tova. *Modernism, Feminism and Jewishness*. Cambridge: Cambridge UP, 2007. 92; 84-97. Print.

"Money, *n*." *OED Online*. 27 Oct. 2009. <http://dictionary.oed.com/cgi/entry/00313968>. Web.

Pridmore-Brown, Michele. "Of Virginia Woolf, Gramophones, and Fascism." *PMLA* 113.3 (1998): 411-12. Print.

See, Sam. "The Comedy of Nature: Darwinian Feminism in Virginia Woolf's *Between the Acts*." *Modernism/modernity* 17.3 (2010). 643. Print.

Skidelsky, Robert. *Politicians and the Slump: The Labour Government of 1929-1931*. 1967. London: Macmillan, 1994. 336. Print.

"Special, *a.*, *adv.*, and *n*." *OED Online*. 16 Jan. 2011. <http://dictionary.oed.com/cgi/entry/50232614>. Web.

"Species, *n*." *OED Online*. 16 Jan. 2011. <http://dictionary.oed.com/cgi/entry/50232637>. Web.

Tate, Trudi. *Modernism, History and the First World War*. Manchester: Manchester UP, 1998. 125. Print.

"Tinker, Tailor." *New Statesman* 3 Mar. 1928. 668. Print.

Wells, H. G. *The World of William Clissold*. 1926. London: Heron Books, 1969. 220-22. Print.

Woolf, Leonard. *Co-operation and the Future of Industry*. London: George Allen & Unwin, 1918. 126-27. Print.

——. "De Profundis." *Political Quarterly* 10.4 (1939): 468-69. Print.

——. *Downhill All the Way: An Autobiography of the Years 1919-1939*. London: Hogarth Press, 1967. Print.

——. "Introduction." *The Intelligent Man's Way to Prevent War*. London: Victor Gollancz, 1933. 16-17. Print.

——. *Quack, Quack!* London: Hogarth Press, 1937. 40; 109. Print.

——. "Utopia and Reality." *Political Quarterly* 11.2 (1940). 181. Print.

——. *The War for Peace*. London: G. Routledge & Sons, 1940. 105; 202; 222; 238-39. Print.

Woolf, Virginia. *Between the Acts*. 1941. Eds. Gillian Beer and Stella McNichol. London: Penguin, 2000. Print.

——. *The Diary of Virginia Woolf*. Ed. Anne Olivier Bell. 5 vols. Vol. 4-5. London: Hogarth Press, 1982-84. Print.

——. *The Letters of Virginia Woolf*. Ed. Nigel Nicolson. 6 vols. Vol. 3-5. London: Hogarth Press, 1977-79. Print.

——. *Pointz Hall: The Earlier and Later Typescripts of* Between the Acts. Ed. Mitchell A. Leaska. New York: University Publications, 1983. Print.

——. *A Room of One's Own/Three Guineas*. 1929/1938. Ed. Michèle Barrett. London: Penguin, 2000. Print.

Zwerdling, Alex. *Virginia Woolf and the Real World*. Berkeley, CA: U of California P, 1986. 308-11. Print.

Woolf's Copernican Shift: Nonhuman Nature in Virginia Woolf's Short Fiction

Diana L. Swanson

Nature is what we know–
Yet have no art to say–
So impotent Our Wisdom is
To her simplicity

—Emily Dickinson, #668

The ecological crisis is not just or even primarily a crisis of technology, but is rather a crisis of rationality, morality, and imagination.

—Val Plumwood, *Environmental Culture: The Ecological Crisis of Reason*

In *Middlemarch*, George Eliot writes that "if we had a keen vision and feeling of all ordinary human life, it would be like hearing the grass grow and the squirrel's heart beat, and we should die of that roar which lies on the other side of silence" (ch. XX). In much of her fiction, Virginia Woolf is intent on capturing "the other side of silence." Critics and common readers have always responded to Woolf's probings and evocations of the ebb and flow of "ordinary human life," of "the things people don't say" as Terence Hewet puts it in *The Voyage Out* (1915). Only recently, however, have critics paid much attention to Woolf's attempts to represent the "other side of silence" of the nonhuman world.

Louise Westling argues in her important article "Virginia Woolf and the Flesh of the World," that over the course of Woolf's career she "increasingly placed human ambitions and systems of meaning against the backdrop of enormous geological forces and vast reaches of time. Increasingly, she sought to portray the non-human, or what David Abram calls the 'more than human' world within which we are tiny and only momentary presences" (856). Among others, Westling, Gillian Beer, Mark Hussey, Elizabeth G. Lambert, and L. Elizabeth Waller have each, in different but interconnecting ways, discussed Woolf's critique of the long and deep tradition of subject/object, mind/matter, culture/nature dualism in Western thought and her evocation of an ecological vision of the world in which human beings are part of "the kinship of the living" (Westling 867).

Critics generally agree that Woolf's experimental short fiction of the late teens and twenties laid the groundwork for her modernist novels. Less generally noted is that Woolf's years of formal experimentation in the late nineteen-teens and early twenties included experimentation with representing nonhuman existence and subjectivity, with evoking the "roar" of nonhuman nature. In this essay, I argue that Woolf's experimental short fiction demonstrates how human language and literary form can be used to undermine the anthropocentrism of Western culture, including the objectification of the nonhuman, as well as to evoke and recognize the reality of other-than-human being in itself rather than as a projection of human desires and conceptions. By comparing Woolf's earliest short stories to her experimental stories and sketches of 1917-1921, I show that the writing of the experimental short fiction effected a Copernican shift for Woolf: the human world is no longer the center of her writerly universe. This paradigm shift (Kuhn, *Copernican*; *Structure*) helped to foster the worldview of her longer works.

1. Solipsism, Otherness, Literature, and Human Knowledge of "Nature"

I suggest that Woolf's short fiction shows her moving toward representing the subjectivities of nonhuman beings, but how can nature "speak" in humans' literature, other than metaphorically and about human concerns? Is it possible for human beings to perceive the subjectivity of nonhuman beings? Does representing nonhuman beings as having knowledge, agency, and subjectivity impute human characteristics to nonhuman beings? The divide and distinction between human and nonhuman seems to many people too wide for humans to cross with any pretension to truth.[1]

While avoidance of anthropomorphism is based on the well-founded concern not to project human concepts and feelings onto nonhumans, the belief that human beings cannot perceive, know, or express the nonhuman as anything other than a projection of our own minds and desires raises both ethical and epistemological problems. First, it produces a profoundly solipsistic view of the world, a human species solipsism. Second, it restricts the power and potential of the human capacity to know to looking into a mirror, to knowing only ourselves, to a species narcissism. Third, it makes the vast other-than-human world not only unknowable but also unknowing and without agency; in this sense, human species solipsism and narcissism objectifies and deadens the rest of the world, as the title of historian

[1] My focus here is on the possibility of literary representation of the nonhuman world as having its own ontological and subjective status; I do not take on the question of the status of humans as animals and animal/human relations. Critical animal studies is a burgeoning area within ecocriticism and ecological scholarship generally. For insight into this field, see, for example, Westling's "Literature, the Environment, and the Question of the Posthuman" (which, among other things, treats Woolf's *Between the Acts*), her "Merleau-Ponty's Human-Animality Intertwining and the Animal Question," Cary Wolfe's *Zoontologies: The Question of the Animal*, and Carrie Rohman's *Stalking the Subject: Modernism and the Animal*.

Carolyn Merchant's book, *The Death of Nature*, underlines. Finally, rejection of the possibility of recognizing and representing nonhuman subjectivity participates in the Western subject/object, mind/matter, culture/nature dualism based on notions of reason as essentially and exclusively human and of nature as a passive object of our knowledge and control (Plumwood). From this perspective, other-than-human nature has been defined out of "personhood." Thus, modern[2] Western forms of knowing the natural world become what ecofeminist philosopher Val Plumwood calls "monological" as they construct a subject/object dualism in the process of knowledge creation. The "object" of knowing becomes, in this view, a "nullity, never itself a reciprocal knower or active in disclosing knowledge, *never itself the subject of a narrative we can hear*" (45, emphasis added). Human knowledge thus becomes a monologue, a soliloquy of the human species rather than an interaction and a dialogue (polylogue?) with the rest of the world.

Plumwood proposes "translation" as a useful way to think about representation of the other and to get out of the epistemological and ethical trap of what I am calling species solipsism. She notes that human cross-cultural and cross-language translation is not rejected out of hand as impossible, but rather requires recognition and discussion of the difficulty and uncertainty of translation. "Cross-species representation, like cross-cultural representation," according to Plumwood,

> is not automatically colonising or self-imposing, and may express motives and meanings of sympathy, support, and admiration. . . . We might expect an appropriate methodology for dealing with cross-species conceptual difference and translation to be one which *stressed corrigibility and open expectations*. Dealing with both human and non-human cases of translation indeterminacy requires openness to the other and careful, sensitive and self-critical observation which actively seeks to uncover perspectival and centric biases. (60, my italics)

Plumwood's emphasis on uncertainty, openness, and self-critique is important for thinking about how literature can function as one human method for recognizing, imagining, and expressing—or, as Plumwood might put it, translating—the nonhuman world as alive, knowing, and possessed of agency.[3]

[2] I use "modern" here in the historical and philosophical sense of post-Renaissance, rather than in the literary and art-historical sense of the aesthetic movement of modern*ism*.
[3] Plumwood's argument echoes philosopher of science Sandra Harding's epistemology and Plumwood, indeed, points out Harding's emphasis on dialogue, as opposed to monologue, as necessary to produce more accurate and less totalizing knowledge (44). In *Whose Science? Whose Knowledge?* Harding argues that, since all knowledge creators operate in a particular time and place, the traditional standard of objectivity as excluding all passions

Literature can help us make the leaps of imagination necessary to move towards understanding of and empathy for experiences and realities different from our own. We see this most readily in cases of human otherness. Whoever we are in the early twenty-first century, when we read of Lord and Lady Macbeth, of Sethe and Paul D, of Anna Karenina, we get glimpses of human otherness. The experience of reading can lead us to recognize profound otherness (rather than to objectify the other) and to know something about an other—whether the otherness is of time, place, culture, or experience. We do not get total, infallible knowledge of the realities of human life in the English Renaissance or in nineteenth-century America or Russia, but we do achieve situated, partial knowledge of experiences and perspectives that are not our own. Paradoxically, literature, a linguistic and cultural production, can help us get beyond the limits of our particular languages, cultures, and times. Similarly, literature can help us recognize and "translate" the profound otherness *and* subjectivities of the nonhuman world.

Woolf's use of architectural metaphors to discuss literary form is of help in understanding this power of literature. For example, in *A Room of One's Own*, she says that "a book is not made up of sentences laid end to end, but of sentences built, if an image helps, into arcades or domes" (80). In "Phases of Fiction," she says that "when the book is finished, we seem to see . . . something girding it about like the firm road of Defoe's storytelling; or we see it shaped and symmetrical with dome and column complete, like *Pride and Prejudice* and *Emma*" (143). Architecture as an art and a technology works with empty physical space. A building is not a home, a classroom, or a parliament. A building is walls, floors, ceilings, stairs, windows, and doors arranged in particular ways to create empty spaces within which

---

and particularities is impossible. By including dialogue with others as well as investigation of our own social locations and biases within knowledge-creation processes, however, we can achieve a standard of objectivity "stronger" than that conventionally defined (Harding, Chapter 6 *passim*). In this way, Harding maintains objectivity as a goal that, while incompletely attainable, is necessary to creating accurate knowledge and redefines knowledge as inevitably situated and partial rather than universal and total. Similarly, we can recognize that human understanding of other-than-human subjectivity is incompletely achievable yet is at the same time a necessary goal in order to create more accurate, ethical, situated, and ecological knowledge. Harding is a leading proponent of feminist standpoint theory which, after four decades of development, is an important and useful school of feminist thought. One of feminist standpoint theory's major contributions has been to offer a workable alternative to positivism's limited definition of objectivity and post-structuralism's tendency toward relativism. For a helpful overview of feminist standpoint theory, see *The Feminist Standpoint Theory Reader*, edited by Harding. For discussion of the application of standpoint theory to literature, see "Postcolonial Fiction and the Outsider Within: Toward a Literary Practice of Feminist Standpoint Theory" by Brooke Lenz. For the application of feminist standpoint theory to ecofeminism, see "Feminism and the Treatment of Animals: From Care to Dialogue" by Josephine Donovan.

people then live and move. By furnishing those empty spaces and by living and interacting in certain ways within them, humans create a home, a classroom, or a parliament. Literature also works with empty space. Through particular arrangements of words and sentences, it creates emotional and mental spaces in which that which is wordless can be made perceivable by active reading. The meeting of the literature and the reader's mind and heart creates a space of feeling. Thus literature gestures towards what cannot be directly articulated, or "exposed" in expository writing. For example, some experiences, such as extreme grief, love, or horror, or the complexity of mourning or of mystical revelation, leave us "speechless." These experiences elude the power of words. Yet, certain poems, novels, essays, or plays can create structures of words, images, and plot that elicit such emotions and lend us insight into our own and others' experiences. As the particular arrangement of the spaces in a building allows and prevents certain kinds of movement and activity, so the particular arrangement of literary components allows and prevents particular modes of feeling and thinking. Thus, works of literature create mental and emotional spaces which give a shape to and therefore render perceivable "unspeakable" experiences and understandings.[4] Literature creates meaning which it does not say, which cannot be said in words, but which it nevertheless enables readers to perceive and feel. As Edward T. Bishop argues concerning "Kew Gardens," "the quality [Woolf] called 'life' or the 'essential thing' refused to be fixed by a phrase, but it could be arrested, briefly, by a net of words, words that evoke as well as indicate, that conspired to produce their own luminous halo, rendering

[4] In *The Reading of Silence: Virginia Woolf in the English Tradition*, Patricia Ondek Laurence explores the ways Woolf gives the "unsaid," the "unspoken," and the "unsayable" presence and meaning in her novels. Laurence discusses the forms of Woolf's novels mainly in terms of music but occasionally also in terms of architecture, saying that "on the structural level, beyond a sight or an emotion expressed in a sentence, there is the flux and flow of certain emotional patterns that are captured in the form of the novel" (178). She asserts that "this architecting—the patterning of sound, silence, and motion—can be found in sentences, chapters, and novels" (184). Laurence argues that Woolf attempts to include the rhythms and voices of nature in her later novels *The Waves* and *Between the Acts*. She asserts that, like composer John Cage, Woolf had a revelation that "humanity and nature, not separate, are in this world together" (Cage quoted in Laurence, 193) and that, like Cage, Woolf incorporates the sounds and silences of nature into her art. In Laurence's view, the sounds and silences of nature function in *The Waves* and *Between the Acts* as "a silent backdrop" to the human narratives (197), as reminders of mortality, time, and human smallness. Important as Laurence's work is for opening up these questions, however, her discussion of nature in Woolf's work remains focused largely on the ways that nonhuman nature frames or represents human concerns. She also seems to assume that "life" (meaning individual human lives) and "nature" are disjunct (180, 196), thus replicating the human/nature binary. See the statements, for example, that "life and nature . . . are in harmony" and "the rhythms of nature prevail over human life in the end" (196).

(by inducing) a process of consciousness rather than a concrete picture" (275). Or, in other words, "the reality Woolf conveys is apprehended through the *experience* of reading" (272, my emphasis).

In this way, literature can be central to our ability to recognize the reality of other-than-human nature. Birds, dirt, rocks, plants, insects, animals do not use words; so how can human beings understand the nonhuman and in turn represent it in human language? Recognizing and writing the nonhuman requires recognizing its otherness, its difference from human beings, while not objectifying it, that is, not making the nonhuman world simply a reflection of human beings or a tool for our use. *It requires disjoining otherness from objectification and finding literary methods to create mental and emotional spaces that enable human recognition of the nonhuman.* In this way, literature can be a powerful tool to help solve the ecological "crisis of morality, rationality, and imagination" (Plumwood).

Woolf writes about this non-objectifying recognition of the otherness of the nonhuman world when she compares the way Dorothy Wordsworth wrote about nature to the way Mary Wollstonecraft did ("Four Figures"). As Jocelyn Bartkevicius points out, "when Woolf wrote about the sky, what often interested her more than any image or symbol was the sky itself. Consider the stark contrast she draws . . . between Mary Wollstonecraft and Dorothy Wordsworth" (246). Woolf says that "Dorothy [unlike Wollstonecraft] never confused her own soul with the sky" ("Four Figures" 149). As Bartkevicius underlines, Woolf was interested in Wordsworth's ability to "look at the sky—and indeed at such 'vegetables' as trees and grass—and see them in themselves . . . not as the other to be subordinated to herself or to social and political needs, interests, and agendas" (247). L. Elizabeth Waller emphasizes what she sees as an "'ecological' dialogue of human characters engaged directly and profoundly with nonhuman characters" in Woolf's novels. Waller suggests that, in *Orlando*, for example, Woolf "created, or *translated*, subjects that speak and act on levels of movement and sensation to produce utterance, presence—'deer stepped nearer'; 'summer clouds stayed'; 'rooks wheeled round'" (143, emphasis mine). Waller's analysis supports the idea that Woolf's work implicitly challenges what Plumwood calls the monological epistemology of Western thought, opening readers, if we are willing, to "conversation" with nonhuman others.[5]

Charlotte Zoë Walker has also investigated what she calls "the presence and

[5] However, Waller speaks of Woolf's writing evoking "subject-object diffusion" and asserts that, in *The Waves* for example, "each human protagonist . . . gains a sense of self only by dissolving identity into the fabric of more-than-human" (149). Merging with nonhuman being can be another way of projecting human desires and goals onto nonhuman beings, making them, once again, into tools for human use by disallowing their profound otherness. Waller, however, does not discuss this ethical problem nor how Woolf may or may not be participating in or avoiding it.

dialogue with nature" in Woolf's short fiction (173). In her article "Letting in the Sky," she argues that Woolf's short stories incorporate nature in four ways: by exploring the "interrelatedness of all forms of life," by "reading the 'text' of nature for answers" to existential questions, by examining the "boundaries between nature and civilization," and by "set[ting] up a dialogue between nature and patriarchal institutions to offer a devastating critique of patriarchy" (174). Walker's article lays out helpful areas for further ecocritical analysis of Woolf's oeuvre but does not distinguish sufficiently between ways in which Woolf's works may use "nature" symbolically as a way to represent the human and ways Woolf's works may open up possibilities for human recognition of nonhuman existence and subjectivity in itself—the necessary foundation for escaping solipsism and monological thinking.

In the quotation from George Eliot which opens this article, "hearing the grass grow and the squirrel's heart beat" is a simile for being keenly attuned to people's feelings, for being fully compassionate. Thus, Eliot is using the grass and the squirrel to represent an aspect of human life. Wollstonecraft's and Eliot's way of writing nature, the way of human species solipsism, is the dominant tradition in English letters. In her modernist push beyond the nineteenth-century literary tradition she inherited and admired, Woolf opened up possibilities for representing the grass and the squirrel as themselves. She makes other-than-human nature "the subject of a narrative we can hear" and thus offers help in the process of developing less objectifying and more vitalizing relationships with the rest of the living world.

2. In the Beginning: Woolf's Earliest Fiction, 1906-1909

Nonhuman nature—in the shapes of earth, sky, water, insects, birds, animals—holds a significant place in Woolf's fiction from the beginning but its function and Woolf's mode of representing it shifts over time. In her earliest fiction written in 1906 and 1909 (Dick 289-290), nonhuman nature serves a traditional literary function; references to nature describe human concerns. In some cases, Woolf's narrators use nonhuman nature through simile or metaphor to describe human beings—usually marginalized people such as women or the lower classes—a metaphorical move consonant with the dominant Western trope of identifying those lower on the social scale with nature and especially animals. In other cases, nature becomes a soothing refuge from human cares or reflects the peace or turbulence of human affairs, again invoking traditional views of the nature/human relationship in the forms of the pastoral and the Romantic.

In "Phyllis and Rosamond," Phyllis feels "like a bird with wings pinioned" while at the Tristrams' party, observing that the young Tristram women enjoy a wider education and greater freedom than she and her sister (24). In this case, the young Virginia Stephen uses bird imagery to suggest women's social suppression as did such earlier writers as Charlotte Brontë, George Eliot, Elizabeth Barrett Browning, and many others. Later in the party, given the chance at a private conversation with Miss Sylvia Tristram, Phyllis "snatched at it like a dog at a bone; indeed her face wore a gaunt ravenous expression" (26). Woolf also uses natural images as metaphors for a woman in "The Mysterious Case of Miss V." The narrator describes the "expedition" to call on Miss V. as like "set[ting] out in an omnibus to visit the shadow of a blue bell in Kew Gardens . . . or to catch the down from a dandelion" (31). Once again, in "Memoirs of a Novelist," a woman is imaged as like a nonhuman being, albeit in this case unflatteringly; Miss Willat is "like some gorged spider at the centre of her web" (72). Finally, the second narrator of "The Journal of Mistress Joan Martyn," the young lady of the manor, uses nature images to describe the lower classes. Joan describes the servant, William, as "so ancient . . . that one might as well ask the pollard willow in the fen to share one's fire, or join one's talk" (46). Similarly, she describes the home of a family of serfs as "more like the burrow of some rabbit on the heath than the house of a man" and doubts whether Beatrice Somers "could have spoken, or whether snarling and howling was her only language." She describes Beatrice and her husband Peter as "pests" bred by her land (52-53). Less brutalizing but still expressing her perception of the other person as alien, is Joan's description of the travelling bard: "he listened to our prayers no more than the owl in the ivy: saying merely, 'I must go on my way.' . . . we felt as though some strange bird had rested on our roof a moment, and flown on" (57). Finally, she uses a well-tended domestic animal to describe herself on a pilgrimage to the local shrine: "start with your spirit fresh like a corn fed horse" (57). In these various examples of simile and metaphor, nonhuman beings function as descriptors of human beings and often as ways to express the narrator's sense that the other person (such as Miss V. or Beatrice Somers) is mysterious and incomprehensible or to express the narrator's trepidatious envy of the other on the one hand (Joan toward the bard) or fear, contempt, and hostility on the other hand (Joan toward the serfs and the narrator toward Miss Willat).[6]

Nature is also envisioned as a sanctuary for or a reflection of humans in these early stories. For example, Joan Martyn describes the land itself as a grandmother and as a sanctuary:

> Norfolk and the parish of Long Winton . . . is to me what my own grandmother is; a tender parent, dear and familiar, and silent to whom I shall return in time. O how blessed it would be never to marry, or grow

[6] In "The Journal of Mistress Joan Martyn," Woolf gives the nature imagery solely to Joan; it may be that Woolf was aware of the class connotations of such "animalizing" of people and was using them to indicate Joan's class-constructed perspective.

> old; but to spend one's life innocently and indifferently among the trees. and rivers which alone keep one cool and childlike in the midst of the troubles of the world! (52)

Here Joan describes her love of the land she has grown up exploring with her father's steward, Anthony, and turns to it as an imagined escape from the uncertainty and anxiety she feels about coming of age and marrying. Her vision both personifies the land and pastoralizes it, creating a typical pastoral scene in which the land, trees, and rivers embody the possibility of an innocent, calm, prelapsarian, "childlike" existence. The narrator of "Memoirs of a Novelist" imagines Miss Willat similarly escaping the pain and awkwardness of a patriarchal rite of passage for young women, the first dance: "she fixed her eyes upon the festoons . . . and tried to fancy that she sat on a rock with the bees humming round her" (66). To Miss Willat bees seemed happier and less intimidating than beaux and the marriage market.

Both "The Journal" and "Memoirs" also use nature to mirror human society. When her father and brothers return from a dangerous journey, to Joan nature reflects the peace of human affairs: "the peace of the nation, and the prosperity of our own small corner of it . . . make a complete circle of satisfaction; you may pass from the smooth dome of sky, to our own roof without crossing any gulf" (57). When Miss Willat suffers from "terrible self-consciousness" and a sense of the evil of the human world, which arises at least in part from the lack of fit between her personality and desires and the conventional expectations for women, she turns to nature imagery to express her situation. "'Am I the only blot upon the face of nature?' she asked in May, 1841. 'The birds are carolling [sic] outside my windows, the very insects are putting off the winter's dross'" (67). Here Miss Willat naturalizes the very social conventions that alienate and marginalize her, using birds and insects to express "normal" happiness in the social activities of courting (it is spring and the birds and the bees are active) and creating heteronormative families.

Thus, in these short stories of 1906 to 1909, Woolf uses nature imagery in a quite traditional literary manner. Similes and metaphors using nonhuman nature—whether birds, insects, plants, animals, or the land itself—serve to either characterize human beings or mirror human society. References to nature on the part of both the characters within the stories and the narrators of the stories remain within the mode of human species solipsism.

3. De-objectifying Nature: Woolf's Experimental Short Fiction of 1917-1921

In the latter half of the 1910s, Woolf turned again to writing short fiction, this time as studies for a new way of writing. In 1930, Woolf described two of these experimental pieces, "Monday or Tuesday" and "Blue and Green," to Ethel Smyth as "the wild outbursts of freedom, inarticulate, ridiculous, unprintable, mere outcries" (*L4* 231). For Woolf, these sketches pushed the boundaries of the unsayable and were the products of moments of freedom and vitality, of seeing past old rules and realities. In these lyrical short stories, Kathryn N. Benzel proposes, Woolf "invents a new type of narrative that disregards the conventional dichotomy between reason and emotion" and that "connects the reader and the writer in a shared moment of creativity" (171, 164). Discussing "Kew Gardens," Alice Stavely also argues that Woolf "devises a new narrative form" (48) and develops "a feminist narratology through her experiments in writing short fiction" (59). Michelle Levy considers nonhuman objects in Woolf's short stories, tracing Woolf's interest in the relationship between "the imaginative powers of the human mind and the facticity of the external world" (140-141). Levy argues, as I do, that Woolf "decenter[s] the human presence in fiction" (145). All three of these studies of Woolf's short fiction emphasize significant connections among Woolf's narrative experimentation, her feminism, her shifting of the center of attention, and her revising of the relations of authority such that the reader becomes a co-artist, connections that are important to my argument as well. All three essays also focus primarily on how the short fiction represents the process of human consciousness. In contrast, I focus in the discussion below on how Woolf developed new ways to represent the nonhuman, ways that enable recognition and translation of the subjectivity and the otherness of the nonhuman while not objectifying it.

Written during World War I, "The Mark on the Wall" (1917) dramatizes this shifting from an old reality to a new one through the musings of the first person narrator. The narrator feels the old certainties slipping away as the experiences of the war, even for those living a domestic life in England, undermine traditional authorities and truths. The story is set in that quintessential Victorian English domestic scene, the parlor at tea-time. More accurately, and significantly, it is set just after tea-time on a winter's day, as it is also set just after the heyday of British global dominance, when the empire is beginning to disintegrate. And, indeed, the story does not create the sense of cozy certainty one expects from a Victorian tea-time scene. The narrator notices a dark mark, marring the whiteness of her wall, and wonders what it is. It could be a nail hole, a small, black rose leaf left over from summer, a nail head; each possibility leads to ruminations about housekeeping, history, and the impossibility of keeping control over the physical world through dusting and cleaning or of pinning down the past through sifting and sorting the fragmentary evidence left. Time is out of our control; physical objects are out of our control—think of how many objects one has unaccountably lost in one's lifetime, the narrator says. She thinks that even if she got up to look at the mark on the wall she probably wouldn't be able to tell what it was, "because once a thing's done, no one ever knows how it happened" (78). This mundane detail of a mark on the wall thus leads the narrator to meditate on the nature of reality and the uncertainty of human knowledge. The narrator's nascent epistemology resembles, humorously, that being created by the new quantum physics in the early twentieth century.[7] The work of Einstein, Heisenberg and others was leading scientists to the conclusion that there is an inherent limitation to the certainty of human knowledge about the physical world.

Woolf's narrator, noticing that the mark looks like it protrudes from the wall, imagines that it would feel like a "smooth tumulus like those of the barrows on the South Downs which are, they say, either tombs or camps" (80). She follows up on this evidentiary and logical problem (are they tombs or camps?), imagining the antiquaries digging for evidence, inclining to the tomb theory or the camp theory. Her imagined antiquary, a retired colonel, prides himself on collecting evidence for both sides of the debate, then writes a pamphlet for the camp side, dies, and his excavated arrowheads are given to the local museum, "proving," the narrator says, "I really don't know what" (81). Her breezy and humorous depiction of the debates over the archaeological evidence echoes contemporary developments in physics. Like Heisenberg, the narrator arrives at uncertainty: "No, no, nothing is proved, nothing is known," she declares (81).[8]

The narrator explicitly connects this uncertainty about reality to the social changes underway in the first two decades of the twentieth century, and specifically to the challenges to the masculinist, classist hierarchy of English society. She says that the word "reality" has a "military sound" and "recalls leading articles, cabinet ministers—a whole class of things indeed which as a child one thought the thing itself, the standard thing, the real thing, from which one could not depart save at the risk of nameless damnation. . . . There was a rule for everything" (80). The narrator thus gestures towards a Victorian world that is passing away, a world of definite rules, procedures, and realities, of prime ministers, newspaper editori-

[7] Westling also connects the influence of the new physics to Woolf's ecological writing but emphasizes the blurring of categories and boundaries, such as time and space and human and nonhuman, "the porous, the metamorphic boundaries between forms and species, and our deep enmeshment within this dynamic, shifting reality" ("Virginia Woolf" 859).

[8] Einstein's relativity theory and Bohr and Sommerfeld's quantum mechanics were famously shaking the foundations of scientific reality in the first two decades of the twentieth century. In the early 1920s, quantum theory was shown to be inadequate and one problem area was the nature of light: is it particle or wave? There was evidence for both theories. Heisenberg, at work on these problems in quantum mechanics, tried to measure the position and the momentum of subatomic particles and discovered that the act of observing changes the observed. The more precise measurement you make of the position of a subatomic particle, the less precise you can be about its momentum, and vice versa. In 1927, he published his paper on the Uncertainty Principle.

als, and the military, of mandatory tea-time and Sunday walks. Discovering that these realities "were half phantoms" is both "shocking" and "wonderful." Yet this freedom from the old standards for reality leaves an absence, an uncertainty about what standards to use, about how to define reality:

> What now takes the place of those things I wonder, those real standard things? Men perhaps, should you be a woman; the masculine point of view which governs our lives, which sets the standard, which establishes Whitaker's Table of Precedency, which has become I suppose, since the war half a phantom to many men and women, which soon, one may hope, will be laughed into the dustbin where the phantoms go, the mahogany sideboards and Landseer prints, Gods and Devils, Hell and so forth, leaving us all with an intoxicating sense of illegitimate freedom—if freedom exists. (80)

In *The Complete Shorter Fiction of Virginia Woolf*, Susan Dick states that "Whitaker's Table of Precedency" probably refers to "The Peerage of the United Kingdom" in *Whitaker's Almanack* (291 n. 2), which, as the narrator tells us later, establishes who has more status than whom and thus who has precedence over whom. The narrator hopes that the upheavals and disillusionment of the war will help to laugh into the dustbin not only the Victorian style of furniture and art but also the hierarchical system of authority, sexism, and social class represented by Whitaker's precedencies.

The narrator imagines an existence without this authority and hierarchy, or as she puts it, "without professors or specialists or house-keepers with the profiles of policemen," a "peaceful" world of "open fields" (81) where one's thoughts can wander. When she realizes that Whitaker's "Table of Precedency" prevents this world, she wants to jump up and see what the mark on the wall is. She speculates that this desire is "Nature once more at her old game of self-preservation" because "this train of thought," she perceives, "is threatening mere waste of energy, even some collision with reality, for who will ever be able to lift a finger against Whitaker's Table of Precedency?" (82). The narrator understands the impulse to jump up and look at the mark to be a way to avoid a disturbing train of thought. However, looking again at the mark on the wall also gives the narrator "a satisfying sense of reality which at once turns the two Archbishops and the Lord High Chancellor to the shadows of shades" (82). In other words, the physical presence of the mark on the wall gives the narrator a glimpse of a reality alternative to that of the seemingly intransigent British social system (a human cultural construction), a sense of "the impersonal world which is proof of some existence other than ours" (82), a sense that the human is not the whole world: "that is what one wants to be sure of" (82).

Thus the narrator's openness to uncertainty and "corrigibility" (cf. Plumwood) leads her to recognize the nonhuman as real: there is "some existence other than ours."[9]

These meditations then lead the narrator to imagine the life experiences of a tree:

> the close dry sensation of being wood; then the grinding of the storm; then the slow, delicious ooze of sap. . . . The song of birds must sound very loud and strange in June; and how cold the feet of insects must feel upon it, as they make laborious progresses up the creases of the bark, or sun themselves upon the thin green awning of the leaves, and look straight in front of them with diamond-cut red eyes. (82-83)

Thus, this narrator imagines the subjectivity of a nonhuman being, taking seriously the possibility that a tree—usually excluded from subjectivity even more than animals and birds—has a perspective on the world. The tree experiences being dry, feels the ooze of sap in the spring, hears the birds, feels the insects and the wind. I suggest that, to borrow philosopher Thomas Nagel's distinction in his classic essay "What is it Like to Be a Bat?," rather than personifying the tree, that is, imagining what a human being would feel like being a tree, the narrator tries to imagine how a tree feels. Note that the phrasing ("must sound," "must feel") indicates the speculativeness of this passage. The narrator thus indicates awareness of the uncertainty of her tree portrait and openness to another view, enacting the corrigibility and uncertainty that Plumwood suggests must accompany our "translations" of nonhumans. In this way, the narrator is starting to imagine the world from a nonhuman perspective, starting to shift the human from the center.

"The Mark on the Wall" ends with the narrator's musings interrupted by her companion who exclaims "'Curse this war; God damn this war! . . . All the same, I don't see why we should have a snail on our wall.' Ah, the mark on the wall! It was a snail" (83). The mark on the wall, which represents nonhuman reality and offers some respite from the social, intellectual, and martial violence of Whitaker's Precedencies and all they represent, is a snail. Thus Woolf pokes fun at her narra-

[9] In "Letting" and "The Book," Walker also notes the story's use of Whitaker's Table of Precedency as representative of patriarchy and hierarchy. Walker argues that in many of her works Woolf suggests an opposition between patriarchy and nature and a "complicity between nature and women with no investment in the Table of Precedency" ("Letting" 183). However, I think that Woolf's representations of the human/nature and man/woman relationships are more complex and nuanced than oppositional and binary. With regard to "The Mark on the Wall," I think Walker's analysis misinterprets the passage about "Nature's old game of self-preservation" and does not sufficiently take note of the functioning of the first person narration; in my view, the main focus of the story is the narrator's (not Woolf's) train of thought and the development of her recognition of the nonhuman world.

tor's musings and debates, while at the same time underlining their seriousness by offering one more example of the other-than-human being of the material world, of the tenuousness of human policing of human-created boundaries and categories like outside (where the snail "belongs") and inside (where clean, painted walls and parlor furniture belong). Even "housekeepers with the profiles of policemen" cannot keep everything in line and in place (81).

"Kew Gardens" (1919) picks up on the use of a snail to represent nonhuman reality and moves the point of view farther from the human. The story begins in "the oval-shaped flower-bed" with its green stalks and red, blue, and yellow petals with the light filtering through them: "The light fell either upon the smooth grey back of a pebble, or the shell of a snail with its brown circular veins" (84). The third-person narrator describes the people walking past only to the extent that they are within ear and eye shot of the flower bed. The narrator reports parts of their ongoing conversations and as they walk on into the distance, they "soon [diminish] in size among the trees and [look] half transparent as the sunlight and shade [swim] over their backs in large trembling irregular patches" (85). The patches of sunlight and shade play over the backs of the human beings as they do over the pebbles and the snail in the flower bed beneath the red, blue, and yellow blooms. The human beings are in the same relation to the sun and Kew and its trees as the snail is to the sun and the flowerbed and its flowers. Thus, the human characters are not the central focus but are treated similarly to the nonhuman beings. Woolf gets the rest of the world into the picture—bugs, plants, snail, thrush, earth, pebbles, sunlight, shade—and has shifted the center of focus away from the human; more than that, she creates a snail's eye view of the world:

> brown cliffs with deep green lakes in the hollows, flat blade-like trees that waved from root to tip, round boulders of grey stone, vast crumpled surfaces of a thin crackling texture—all these objects lay across the snail's progress between one stalk and another to his goal. Before he had decided whether to circumvent the arched tent of a dead leaf or to breast it there came past the bed the feet of other human beings. (85-86)

And again we hear bits and pieces of conversation, see a few moments of these people's walk through Kew.

Thus, the rhythm of the story goes back and forth between the human wanderers in Kew and the nonhuman. The narration alternates between describing the humans and their movements and conversations and describing the flowers, the leaves, and the snail, the thrush, the insects, and their movements. This narrator is very different from the narrator of "The Mark on the Wall"; the third-person narrator reports and describes rather than interprets and searches for meaning.

The narrator seems to be sitting still by the flowerbed and paying attention to everything happening on that one piece of earth. Readers "hear" parts of human conversations but do not get to follow any of the human characters to any sense of resolution. In this way, the story frustrates traditional narrative expectations. The story asks us as readers to give up our focus on people and their desires and goals which are implicitly compared to the snail's goal, and the thrush's and the butterflies'. Instead of giving us insights into and resolutions of the human beings' relationships and problems, "Kew Gardens" asks us to be open to the possibility that the other-than-human beings present in the same place as the human characters also have goals and problems and make decisions. The snail "decided" whether to go around or over the leaf (86); the thrush "chose to hop" (89). The story also asks us to experience rhythm, shape, color, light, texture, and to experience them from the snail's perspective as much as from the perspective of the human beings; it focuses on sensuous experience rather than the pursuit of a linear narrative or the fate of a character. As Benzel argues concerning "Blue and Green" and "Monday or Tuesday," "to read these pieces is not to accumulate details in the conventional narrative sense of plot and characterization, but to experience a visionary moment . . . one that replicates an immediate emotion, a sense perception, some heightened sensibility or cognition" (157-158). In this story, Woolf asks us to sit still and pay attention to the nonhuman as well as the human and to pay attention to our bodily senses, especially to sight and sound, and the experiences and thus the knowledge our senses give us. She asks us to *be in* Kew Gardens rather than to go through Kew Gardens.

The story pans out in a wide-angle shot, so to speak, just at the end, placing Kew Gardens in the context of the city, where "the motor omnibuses were turning their wheels and changing their gears; like a vast nest of Chinese boxes all of wrought steel turning ceaselessly one within another the city murmured; on the top of which the voices cried aloud and the petals of myriads of flowers flashed their colours into the air" (89). This final paragraph both continues and disrupts the sensuous experience of "Kew Gardens"; continues it in the sense that the emphasis remains on the sensuous experiences of sight and sound, disrupts it in the sense that the reference to the city is a reminder that Kew Gardens is part of a city—London—which is like a vast machine, "like a vast nest of Chinese boxes all of wrought steel turning ceaselessly one within another," a city of industry and empire.

"Kew Gardens" begins with the flowers and the snail and ends with the city, with human commerce and government. In the short sketch "Monday or Tuesday" (1921), the hectic human city and human pursuits are framed at beginning and end by the sky and a heron. The body of this short sketch is composed of choppy sentences in which prosaic snippets of everyday urban human life weave in and out of a questioning search for "truth":

> Desiring truth, awaiting it, laboriously distilling a few words, for ever desiring–(a cry starts to the left, another to the right. Wheels strike divergently. Omnibuses conglomerate in conflict)–for ever desiring–(the clock asseverates with twelve distinct strokes that it is midday; light sheds gold scales; children swarm)–for ever desiring truth. Red is the dome; coins hang on the trees; smoke trails from the chimneys; bark, shout, cry 'Iron for sale'–and truth? (131)

This hectic rush of the business of human life and this anxious and unsatisfied search for truth contrast with the peace and presence of the heron and the sky. The sketch begins thus: "Lazy and indifferent, shaking space easily from his wings, knowing his way, the heron passes over the church beneath the sky. White and distant, absorbed in itself, endlessly the sky covers and uncovers, moves and remains" (131). And it ends: "Lazy and indifferent the heron returns; the sky veils her stars; then bares them" (131). The heron's certainty contrasts with the frenetic pace of the human beings and both the heron and the sky, we are told, are indifferent to the human activities below: what is so important and central to human beings is nothing to these representatives of the vast nonhuman world. The heron has his own reason for flying and its own destination. The sky and the heron do what they do without the attention or instigation of human beings, on their own accounts. And have the human beings noticed the sky and the heron? What is the truth they—or is it the narrator?—seek, particularly if this truth does not include what is around them all day? The framing of the story also contrasts the knowledge of the heron—"knowing his way"—with the anxious search for knowledge of the human beings, implying that, indeed, the heron is capable of knowing. The framing of the story, like the framing of a building, creates the space for raising these questions and thoughts. Once again, though through a different device than in "Kew Gardens," Woolf questions the centrality of human concerns, the human point of view, and the exclusive ownership of subjectivity by humans.

Although each of these three short stories works somewhat differently, they share some techniques for evoking, and attempting to translate, the reality, the presence, the subjectivity of the natural world which goes on around and in spite of us: reporting, selective use of synecdoche, juxtaposition, and odd points of view.

By reporting I mean description that refrains from comparing the nonhuman to the human, that focuses on the experience of the senses, on what is perceived, and that refrains from turning the perceived into something else by making it symbolic. Reporting is language that strives to describe not the feelings and desires of a perceiver but "the thing itself." Note that I use the words "refrains," "focuses," "strives." I am not saying that reporting captures that which is perceived in an absolute or transparent way but that the goal of reporting is to perceive and represent as accurately as possible the world of beings and objects external to the human mind. Reporting, in this sense, puts into action the "corrigibility and open expectations" that Plumwood calls for in attempts at cross-cultural and cross-species "translation." Reporting in this sense is the technique Woolf describes Dorothy Wordsworth using:

> This '*I* so much alive' was ruthlessly subordinated to the trees and the grass. For if she let 'I' and its rights and its wrongs and its passions and its suffering get between her and the object, she would be calling the moon 'the Queen of the Night'; she would be talking of dawn's 'orient beams'; she would be soaring into reveries and rhapsodies and forgetting to find the exact phrase for the ripple of moonlight upon the lake. ("Four Figures" 149)

Woolf argues that Dorothy's "plain statement[s]" and "brief notes unfurl in the mind and open a whole landscape before us" (151). Similarly, in "Kew Gardens," Woolf's plain reporting of "brown cliffs," "blade-like trees," "vast crumpled surfaces" opens a snail's whole landscape before us. In "The Mark on the Wall," the narrator tries to describe the mark simply and accurately but her associational cast of mind leads her to all sorts of speculations, ruminations, storytelling, and meaning-making. One can read this as a parody of Romantic musings on views of landscapes or appearances of objects. In effect, the story ends up being about the "I" telling it rather than about the mark on the wall. The narrator admits that "I want to think quietly, calmly, spaciously, never to be interrupted, never to have to rise from my chair, to slip easily from one thing to another, without any sense of hostility, or obstacle. I want to sink deeper and deeper, away from the surface, with its hard, cold facts" (78-79). "The Mark on the Wall" raises the issue of reporting vs. symbolizing and shows the narrator becoming more and more abstracted from sensory perceptions of her environment and falling into the mode of projecting human thoughts, questions, and symbols onto the external world.

"The Mark on the Wall" also shows the untenability of human solipsism and narcissism by the revelation at the end of the story that the mark is a snail. This discovery jerks the narrator out of her musings and requires her to pay attention to the material world around her and realize the impossibility of human control of the other-than-human world. She cannot control where snails go nor entirely what they mean. In this way, the snail becomes a representative of nonhuman being and reality; the snail is a synecdoche for the nonhuman. The use of synecdoche, however, does not require that the snail become *merely* a symbol. The snail does not lose its snailness, as neither do the snail, thrush, flowers in "Kew Gardens" or the heron in "Monday or Tuesday." Although they create meanings in these stories through representing the vast and various reality of other-than-human being, they are still individual snail, thrush, flowers, heron. The stories represent the material presence and subjectivity of the individual nonhuman beings at the same time as those beings operate as synecdoches. In fact, the synecdoches could not work and mean as they do without the snail, thrush, flowers, heron retaining their otherness and subjectivity.

By juxtaposition, I mean the placing of human and nonhuman side by side without direct narratorial comment, as Woolf does in "Kew Gardens" and "Monday or Tuesday." This technique allows new views of reality, of existences and relationships, to unfurl for the reader. "Kew Gardens," as discussed above, places the snail beneath the flowers side by side with the humans beneath the trees, implying parity between the snail and the humans. The people are also implicitly compared to the thrush. During the hot afternoon, the people "wavered and sought shade beneath the trees, dissolving like drops of water in the yellow and green atmosphere." Similarly seeking shade, the thrush "chose to hop, like a mechanical bird, in the shadow of the flowers, with long pauses between one movement and the next" (89). Walker points out that the humans are also shown behaving similarly to the butterflies in the garden: "The gait of the strolling humans is compared to 'that of the white and blue butterflies who crossed the turf in zig-zag flights'" (178). Finally, the humans' repeated searches for tea also echo the search of the snail, the thrush, and the insect for some goal—presumably also food. These juxtapositions develop a parity between the human and nonhuman beings, implying that the nonhumanbeings have consciousness and agency while the human beings are motivated by physical sensations of heat and hunger.

Finally, Woolf plays with point of view in these sketches, twisting the reader's metaphorical neck into unfamiliar positions, asking her reader to view the world from odd angles, and thus to recognize and consider unfamiliar perspectives on what is real. In "The Mark on the Wall," she asks readers to sit with a narrator who never gets up out of her chair, to follow that narrator from visions of the after-life and of the life of a tree to the vertigo of interruption: "I can't remember a thing. Everything's moving, falling, slipping, vanishing. . . . There is a vast upheaval of matter. Someone is standing over me and saying–"I'm going out to buy a newspaper'" (83, ellipses in original). In "Kew Gardens," she asks readers to lie on the earth of a flower bed, seeing the soil, flowers, and sunlight from the vantage point of a snail. In "Monday or Tuesday," she asks readers to step back from the street level of the city to take a living snapshot that includes not just sights but sounds and feelings and thoughts, a snapshot taken from about the height of a heron's flight.

In these ways, Woolf's stories make mental and emotional spaces, or vessels, for something which they cannot *say*, but which they allow to be seen and felt: the stories open up spaces in which the presences of flowers, trees, and sky resonate, snails search, thrushes choose, and herons know. Other-than-human subjectivities make themselves felt—incompletely accessible but there, present to be noted, and to make us pause in the midst of taking our anthropocentric ways through the world.

4. Woolf's Copernican Shift

The writing of her experimental stories and sketches of 1917-1921 effected a Copernican shift for Woolf; she came to see the human world as no longer the center of the universe. Whitaker's precedencies, the hierarchies of a masculinist, classist, humanist society, lose their aura of solid, inevitable reality placed in this new cosmology. I suggest that Woolf's new way of seeing and writing the nonhuman world formed part of her challenge to the worldview she inherited from her Enlightenment and Victorian forebears and enabled Woolf's reframing and defamiliarizing of the human world in her later novels and in *A Room of One's Own* and *Three Guineas*. Following trajectories first sketched in the earlier stories, the sky, birds, the moon, the sea, the wind, make ways of their own through Woolf's later texts. As in "Monday or Tuesday" the unending human search for "truth" is framed by the sky and the "indifferent" heron who "know[s] his way," so in *Jacob's Room*, *To the Lighthouse*, *The Waves*, *The Years*, and *Between the Acts* the human world is framed and/or intersected by the nonhuman world. In this way, Woolf uses reporting, synecdoche, and point of view to create experiences of other-than-human presence and to imagine and "translate" other-than-human subjectivity. She creates telling juxtapositions between human feelings and doings and the other-than-human world which goes on, as the narrator of "The Mark on the Wall" puts it, "without paying any attention to us" (82).

Works Cited

Bartkevicius, Jocelyn. "'In Relation to the Sky': Virginia Woolf's Other Real World." *Virginia Woolf and Her Influences: Selected Papers from the Seventh Annual Conference on Virginia Woolf.* Eds. Laura Davis and Jeanette McVicker. NY: Pace UP, 1998. 244-250. Print.

Beer, Gillian. "Virginia Woolf and Prehistory." *Virginia Woolf: The Common Ground.* Edinburgh: Edinburgh UP, 1996. 6-28. Print.

Benzel, Kathryn N. "Verbal Painting in 'Blue and Green' and 'Monday or Tuesday'." In *Trespassing Boundaries: Virginia Woolf's Short Fiction.* Eds. Kathryn N. Benzel and Ruth Hoberman. Gordonsville, VA: Palgrave Macmillan, 2004. 157-174. Print.

Bishop, Edward T. "Pursuing 'It' Through 'Kew Gardens'." *Studies in Short Fiction* 19.3 (1982): 269-275. Print.

Dick, Susan, ed. *The Complete Shorter Fiction of Virginia Woolf.* NY: Harcourt Brace Jovanovich, 1985. Print.

Donovan, Josephine. "Feminism and the Treatment of Animals: From Care to Dialogue." *Signs* 31.2 (2006): 305-329. JSTOR. Web. 12/19/2011.

Eliot, George. *Middlemarch: A Study of Provincial Life.* NY: Signet/New American Library, 1964, 1981. Print.

Flax, Jane. *Thinking Fragments: Psychoanalysis, Feminism, and Postmodernism in the Contemporary West.* Berkeley: U of California P, 1990. Print.

Harding, Sandra G. *Whose Science? Whose Knowledge? Thinking from Women's Lives.* Ithaca, NY: Cornell UP, 1991. Print.

Harding, Sandra G., ed. *The Feminist Standpoint Theory Reader: Intellectual and Political Controversies.* NY: Routledge, 2004. Print.

Hussey, Mark. *The Singing of the Real World: The Philosophy of Virginia Woolf's Fiction.* Columbus, OH: Ohio State UP, 1986. Print.

Kuhn, Thomas. *The Copernican Revolution: Planetary Astronomy in the Development of Western Thought.* Cambridge: Harvard UP, 1957. Print.

——. *The Structure of Scientific Revolutions.* Chicago: U of Chicago P, 1962. Print.

Lambert, Elizabeth G. "'and Darwin says they are nearer the cow': Evolutionary Discourse in *Melymbrosia* and *The Voyage Out*." *Twentieth Century Literature* 37.1 (1991): 1-21. JSTOR. Web. 5.5.2006.

Laurence, Patricia Ondek. *The Reading of Silence: Virginia Woolf in the English Tradition.* Stanford, CA: Stanford UP, 1991. Print.

Lenz, Brooke. "Postcolonial Fiction and the Outsider Within: Toward a Literary Practice of Feminist Standpoint Theory." *NWSA Journal: National Women's Studies Association Journal* 16.2 (2004): 98-120. Print.

Levy, Michelle. "Virginia Woolf's Shorter Fictional Explorations of the External World: 'Closely United . . . Immensely Divided'." In *Trespassing Boundaries: Virginia Woolf's Short Fiction.* Eds. Kathryn N. Benzel and Ruth Hoberman. Gordonsville, VA: Palgrave Macmillan, 2004. 139-155. Print.

Merchant, Carolyn. *The Death of Nature: Women, Ecology, and the Scientific Revolution: A Feminist Reappraisal of the Scientific Revolution.* San Francisco: Harper and Row, 1980. Print.

Nagel, Thomas. "What Is it Like to Be a Bat?" *The Philosophical Review* 83.4 (1974): 435-50. JSTOR. Web. 4.19.2006.

Plumwood, Val. *Environmental Culture: The Ecological Crisis of Reason.* London and NY: Routledge, 2002. Print.

Rohman, Carrie. *Stalking the Subject: Modernism and the Animal.* NY: Columbia UP, 2009. Print.

Staveley, Alice. "Conversations at Kew: Reading Woolf's Feminist Narratology." In *Trespassing Boundaries: Virginia Woolf's Short Fiction.* Eds. Kathryn N. Benzel and Ruth Hoberman. Gordonsville, VA: Palgrave Macmillan, 2004. 39-62. Print.

Walker, Charlotte Zoë. "The Book 'Laid Upon the Landscape': Virginia Woolf and Nature." *Beyond Nature Writing: Expanding the Boundaries of Ecocriticism.* Eds. Karla Armbruster and Kathleen R.Wallace. Charlottesville, VA: UP of Virginia; 2001. 143-161. Print.

——. "Letting in the Sky: An Ecofeminist Reading of Virginia Woolf's Short Fiction." *The Environmental Tradition in English Literature.* Ed. John Parham. Aldershot, England: Ashgate, 2002. 172-185. Print.

Waller, L. Elizabeth. "Writing the Real: Virginia Woolf and an Ecology of Language." *New Essays in Ecofeminist Literary Criticism.* Ed. Glynis Carr. Lewisburg: Bucknell UP; London and Toronto: Associated University Presses, 2000. 137-156. Print.

Westling, Louise. "Literature, the Environment and the Question of the Posthuman." *Nature in Literary and Cultural Studies.* Eds. Catrin Gersdort and Sylvia Mayer. Transatlantic Conversations on Ecocriticism. Amsterdam, Netherlands: Rodopi, 2006. 25-47. Print.

——."Merleau-Ponty's Human-Animality Intertwining and the Animal Question." *Configurations: A Journal of Literature, Science, and Technology.*

——. "Virginia Woolf and the Flesh of the World." *New Literary History* 30.4 (1999): 855-875. Project Muse. Web. 5.29..2001.

Wolfe, Cary. *Zoontologies: The Question of the Animal.* Minneapolis: U of Minnesota P, 2003. Print.

Woolf, Virginia. "Four Figures: Dorothy Wordsworth." (1929) *The Common Reader. Second Series* (1932). NY: Harcourt Brace Jovanovich, 1960. 148-155. Print.

——. "The Journal of Mistress Joan Martyn." In Dick, ed. 33-62. Print.

——. "Kew Gardens." (1919) In Dick, ed. 84-89. Print.

——. *The Letters of Virginia Woolf.* Vol. 4. Ed. Nigel Nicolson and Joanne Trautman. NY: Harcourt Brace Jovanovich, 1978. Print.

——. "The Mark on the Wall." (1917) In Dick, ed. 77-83. Print.

——. "Memoirs of a Novelist." In Dick, ed. 63-73. Print.

——. "Monday or Tuesday." (1921) In Dick, ed. 131. Print.

——. "The Mysterious Case of Miss V." In Dick, ed. 30-32. Print.

——. "Phases of Fiction." (1929) *Granite and Rainbow: Essays.* NY: Harvest/ Harcourt Brace Jovanovich, 1958. 93-145. Print.

——. "Phyllis and Rosamond." In Dick, ed. 17-29. Print.

——. *A Room of One's Own.* (1928) NY: Harvest/Harcourt Brace Jovanovich, 1957. Print.

Virginia Woolf's *Orlando* Preface, the Modernist Writer, and Networks of Cultural, Financial and Social Capital[1]

Helen Southworth

Virginia Woolf did not include the maps in *Orlando* (1928) that she suggested she might in a letter to Vita Sackville-West, or the "poem. Something about an island. landscape. dream. people with canoes. the trees" that she projected in an earlier version of the novel (Sackville-West 240; Clarke 2). Nevertheless, *Orlando* tempts the reader to map it, literally in terms of the geography described in the work or figuratively in terms of the many allusions woven into its pages. This essay focuses on Woolf's *Orlando* Preface as a map of sorts. The names contained therein constitute a virtual gathering and reveal much about the networks of cultural, financial and social capital in which Woolf was enmeshed. Woolf's coterie, partly identified in the Preface, suggests how such groups formed and functioned at the time. Analysis of the *Orlando* Preface from this perspective demonstrates what a literary historical approach can tell us about how a key modernist text developed.

The *Orlando* Preface draws on a long tradition of parodic prefaces such as Miguel de Cervantes's preface to *Don Quixote* and Laurence Sterne's preface to *Tristram Shandy*. In this instance, however, I take my cue from a later manipulation of the preface form or acknowledgments page by Paul Theroux. In an interview, Theroux explains that he often finds acknowledgment lists "more interesting and revealing than the books themselves—nearly often they have a plot, and a little drama" (333). Indeed, in Theroux's short story entitled "Acknowledgments" we follow the narrator-author's research trip in quest of the fictional minor West Country dialect poet Matthew Casket, his own successes and failures, as well as those of Casket, via a list of the names of the people who have helped him and in many cases the services rendered.[2] I want to read Woolf's list of names in a similar spirit, for the plot and the drama and in terms of her life as a modernist writer.

[1] I would like to thank the following people for help with the research for and writing of this paper: Stephen Barkway, Caleb Southworth, Darlene Southworth, Alice Staveley, Carmen Königsreuther Socknat, Barry Eigen, Amy Elkin, Trevor Bond, Stuart Clarke, Toral Gajarawala, and several astute anonymous reviewers.

[2] An extract from Theroux's story reveals similarities. "Special thanks must go to the staff of Broomhill Hospital, Old Sarum, and particularly to Miss Francine Kelversedge, S.R.N., for encouraging me in my project during a much needed rest from exhausting weeks of research. Colonel and Mrs. Hapgood Chalke came to my rescue at a turning point in my Broomhill sojourn; to them I owe more than I can adequately convey, and to their dear daughter, Tamsin, my keenest thanks for guiding my hand and for her resourcefulness providing explanations when they were in short supply" (Theroux 34).

With the publication of *Orlando* Woolf ascended into the realm of bestselling writers: "[t]he reception, as they say, surpassed expectations. Sales beyond our record for the first week," Woolf wrote of *Orlando* in her diary (*D*3 200). In this sense 1928 represented an interesting moment for Woolf to assess her career as a writer. In his book about literary celebrity Loren Glass uses Pierre Bourdieu's categories to consider Gertrude Stein's move from an autonomous to a heteronomous field of cultural production with the publication of *The Autobiography of Alice B. Toklas* in 1933. He argues that as Stein moved from a place "where the symbolic value of art is seen to derive from a resistance to economic value" to one "where the intimate relation between symbolic and economic capital is no longer disavowed," her identity as a modernist writer changed (131). Paradoxically the confidence Stein had in her genius before *The Autobiography*, despite little success in terms of publication, was shattered when she gained the recognition she had always felt she deserved. If we consider *Orlando* as marking a similar turning point in Woolf's career, the Preface represents an extraordinarily prescient statement on Woolf's part about the paradoxical and precarious status of the modernist writer whose work lost prestige as it gained popularity and financial viability. The coincidence of *Orlando*'s success with the height of the Hogarth Press's success in terms of number of titles published suggests that Woolf was also celebrating with her Preface the freedom the publishing operation afforded her.

Woolf and Dedications

Orlando's Preface is Woolf's most elaborate acknowledgment page or preface. Suggesting that she felt indebtedness important, Woolf had dedicated many of her works previous to *Orlando*: *The Voyage Out* (1915) is dedicated to L.W. [Leonard Woolf], *Night and Day* (1919) to her sister Vanessa Bell ("To Vanessa Bell/but, looking for a phrase, /I found none to stand beside your name"), and the first *Common Reader* (1926) to Lytton Strachey, in return for his dedicating his *Queen Victoria* to her in 1921 (in which instance she "insisted, out of 'vanity,' on having her full name on the page" [Lee 462]). Although there is no dedication in *Mrs. Dalloway* (1925), Woolf's decision to send the manuscript of the novel to the dying French painter Jacques Raverat in France suggests a dedication of sorts, and Woolf's comments regarding *To the Lighthouse*'s (1927) status as an elegy to her parents' memory the same. Woolf had considered dedicating *To the Lighthouse* to Roger Fry, but, doubting the quality of the work, she decided against it (Spalding, *Roger Fry* 259). Thanking Fry for his praise of the book, anticipating her thanking him in *Orlando*, saying in private what she will later have the courage to say in public, Woolf wrote:

> Now I wish I had dedicated it to you. But when I read it over it seemed to me so bad that I couldn't face asking you. And then, as it happened, that very day, I met you somewhere, —was so overcome (did you guess it?) by your magnificence, splendour and purity (of intellect, not body) that I went home and was positive it was out of the question—dedicating such a book to such a man. Really therefore the not-dedication is a greater compliment than the dedication would have been—But you shall have a private copy, if you'll accept it. What I meant was (but would not have said in print) that besides all your surpassing private virtues, you have I think kept me on the right path, so far as writing goes, more than anyone—if the right path it is. (*L*3 385)

Similar "not-dedication[s]" exist for *Jacob's Room* (1922) and *The Waves* (1931). When completing her seventh novel, Woolf contemplated writing the name and dates of her brother "Julian Thoby Stephen 1881-1906," who had died tragically young of typhoid, on the first page, as she had done in her notebook when completing her third novel, but decided against it (*D*4 10; Hussey 126). In the case of *The Waves*, Woolf feared she was being too sentimental. Vanessa Bell responded to Woolf's concern by telling her sister, with a quotation from *Hamlet*, that she felt that with *The Waves* Woolf had "found the 'lullaby capable of singing [Thoby] to rest'" (*L*4 390-1 n1).

Dating the Preface

It is unclear when Woolf conceived of *Orlando*'s Preface. The Preface is not included in the holograph draft of *Orlando* completed, according to Stuart Clarke, between March 17 and March 22, 1928. The holograph does contain a dedication, to "Vita from Virginia/ Dec. 6th 1928," likely added when Woolf took the bound manuscript to Sackville-West at Long Barn. This took the form of the gender neutral and more formal "To V. Sackville-West" in the published version (October 2, 1928). Woolf does mention the Preface in private letters, to her nephew Quentin Bell, to the popular novelist and her sometime antagonist Hugh Walpole and to longtime family friends Nelly Cecil and the legal scholar and recent Hogarth Press author (*The Structure of Wuthering Heights* 1926) C.P. Sanger, all of whom are acknowledged in the Preface. On May 6, 1928, relatively late in the writing process, Woolf wrote to the eighteen-year-old Quentin Bell, "I am scribbling away to finish my nonsense book. Have I your permission to mention you in the Preface? Because I've done it" (*L*3 493); she mentioned it again in a letter to Quentin on June 5. Five months later, on October 21, 1928, following publication, she responded to Walpole in a mockingly hyperbolic tone: "I am very glad that being in Orlando's preface did not annoy you. It is very good indeed of you to be so generous about it. I am deep in your debt, deeper and deeper" (*L3* 547). On the same day, Woolf assures Nelly Cecil "with [her] hand on [her] heart, if that is the correct position, that my motives in dragging you so impudently into my preface (Violet [Dickinson] says she doesn't like keeping such low company at all) were honourable affection, gratitude, esteem: Ought I to have asked your permission?" (*L3* 553). Also in October 1928, Woolf replied to Sanger in a more respectful tone than that used for Walpole: "My dear Charlie, It is very good of you to write—especially when I had taken such liberties with your venerated name (which I do seriously venerate). Orlando was meant as a joke; and I daresay it gives a view of life which is not at all my own—if it gives a view of life at all" (*L3* 554).[3] These letters set the stage for a reading of the preface as multi-functional: Woolf acknowledges family ties with Quentin and old friendship with Cecil and Sanger; she recognizes real intellectual and professional debts with Sanger and Quentin and, at the same time, pokes fun at the literary establishment as embodied by newer acquaintance Walpole.

Reactions to the Preface

Contemporary public reaction to the *Orlando* Preface was mixed. In his condemnatory review of *Orlando,* "A Woman's High Brow Lark," Bloomsbury antagonist Arnold Bennett wrote: "It is a very odd volume. It has a preface, in which Woolf names the names of 53 people who have helped her with it. It has, too, an index. I admit some justification for the preface, but none for the index" (Majumdar and McLaurin 232). In a review of the almost simultaneously released *Elizabeth and Essex* by Lytton Strachey and Woolf's *Orlando* for *The Bookman,* ally Raymond Mortimer, who is himself among those listed in the Preface, described *Orlando* as "a lark": "the preface is a parody of prefaces and the whole book is written in tearing high spirits" (Majumdar and McLaurin 241).

Leonard Woolf's comments in a 1966 letter to actor Robert Speaight provide support for readings of the Preface as "ironical," as a parody, as does Leonard's *Hunting the Highbrow*, published as part of the Hogarth Essays Second Series in March 1927 as Woolf wrote *Orlando*. Leonard Woolf had read in Speaight's obituary of middlebrow writer Clemence Dane that Dane saw the *Orlando* Preface as "'an unpardonable piece of snobbery' and as an example of the 'central heating of Bloomsbury.'" Leonard repurposes Dane's comment to assert that in fact the Preface was "*a skit* on the unpardonable snobbery of so many learned and unlearned writers who write prefaces spattered with well known people to whom they ladle

[3] This is backed up in a second letter to Sanger's wife, Dora, who had written to say she liked *Orlando*: "I hope Charlie didn't mind my using his name—it was a great support to me …" (*L3* 554).

out their thanks" (my emphasis, Spotts 543). Later literary critics have read the Preface in vastly different ways. David Daiches takes Woolf's Preface seriously, calling it "illuminating" (98). He ties Woolf's listing of literary antecedents to what he considers a central issue in the novel, that is, an "interest in the relation of the present moment to the flux of experience in general" and he understands her list of contemporaries, "friends, scholars, historians, critics," as an indication of "the seriousness with which Virginia Woolf took her job of historical reconstruction." Daiches suggests that Woolf's choice of writers is relevant to "modern writing," her "the first that come to mind" tongue in cheek (98-99). Beverly Ann Schlack acknowledges the "mock-solemn" quality of the work, but at the same time, like Daiches, asserts that the names are "more than token acknowledgement of literary debts," rather that "they are evidence of the considerable tradition out of which even so singular a work as *Orlando* springs" (79). J. J. Wilson, however, incredulous at Daiches' interpretation (she says she read it "with the kind of horrified fascination one feels watching someone slip on a banana skin") categorizes the "spite-full" Preface as part of the *Orlando* author's subversive anti-novelist arsenal: "the mask drops, the hoax is obvious; the arbitrariness and acerbity of sentiment and tone are unmistakable to anyone accustomed to the habits of the rabid anti-novelist" (176-77).

More recently, Caroline Webb has compared Woolf's Preface with James Joyce's list of "Irish heroes" in the Cyclops chapter of *Ulysses* in terms of the humor each one generates and the different "perspectives on notions of linguistic and literary authority" that result (191). Arguing, like Wilson, that the work dictates an analysis of the Preface, Webb contends that the list of names, while appearing initially "self-consistent and appropriate," shows its true parodic colors when juxtaposed with the novel, "a subversive impersonation of a...scholarly biography" (196). Thus, for example, Webb argues that while thanking Sanger in a story about inheritance initially makes sense because of his legal expertise in this area, the throwing out of property law in the novel, with the female Orlando able to inherit the family house, negates Woolf's deference to authority (193). Running counter to Webb's reading, Susan Dick, in an analysis of the generic status of the novel itself, suggests that "the index, [fulsome] preface and illustrations contribute to the 'truth' side of the equation in this mock-biography" (63). And, in a similar vein, Karyn Z. Sproles argues that "[t]he preface and photographs are jokes that remind us that Woolf was a real person who had a life and a lover...The preface, the photographs, and the intertextuality of the jokes intrude the real world into the fictional" (106-7).

The Preface was undoubtedly meant to amuse and to challenge, and indeed Woolf was famous for her cutting wit. However, like Daiches and Schlack and Dick and Sproles, I want to highlight the real side of it with a focus on what it says about Woolf's career as a writer. Wilson is certainly right in describing the list as acerbic; however its contents are not arbitrary. Rather, they represent a serious engagement with issues related to the importance of networks and collaboration to the modernist writer and a celebration of the diverse coteries with which Woolf was involved in 1928. In this sense, my reading extends Leonard Woolf's description of the Preface as a "skit on the unpardonable snobbery" of many of Woolf's contemporaries. While Alex Zwerdling argues that the *Orlando* Preface suggests a narrowness to Woolf's affiliations which was actually counter to her own and Leonard Woolf's engagement in a much "wider culture" (28), I argue that the *Orlando* preface actually confirms that broad cultural engagement. Departing from earlier readings that consider the Preface mostly from the perspective of Woolf's indebtedness to the past, my analysis focuses instead on what it tells us about her cultural, financial and social networks of 1928.

Provocations

With her acknowledgments page Woolf was certainly poking fun on a personal level at the pretensions of her dedicatee Sackville-West.[4] Sackville-West's autobiographical *Knole and the Sackvilles* (1922), on which *Orlando* is in large part based, is prefaced with a chronological table, a table of descent and a poem (see Schlack 77-78). Sackville-West's *Challenge* (1923), which in its capacity as a *roman à clef* and as a love letter from Sackville-West to Violet Trefusis anticipates *Orlando,* is dedicated to Trefusis with a Romany inscription, a private language adopted by the two women. Significantly, in terms of its centrality to *Orlando* as model for Orlando's poem the "The Oak Tree," Sackville-West dedicated "The Land" (1926) to her friend, the socialite and literary patron Dorothy Wellesley, who also appears in the *Orlando* Preface. Woolf's inclusion of her own much less eminent family and friends acts as a playful response to Sackville-West's promotion of the same. Sackville-West's dedication to Woolf of her first Hogarth Press publication, *Seducers in Ecuador* (1924), represents a first acknowledgment of debt which Woolf's dedication of *Orlando* to Sackville-West (set apart from the Preface) reciprocates.

On a more public level, Woolf's *Orlando* Preface engages with critics and the larger literary establishment. These were people from whom she anticipated what she termed "blast[s]" in a 1928 letter to Hugh Walpole written subsequent to *Orlando*'s publication (*L3* 552). Among Woolf's and Bloomsbury's most hos-

[4] Another possible source is Leslie Stephen's preface to his biography of his brother James Stephen. Here Leslie Stephen thanks family members and experts and deploys a similarly self-deprecating tone to that used by Woolf. The fact that Leslie Stephen's work is a piece of family history suggests Woolf is signaling *Orlando* as such.

tile critics, and the most famous "blaster" of all, was P. Wyndham Lewis; while Woolf's use of "blast[s]" cannot be definitively linked to Lewis, it is likely that she had him in mind when she deployed the term. I consider two of Lewis's pieces as examples of the kind of attacks to which Woolf's Preface responds. First, Lewis's "Bless" and "Blast" lists (*Blast* manifesto 1914) suggest themselves as precursors to Woolf's *Orlando* Preface in their deployment of similar formats and their inclusion of similar content, prompting an examination of Woolf's acknowledgments from the perspective of coterie culture. Second, Woolf's response in correspondence with T. S. Eliot to Lewis's 1924 *Criterion* article "Apes of God" sees her playfully engaged with an overt attack on Bloomsbury in terms that anticipate the Preface. While Lewis does not appear on Woolf's list, other similar figures are represented there. Although the two Lewis pieces discussed precede *Orlando*, "Apes of God" by just four years and *Blast* by fourteen years, they nonetheless illustrate well the frequently hostile environment in which Bloomsbury existed.

Lewis's "Bless" and "Blast" lists formed part of the Vorticist Manifesto, published in *Blast* 1 on June 20, 1914. They were modeled on Guillaume Apollinaire's "Mer . . de . . . aux" and "Rose aux" lists (*Manifeste-Synthèse, L'Antitradition Futuriste,* June 29, 1913). These lists were not themselves without precedent, a possible forerunner the Pre-Raphaelites' "slightly absurd" list of "Immortals"(compiled in 1884), which included "Joan of Arc, the Prophet Isaiah, Hogarth, Cervantes, Leigh Hunt and Washington, with Jesus Christ at the head" (Windsor 86).[5] Douglas Goldring, who was with Lewis when the list was created, explains that the "blasted" names consisted of "eminent figures whose publicity was considered boringly excessive," and the "blessed" were "either members of the South Lodge circle, 'blessed' to please Ford and Violet [Hunt] or popular public figures" (68). As Michael North has suggested more recently in terms that anticipate Woolf's Preface, "*Blast* itself emerged from a mechanically comical duet with the public it was supposed to affront" (127). Despite its apparent lack of rationale, Lewis's list of people and things, composed amidst "knowing grins" and "irreverent giggles" according to Goldring, reflects Lewis's general scorn for networking and patronage (68). Woolf's *Orlando* Preface has a similar double edge; like Lewis's lists it is at once a playful skit on and a serious indictment of the contemporary literary scene.

Among those Lewis considered most guilty of the self-promotion and cliquish behavior attacked in the "Bless" and "Blast" lists were members of the Bloomsbury Group. Suggesting that it may have directly prompted Woolf's Preface, Lewis's list included Bloomsberries, as did Apollinaire's. Roger Fry was among those in-

[5] Another comparison (although published simultaneously with *Orlando*) might be made with Louis Zukofsky's poem "Poem Beginning 'The'" in Ezra Pound's magazine *The Exile* (no. 3, Spring 1928) in which Zukofsky includes an acknowledgments page that lists Woolf's *Mrs. Dalloway.*

cluded under the "Rose aux" category in Apollinaire's list; Apollinaire told Fry he had been included for his "valiance d'esprit d'avant-garde" (qtd in Windsor 93). "Clan Strachey" and Bloomsbury associate Fabian Sydney [*sic*] Webb are on the "Blast" list; although not included on Lewis's lists, Fry was subject to his attacks elsewhere at this period after he fell out with Lewis over a misunderstanding involving Omega Workshop commissions for design work sold at the Ideal Home Exhibition of 1913 (see Bell and Chaplin).

Woolf does not mention *Blast* in her letters and diaries. Her comments about Lewis appear mostly after 1930, once he launched his major offensive against Bloomsbury, with his *roman à clef The Apes of God* published in 1930, his *Men without Art* in 1935, *The Roaring Queen* written in 1936 (published in 1973), in which Woolf figures as Rhoda Hymen, and his 1937 novel *Revenge for Love*, all of which appeared after *Orlando*. Woolf does however mention Lewis in a letter of May 1924 in which she responds to a letter from T. S. Eliot about Lewis's "Apes of God." This was the second piece of Lewis's later novel of the same name to appear in Eliot's *Criterion* in late April 1924. Woolf's response to Lewis sets the stage for a reading of Woolf's Preface as in dialogue with Lewis's commentary on networking, name-dropping and patronage and lends support to a consideration of it as mimicking Lewis's "Bless" and "Blast" lists.

In his second *Criterion* article, Lewis introduces the term "Ape of God," the moneyed aristocrat who "apes" the artist, a concept central to the later novel of the same name. Lewis categorizes different sorts of "apes"—the most dangerous being the productive ape, he or she who engages in "more than the inconsequent daubing and dabbing … but less than the 'real thing'" (305-6). "The Ape of God proper," according to Lewis, his/her ego implicated in the production of art, is the most likely to defame and do damage to the work of real artists. While in this essay he does not name Bloomsbury explicitly, as he does in his later novel, the implication is obvious:

> [In London] it [amateurism/the Ape of God art-type] has taken the form of a very select closed club. Its members consist of moneyed descendants of Victorian literary splendour, for the most part. Where they approximate to the citizens of this new Bohemia is in their substitution, to begin with, of money for talent as a qualification: in private means being the almost invariable rule: in their discouragement of too much unconservative originality: and in the tone of 'society,' of an affectation of social elegance, prevailing among them. Where they have always *differed* is in their *all* being Apes of God, in the first place—all "geniuses," before whose creations the members of the group, in an invariable ritual, would swoon with appreciation (307).

In comments that provide a framework for the *Orlando* Preface, Lewis goes on to attack Bloomsbury's insularity: "They naturally exercise their influence in the interests of what is virtually their club: a certain network of not very remunerative patronage extending over outsiders who are not too important" (308).

Woolf knew Eliot well by the time Lewis's piece appeared. The Hogarth Press had published Eliot's work and Eliot had printed Woolf's work in the *Criterion*.[6] Eliot would publish Woolf's "Character in Fiction" in June 1924, in the issue subsequent to that in which Lewis's "Apes of God" appeared.[7] Significantly in terms of establishing a link between Lewis's article and Woolf's views on patronage, Eliot also expressed regret in response to "a card" from Virginia Woolf (May 1, 1924), which seems to have been lost, that he did not publish Woolf's own discussion of literary patronage, "The Patron and the Crocus," in the *Criterion*: "Yes, I wished that we could have had that essay [identified in a footnote as "Patron"] in the *Criterion*" (Eliot, *Letters* 2 388). Woolf had perhaps pointed out to Eliot how germane her ideas about how to choose between the "unexampled and bewildering variety" of current patrons would have been to the issues raised by Lewis in "Apes" (212). "Patron" had instead appeared on April 12, 1924 in the *Nation & Athenaeum* a few weeks in advance of Lewis's piece.

What is interesting in terms of the subsequent Preface is Woolf's apparent involvement in the licensing of the publication of Lewis's negative view of Bloomsbury, albeit undertaken in ignorance, and her subsequent reaction to the attack. Having received complaints about Lewis's "Apes of God," Eliot writes to Virginia Woolf reminding her that she, in her capacity as "[his] oracle and counsel in matters journalistic," "(with the supporting opinions too of Leonard and Clive as junior counsel)," had sanctioned his decision to let "one contributor say what he likes about another" in the spirit of "'the best British journalism'" (Eliot, *Letters* 2 412-13). However to Eliot's claim that when he had asked Virginia Woolf this question he was referring to Lewis, Woolf responds that she and Leonard thought he meant Murry, whose article appeared in the same issue as Lewis's.[8]

[6] Eliot had published S. S. Koteliansky's translations from the Russian and Woolf's short story "In the Orchard."

[7] Here we see the degree to which the *Criterion* functioned as an arena for dialogue among modernist writers and artists, among whom Bloomsbury was well represented.

[8] Eliot claims that he did not have time to read the article before publication "there being only twenty-four hours in a day." Letters to Lewis, however, suggest Eliot had in fact read the article. On March 19, 1924, Eliot tells Lewis that he has "surpassed [him]self and everything. It is worthwhile running the Criterion just to publish these" (*Letters* 2 344). On April 6, he writes to Schiff: "If I find that I am 'reproached' with having published such a justifiable article as Wyndham Lewis's 'Apes of God', I fancy that I shall know from what sources the trouble has sprung. Had I been in London, I do not imagine that there would have been such a hue and cry set up about it. In fact, my absence from London at this moment has given the most excellent opportunity to all those people who

Uncharacteristically good humored about the attack, for which she suspects Eliot will be forgiven due to the ignorance of many of those targeted, Woolf relays the reaction of some of her friends to Lewis's article: she is distracted, she says, because "everyone—that is Lytton [Strachey], Osbert Sitwell, Mary Hutchinson is claiming to be an Ape of God and identifying the rest of the pack" (*L*3 108).[9] That all three of those identifying themselves as "Apes" appear on Woolf's list might be explained by the fact that they were Woolf's friends and associates. However, the spirit of Woolf et al.'s reaction to Lewis's attack prompts one to consider the *Orlando* Preface as an extension of this "Apes of God" naming-game and as a challenge to critics like Lewis.

Woolf and the Literary Marketplace

John Carey and Sean Latham, among others, have explored the complex nature of Woolf's snobbery. As both note, Woolf favored elites and rankings, a tendency exacerbated during the tenure of her relationship with the blue-blooded Sackville-West. As her success as an author grew, Woolf found herself with a packed social calendar peppered with titled names. She frequently made disparaging remarks about the "thick dull middle class of letters": just prior to *Orlando*'s publication, in June 1927 when Sackville-West was awarded the Hawthornden prize for her poem "The Land," Woolf calls the awards ceremony "[a] horrid show up … chattering writers … it was the thick dull middle class of letters that met; not the aristocracy" (*D*3 139-40). However, as Latham demonstrates, this arrogance was rarely unaccompanied by an awareness of the flimsiness of her own pretensions, one compounded by bouts of low self-esteem.

Highlighting the ambiguity of Woolf's relationship with the literary marketplace and the aristocracy, Latham uses letters and diaries from the late 1920s

bear a grudge for one reason or another, to gather together and vent their spleen in a cause which, being impersonal, will seem to them to conceal their personal malice. In short, I have played into the hands of my London 'friends' and given them the opportunity to display the hostility to the Criterion which without exception they have most obviously felt since it first made its appearance. Fortunately I am editing the paper for a woman of the world and a cosmopolitan, who is not interested in petty tribal vendettas, and whose idea of a quarterly is of one which will appeal not only to London but to England, to America and perhaps to other countries" (356-7).

[9] As early as 1925, Virginia Woolf expresses her suspicions of Eliot. While Eliot is asking Woolf to contribute to his quarterly, Woolf says he is too cowardly to admit that he is having Faber & Gwyer reprint *The Waste Land* instead of the Hogarth Press. "The Underworld—the dodges & desires of the Underworld, its shifts & cabals are at bottom of it. He intends to get on by the methods of that world; & my world is really not the underworld. However, there is a kind of fun in unraveling the twists and obliquities of this remarkable man" (*D*3 41).

to argue that Woolf rather incongruously imagines an aesthetic autonomy for the modern writer in terms of an independence available only to the aristocracy. "Already at the very top of the social ladder and thus freed from art's anti-economy economy, [the aristocracy] alone [possesses] the material means to sustain their artistic pursuits and the self-confidence to reject either the acclaim or the dismay of the reading public" (106). Latham asserts that in embracing such a perspective Woolf "exploits the very economies of sophistication that Orlando finally escapes" (109). Reading around this assessment, I argue that the Preface, which Latham does not take into account, constitutes a different response to the literary marketplace and the reading public. Woolf's Preface celebrates community and collaboration, as opposed to autonomy, as it acknowledges the layers of infrastructure and the variety of actors required to make a bestselling book and a bestselling modern writer.

Woolf was not subject to financial humiliations such as those suffered by T. S. Eliot suggested by numerous attempts to buy him out of his Lloyds Bank day job. These buy-out efforts included Woolf and Lady Ottoline Morrell's Eliot Fellowship Fund, where Woolf, significantly, becomes the patron, and Natalie Barney and Ezra Pound's Bel Esprit (*L2* 590). However, Woolf knew how important material comforts were to the artist, a topic she famously took up just after *Orlando* in *A Room of One's Own* (1929). As I asserted earlier, Woolf understood the vicissitudes to which the modernist writer was subject in terms of economic and symbolic capital. Indeed, as Patrick Collier has shown, the ambiguous relationship of the author to the literary marketplace is a central theme in *Orlando*, as well as in Woolf's journalism of the 1920s (and in many ways this essay seconds Collier's analysis of the novel as it extends its focus to the Preface).[10] Woolf mockingly undermines the clout of her connections in the *Orlando* Preface, with John Maynard Keynes, for example, listed as husband of Lydia Lopokova, and with servant "Miss Nellie [*sic*] Boxall" placed between Sybil Colefax and Keynes, "a jokey snub to all three," according to Alison Light (174). However, Woolf simultaneously reminds us that her network was a powerful and influential one and that success was earned only with the help of a variety of people, both upstream and downstream of the book, to borrow

[10] "[*Orlando*] puts into play the opposing impulses of the longing for cultural centrality—'as large and miscellaneous an audience as possible' (Eliot, *Prose* 94) and the desire to write a radical language that stretches or subverts the boundaries of signification and whose inaccessibility to most readers can be claimed as a mark of its authenticity. *Orlando* raises the tension between the urge to decry the institutions of the literary marketplace and the need to master and manipulate those institutions, for prestige and cultural capital if not for popularity per se—between the writer's wish to be heard and her desire to remain true to her artistic ambition, expressed in *Orlando* as the wish to refine language into an instrument so efficient, capable of conveying such a dense load of meaning, that it can be understood only by the writer herself and a few select others" (Collier 376).

Aaron Jaffe's terms.[11] These are Woolf's credentials; she is not afraid to lay them out for all to see. Woolf had a much better business sense than she let on, as J. H. Willis asserts in terms of the working of the Hogarth Press and as recent scholarship on Woolf and the literary marketplace affirms; this includes Jeanne Dubino's *Virginia Woolf and the Literary Marketplace*, which incorporates several chapters on Woolf's work for literary magazines, and my *Leonard and Virginia Woolf, The Hogarth Press and the Networks of Modernism*, which highlights the range of authors and work promoted by the Woolfs at their press between 1917 and 1941 (78).

In an interview just after Woolf's death, T. S. Eliot describes Woolf's centrality to what he calls a "whole pattern of culture" in terms that provide a framework for considering the Preface as a statement about networks of cultural, social and financial capital. Eliot's assessment is useful because it provides a view of Woolf's engagement with modernist literary culture from the perspective of a historical contemporary who, in his role as editor at Faber and for the *Criterion*, was enmeshed in the writing business. Although published over a decade after *Orlando*, Eliot's statement is particularly pertinent to the publication of Woolf's 1928 novel and to the Preface in that it saw her most audaciously bringing her private life into the public eye:

> I am well aware that the literary-social importance which Virginia Woolf enjoyed, had its nucleus in a society which those people whose ideas about it were vague—vague even in connection with the topography of London—were wont, not always disinterestedly perhaps, to deride. The sufficient answer *ad hoc*—though not the final answer—would probably be that it was the only one there was: and as I believe that without Virginia Woolf at the centre of it, it would have remained formless or marginal, to call attention to its interest to the sociologist is not irrelevant to my subject. Any group will appear more uniform, and probably more intolerant and exclusive from the outside than it really is; and here, certainly, no subscription of orthodoxy was imposed. Had it, indeed, been a matter of limited membership and exclusive doctrine, it would not have attracted the exasperated attention of those who objected to it on these supposed grounds … I only mention the matter in order to make the point that Virginia Woolf was the centre not merely of an esoteric group, but of the literary life of London … With the death of Virginia Woolf a whole pattern of culture is broken: she may be, from one point of view, only the symbol

[11] Jaffe defines the "upstream" and the "downstream work" involved in modernist literary production respectively as "composition, editing, and collaboration" (90) and "critical and journalistic essays, autobiographies, pensées, and memoirs as well as setting up bookshops, publishing houses, little magazines, and artistic salons" (161).

> of it; but she would not be the symbol of it if she had not been, more than anyone in her time, the maintainer of it. (Eliot in Noble 121-2)

Eliot's rarely quoted, but richly suggestive statement is important because it gets at the dilemma inherent in a desire on the part of the writer or artist to reach a broader public and the need, when one is producing radically different art, for a small, supportive group of friends (this something that Eliot believes Woolf alone has been able to negotiate successfully). As Michael Levenson has argued, using a description of a social event from Woolf's diaries to illustrate his point, clustering behavior and "[t]he circles forming around Stein, Woolf, Pound and DuBois ... were as much the condition of Modernism as any set of formal gestures" (5). Although he confirms the need for a close group of supporters, Eliot asserts that, contrary to popular opinion, the Bloomsbury Group was not closed and "no subscription of orthodoxy was imposed." (This idea is echoed later by Raymond Williams in his analysis of the "anti-system" quality of the Bloomsbury Group.) According to Eliot, Woolf functioned as a necessary "maintainer" of *both* "an esoteric group [*and*] the literary life of London," a point that the *Orlando* Preface illustrates clearly.

56 (or 57) Friends, the Staff of the British Museum and Record Office and an American

In the spirit of Theroux's short story, in what follows I chronicle Woolf's writing life up to 1928 and the publication of her most commercially successful novel to date by filling in the reasons for inclusion of names on the *Orlando* Preface. I show first how Woolf uses the multi-functionality of those listed to emphasize the interconnectedness of her personal life and her writing life: although most of those included are family and friends, they had considerable influence on her work. I highlight in particular the predominance of Hogarth Press-related names to demonstrate how densely the list is populated by professional ties. I then explore how Woolf challenges the conventions of the literary marketplace and prevailing beliefs about Bloomsbury's lack of involvement in it with the addition of numerous unexpected names to the Preface.

At the core of the *Orlando* Preface is Woolf's acknowledgment of debt to family and friends, prefigured by her earlier acknowledgments discussed above. Family ties constitute a large portion of the list as do close social ties, to the point that one might read past or fail to see some of the stranger inclusions as a result. However, with very few exceptions, family and friends are not just family and friends, but they represent a more complicated piece of the puzzle that is Woolf's writing life. This double role-playing is anticipated by Woolf's opening statement in which she alludes to her literary ancestors as "friends." In this way, Woolf makes a conventionally formal relationship informal before giving the informal ties of family a formal side. "Many *friends*," she begins, "have helped me in writing this book. Some are dead and so illustrious that I scarcely dare name them, yet no one can read or write without being perpetually in the debt of [...]" (my emphasis). By highlighting the narrow line dividing her professional from her personal life, Woolf challenges conceptions of her writing life as insular and self-focused (responding to Lewis's comments about "a very select closed club") and at the same time confirms the modernist writer's need for a tight-knit, supportive community (Eliot; Levenson). The "eccentric" quality of Woolf's literary genealogy, to borrow Maria DiBattista's term for the list of literary antecedents, asserts a freedom "to select her ancestors and to fashion an artistic lineage" unavailable to Sackville-West and many of her other more formally trained associates (liv). The list's randomness—Woolf lists "the first that come to mind"—flies in the face of those who ascribe to Woolf in her capacity as "a descendant[] of Victorian literary splendour" (Lewis) a more conventional and predictable literary heritage.

Thus, when Woolf includes family, she frequently, half-playfully, half-sincerely, includes the formal reasons for which she has chosen to thank them. Although there is a hyperbolic quality to the expressions of gratitude, and perhaps a desire to throw Lewis's accusations of nepotism back at him, most of the family members named have contributed to her growth as a writer and/or specifically to the production of *Orlando*. Weaving work and life, she thanks "my husband," Leonard Woolf for "the profound historical knowledge to which these pages owe whatever degree of accuracy they may attain." Woolf thanks her nephews, her niece and her brother-in-law: twenty-year old Julian for his "singularly penetrating, if severe, criticism," Quentin, then just eighteen, whom she addresses as "an old and valued collaborator in fiction," for his help making up satirical portraits of Woolf's friends (*L*3 292, 481), the ten-year old Angelica Bell, who had posed as Sasha for *Orlando*, "for a service none but she could have rendered," and Clive Bell in his capacity as "that most inspiriting of critics." While Woolf is clearly having fun here, we are reminded of her assurance to close family friend Sanger that she does seriously venerate his name, although she has taken liberties with it by including it on her list. Thus, while the specific reasons for thanking Leonard, her nephews, her niece and Bell might be cryptic or exaggerated (although in the case of Quentin and Angelica, and certainly, of course, Leonard, there is truth to her statements) there is in any case a familial debt to be acknowledged. In this same category, Woolf also thanks her brother Dr. Adrian Stephen, and Duncan Grant, father of her niece Angelica Bell, without specifying reasons, although Duncan has professional connections via the Hogarth Press.[12] Woolf thanks her sister, Vanessa

[12] Adrian also published with the Hogarth Press, but his *The "Dreadnought" Hoax* (1936) postdates *Orlando.*

Bell, again without offering a reason, suggesting a general debt and echoing her earlier dedications.[13]

A similar double debt in terms of social and cultural (intellectual) support is acknowledged with Woolf's inclusion of members of the groups, salons and clubs with which she was associated. Prominent among these is the Apostles, a Cambridge University secret society founded in 1820, which included Lytton Strachey, Saxon Sydney-Turner, Leonard Woolf, E. M. Forster, Desmond MacCarthy, Roger Fry, John Maynard Keynes and C. P. Sanger (all named). The classical scholar, Mr J. T. Sheppard, who was an Apostle, is also included. Sheppard appears to have had some direct influence on the novel. At the Keynes's house in Tilton, Sheppard acted the part of an Italian prima donna—at this same party Woolf, reports Quentin Bell, became fascinated with a press cutting about a girl who had become a boy (1.32). Woolf includes all of the Memoir Club members, in so doing acknowledging more recent affiliations: Clive and Vanessa Bell, Adrian Stephen, Duncan Grant, Maynard Keynes, Sydney-Turner, Leonard Woolf, Strachey, Fry, Forster, and Desmond and Molly MacCarthy who also made up the Old Bloomsbury thirteen. New Bloomsbury, or many of those whom Frances Partridge identifies as "fringe Bloomsbury" in a discussion not pertaining to the Preface, also figure prominently—"some from Oxford, like Raymond Mortimer [and] Eddy Sackville-West ... some from Cambridge, like the Davidson brothers and Dadie Rylands ... Arthur Waley; the sculptor Stephen Tomlin ... young Bells, young Stracheys, young MacCarthys, Slade students and many, many more" (Partridge 90). In order to reflect the difficulties of accessing these groups in her capacity as a woman, or to suggest that these people functioned as individuals as well as members of groups, Woolf does not put the names associated with each of these groups together, but disperses them across the list.

The appearance on the list of Janet Case illustrates well the sense in which those acknowledged functioned both culturally and socially in Woolf's life. Case began teaching Woolf Greek in 1902 and later played many roles for Woolf including feminist icon and confidante. The social reason for inclusion of Case is signaled by the addition of Case's older sister, Emphie, whose appearance supports the importance of family ties. Emphie is listed separately from Janet; she sits between Lady Gerald Wellesley and Raymond Mortimer. Emphie's inclusion also indicates that this is a thank you for a visit Leonard and Virginia had made in June of 1928 to see the Case sisters in their New Forest home. On her return from the visit Woolf wrote to Janet Case thanking her for her hospitality: "Leonard and I have been saying at intervals it was one of the few week ends we enjoyed;

[13] In an interesting twist, marking perhaps a deliberate, because counterintuitive, break from Bloomsbury circles, *Orlando*'s cover is one of only two covers of Woolf's Hogarth Press novels not designed by Vanessa Bell; the other is *Flush*.

you and Emphie are some of the only people we envy etc etc. I think instead of garden notes, (which must in time exhaust even your garden) you should write notes on how to live, for the Manchester [Guardian]" (*L3* 509). Woolf's response complicates the question of work and life: Case had done more than contribute to Woolf's intellectual development; she also serves as an example of how "to live."

Violet Dickinson, Woolf's somewhat conventional, but eccentric childhood friend (seventeen years her senior), falls into the same category as Case. Dickinson provided support and refuge at many important moments for the young Virginia Stephen. As Hermione Lee has suggested, "[Dickinson] became indispensable to Virginia for about five years, and played a crucial enabling part in her early writing" (166). Dickinson's response to her appearance in the Preface, where she is lodged between "the Hon. Edward Sackville-West" and Hugh Walpole (Woolf tells Nelly Cecil that Dickinson, obviously facetiously, "says she doesn't like keeping such low company at all" [*L3* 553]), suggests that she understood Woolf's satirical intent. Dickinson and Woolf had drifted apart long before *Orlando;* this indicates the temporal range of Woolf's indebtedness.

Woolf also acknowledges prestige, also a form of cultural capital, as she simultaneously recognizes friendships. Woolf includes many prominent families and a number of titled people on the list. She thanks members of the Strachey family who, according to Leonard Woolf, represented "an intellectual aristocracy of the middle class" (qtd in Hussey 275). Mme. Jacques Raverat (Gwen Darwin) represents the Darwins, and here Woolf implicitly includes via Gwen the late Jacques Raverat who had died in 1925. Some of these names would provoke the wrath of Bloomsbury critics like Lewis, and in this sense she is careful to raise the ire of opponents by including titles. Woolf also includes them as a challenge to middlebrow critics to object to the presence of people who had become essential in their role as facilitators, and frequently financial backers, in the world of art and culture.

Indeed, many people on the list are both friends and important patrons of the arts; they represent both social and financial capital. The inclusion of patrons shows Woolf engaged with the practicalities of the book business and with the controversial subject of how money dictates what gets published about which Woolf had written, most notably in "The Patron and the Crocus" (1924). Among patrons named is Ottoline Morrell, who at the time of *Orlando*'s publication was organizing get-togethers in London, having recently moved from Garsington. During World War One, Morrell's Garsington farm provided a refuge for conscientious objectors, artists and writers, including Duncan Grant, Clive Bell, Aldous Huxley, Siegfried Sassoon and also D.H. Lawrence, for whom Morrell and husband Phillip raised funds for his passage to Florida in 1915, (Seymour 223; Hussey 167). Morrell supported young artists by finding buyers for their work, and in 1909 she joined Roger Fry and Dugald MacColl in setting up the Modern Art Association, a fund for purchasing and exhibiting the work of contemporary artists. She bought Duncan Grant's paintings and provided a studio for Henry Lamb. Frequently the butt of jokes, the eccentric Morrell did not escape the character assassinations at which Bloomsbury and others, such as Lawrence, who parodies Morrell as Hermione Roddice in *Women in Love*, excelled. However, she played a very significant role in the promotion of the arts in the early twentieth century.

Other patrons include Viscountess Lady Robert Cecil, Nelly, who was an old friend and, at an early stage, a collaborator for Woolf: the two women "shared a column at the *Cornhill Magazine* called 'The Book on the Table'" (Lee 164). Cecil was "an early supporter of [the Stephen sisters'] art, commissioning a portrait from Vanessa that was her first to be exhibited" (Hussey 54). She tried unsuccessfully to get conscientious objector status for Duncan Grant and David Garnett in World War I (Bell 2.31). Woolf's playful letter to Cecil about her inclusion in the Preface (cited above) reflects the intimacy the two women shared. Also a friend of Woolf's, Sibyl Colefax, addressed by Woolf in her preface as "Lady Colefax," was central, along with Christabel McLaren, to the "Desmond fund," money gathered in 1927 to help send Desmond and Molly MacCarthy on holiday (*L*3 354; *D*3 130, 137). Woolf describes her contradictory relationship with Colefax, socialite and London hostess, in "Am I a Snob."[14] Woolf met Lady Gerald Wellesley, Dorothy or Dottie, also listed, via Vita Sackville-West. Perhaps best known for her later relationship with W. B. Yeats, Wellesley became a Hogarth Press patron with her financing of the Press's Living Poets Series (1928-1932).

A similar overlap of the social and the financial (personal and business) sides of Woolf's life as a writer, is seen in the rarely noted predominance on Woolf's list of Hogarth Press authors, most of them active in 1928-1929. The Hogarth Press, which, beginning with *Jacob's Room* in 1922, published all of Virginia Woolf's books, was at its peak in 1927 in terms of output as Woolf wrote *Orlando*, publishing the highest number of volumes ever—38 in 1927 and 36 in 1928. Making clear Woolf's attention to the practicalities of the literary marketplace, included are press authors, artists, and workers. While many of these people were also social ties, a number were not. In this sense, *Orlando*'s Preface constitutes a celebration of the Hogarth Press and the freedom it accorded to the Woolfs, and to a number of their friends, including the novel's dedicatee, Sackville-West, fifteen of whose books were published by the press.[15]

[14] For an excellent analysis of the relationship of Woolf and Colefax, see Stephen Barkway's "'I'm a bat and your [sic] a butterfly': Sybil Colefax and Virginia Woolf" presented at the 21st Annual Conference on Virginia Woolf in Glasgow (June 2011).

[15] Stephen Barkway's chapter on Sackville-West's professional relationship with the Woolfs at the Hogarth Press (in Southworth) illustrates the way the Woolfs' social life overlapped with their professional lives.

Among authors acknowledged we find Edward Sackville-West, whose *The Apology of Arthur Rimbaud: A Dialogue* was published in 1927 in the same Hogarth Essays series as *Hunting the Highbrow*; Harold Nicolson, whose *The Development of English Biography* appeared in 1928; and T. S. Eliot, whose *Poems* were published by the Hogarth Press in 1919, and *The Waste Land* in 1923. Also listed are Roger Fry, whose *Twelve Original Woodcuts* was published in 1921, *A Sampler of Castile* in 1923, *Duncan Grant* in 1924, and *Art and Commerce* as part of the first Hogarth Essays series in 1926; E. M. Forster, whose *Anonymity, An Enquiry* appeared in 1925; and Sanger whose *Structure of Wuthering Heights* appeared with the press in 1926. Fry also contributed cover artwork to the press, as did Duncan Grant and Vanessa Bell.[16]

Reflecting the promotional activities of the press, while many of the authors on Woolf's list were already established, others are first timers. Newer authors include several Hogarth Press women writers such as Mrs. (Mary) Hutchinson and Dottie Wellesley. The Hogarth Press published Hutchinson's short stories, *Fugitive Pieces*, in 1927. The first of a number of Wellesley's poetry collections, *Matrix*, was published in 1928. Also listed is "Miss Hope Mirrlees"; her *Paris: A Poem* appeared in a 1919/1920 imprint. Mirrlees was a "favourite pupil" and collaborator of the then recently deceased classicist and Newnham lecturer and Woolf mentor Jane Harrison, who is not mentioned (*L*2 385). Among several Hogarth Press authors-yet-to-be appearing on the acknowledgments list is "Mrs. Stephen Tomlin," Julia Strachey, Lytton's "flamboyant and temperamental" niece whose first novella, a comedy of manners, *Cheerful Weather for the Wedding*, was published by the Woolfs in 1932 (Lee 615; see Willis 206-7).

Hogarth Press workers on the list vary in their degree of social connectedness to the Woolfs. Although Apostle G. H. 'Dadie' Rylands stayed with the Woolfs for only six months, July to December of 1924, when he left for a Fellowship at King's, he returned to the press as an author. His *Russet and Taffeta* was published in 1925 and his *Words and Poetry* in 1928. It was lunch in his rooms that formed the basis of Woolf's description of lunch at an Oxbridge college in *A Room of One's Own* (1929)—significantly in a scene tightly tied up with questions of financial support and access to writing.

Hogarth Press workers of longer tenure acknowledged by Woolf include "Mr. Angus Davidson" and "Mrs. Cartwright." Davidson was an author, editor, and prizewinning translator and is usually identified as a member of the new

[16] Fry's presence on the list is particularly important when it is read in terms of Lewis (as is Eliot's). Lewis disparaged Fry as an art critic after the Ideal Home Rumpus and therefore to praise him in particular for his knowledge of painting constitutes a jab at Lewis. Furthermore, Woolf did seriously venerate Fry (as she did Sanger) as her "not dedication" of *To the Lighthouse* reveals.

Bloomsbury Group. He began work at the press in 1924 but was fired in 1927 by the notoriously difficult Leonard. Like Rylands, after leaving the press, Davidson maintained ties with the Woolfs, and thus he was still active in 1928, editing, along with Leonard Woolf, the Hogarth Lectures on Literature (1927-1933). Significantly, and lending support to the argument that Woolf is sincere in her acknowledgments, Woolf sent Davidson a check of 10 or 20 pounds in late December 1928 calling it "a small slice of Orlando, which I always feel owed a great deal to you" (*L*3 564). Woolf does not indicate how Davidson contributed specifically to *Orlando*; it is likely that she is acknowledging how his assistance at the Hogarth Press freed her up to write.

When Davidson left the press, according to Willis, the Woolfs approached another younger generation figure from the Bloomsbury peripheries, Francis (Frankie) Birrell, also acknowledged, as a possible Hogarth Press partner and helper in the establishment of a new journal provisionally titled the *Hogarth Miscellany*. Birrell was experienced in the literary marketplace: in the 1920s he co-owned a Bloomsbury bookstore with David Garnett, located in Taviton Street then in Gerrard Street, which sold Hogarth Press titles. The Woolfs ordered books from Birrell's and Garnett's bookstore on occasion and even considered buying it as Woolf wrote *Orlando* in 1927 (Hussey 33; also see Partridge). While Birrell did not ultimately join the press, the Woolfs published his work. Along with F. L. Lucas, also acknowledged by Woolf, and constituting one example among many of a collaborative relationship on the list, although one which postdates *Orlando*, Birrell edited *The Art of Dying: An Anthology*, published by the Hogarth Press in 1930; his *A Letter from a Black Sheep* also appeared with the Hogarth Press in 1932.

Mrs. Cartwright was the Hogarth Press office manager-secretary from late 1925 until 1930, working "[i]n the peak years of 1927 and 1928" alongside "a secretary (Peggy Belsher) and a sixteen-year-old apprentice (Richard Kennedy)" (Willis 363). In a different category than the other press workers named in that she was not otherwise connected with the Woolfs, Cartwright's inclusion confirms Woolf's acknowledgment of the professional contribution of the press to her work as a writer. Willis suggests that Cartwright might have been responsible for the more professional approach adopted by the press in the late 1920s, indicated by a shift to massive ledgers in 1926 (388). Supporting this assessment of Cartwright's contribution, when Woolf gives information to Vanessa Bell about "the basement world," a favorite topic, in a letter at the end of April 1928, she remarks that "[t]he Press has revived astonishingly with Cartwright only" (*L*3 490). Davidson and Cartwright are often referred to together as constitutive of the Hogarth Press; the fact that Vanessa Bell held Davidson responsible for the failures and successes of the press suggests how indispensable he was to the Woolfs' professional endeavors (Spalding, *Vanessa Bell* 207).

Although she was not a press employee, the inclusion of the most infamous of Woolf's servants, "Miss Nellie [*sic*] Boxall," underscores the material side, and the economic and practical concerns of Woolf's work. Her name reminds us that the Hogarth Press was in part a domestic operation, the printing undertaken initially at the heart of the house, in the larder and in the dining room. As Lois Cucullu has argued, this intrusion of the commercial into the domestic space represented a bold and transgressive move on the part of the Woolfs, a displacement of the ideal Victorian woman or the "Angel in the House" as Woolf called her in "Professions for Women," one central to modernist art and modernist production. The inclusion of Boxall also underscores the degree to which servants played an important role in Bloomsbury's day-to-day existence, as Ann Stephen has suggested, and as Alison Light's *Mrs Woolf and the Servants* confirms. "The servants of Bloomsbury were a community of their own and gossip passed from one house to another largely on the lips of charwomen" (Stephen in Noble 15). Boxall worked for the Woolfs for eighteen years; Woolf attributed some of Boxall's belligerence to Bloomsbury's influence: Nelly "[w]on't be dictated to: must do as other girls do. This is the fruit of Bloomsbury," she writes in her diary (*D*3 3). Suggesting the proximity in which the Woolfs and their servants lived, Woolf describes herself writing *Orlando* "500 words to a minute with Leonard looking on suspicious in the arm chair, Pinker [the dog] snoring and Nelly [Boxall] playing fox trots on the gramophone upstairs" (*L*3 430).

The appearance on the list of Boxall and Cartwright alerts the reader to several other less recognizable names. These names are unexpected in the sense that these are not people we usually consider part of Woolf's inner circle. In terms of family ties these include Cory Bell, Vanessa Bell's brother-in-law, Mrs. Sidney Woolf, Woolf's mother-in-law, and Margery Snowden, Vanessa Bell's friend and not a particular favorite of Woolf's. In terms of social connections, less obvious mentions include the actress Valerie Taylor and socialite Mary Hutchinson, mentioned above as one of those who identified herself as an "Ape of God." The inclusion of these people undercuts the notion that this is a tight family or social network and authorizes a consideration of the list as more polemical than it at first appears. As I will show, the presence on the list of Cory Bell, Mrs. Woolf, Snowden, Taylor, and Hutchinson counters conceptions of Bloomsbury as conservative and insulated from the real world as it sees Woolf engaged outside of her Bloomsbury network.

Clive Bell's older brother, "Colonel [William] Cory Bell," Unionist MP for Devizes 1918-1923, was the only member of Clive's family, according to Frances Spalding, with whom Vanessa Bell made friends. According to Spalding, Bell "was intelligent and could have succeeded in a number of professions, but he chose the life of an artilleryman as it suited his unashamedly hedonistic temperament" (*Vanessa Bell* 68). The pretensions of the Colonel title must have appealed to Woolf in terms of flaunting the pedigree of her connections in the Preface, as would his notorious love of pleasure. Woolf mentions Bell as an "anti-bugger," as anti-homosexual, in her diary in April 1925 in terms of her own anti-buggery (*D*3 10). This reference suggests that Bell was a mischievous addition as he is thrown among the liberal Bloomsbury "buggers," many of whom had been involved in homosexual relationships (a number of the couples appearing on the list). The addition of Woolf's mother-in-law, "Mrs. Sidney Woolf," with whom she had mixed relations, introduces antagonism to the list, a reminder that not all family relations are necessarily positive ones. Her inclusion may have been designed as a jab at Sackville-West's mother, Victoria or B. M. (Bonne Mama), who disapproved of Vita's lesbian liaisons and was appalled by the publicity Woolf's *Orlando* brought her daughter. Both Cory Bell and Mrs. Sidney Woolf show Woolf tied to families less well-connected and less eminent than her own Stephens and Thackerays, a point Woolf might have wanted to make to those who accused her of privilege resulting from her own ancestry.

Further questions of antagonism and rivalry are introduced to the list with the naming of "Margery Snowdon [*sic*]" (the correct spelling is Snowden), a painter, a member of the Cheltenham Group of Artists and an art school friend and correspondent of Vanessa Bell (*D*3 290). Woolf thanks Snowden for "indefatigable researches in the archives of Harrogate and Cheltenham … none the less arduous for being vain."[17] Spalding describes Woolf's ambivalent feelings about Snowden "whose Harrogate background differed from that of the Stephens": "Virginia, again critical, thought her a commonplace, tragic creature and felt slightly incredulous that Vanessa should take obvious pleasure in her company" (*Vanessa Bell* 39). A portrait of Snowden at fifty written by Woolf in her diary in February 1930 subsequent to *Orlando* reveals that Snowden, who had remained in Cheltenham to care for her elderly mother, felt that her life had been impoverished as a result: "I have had no life & life is over" she tells Woolf (*D*3 289). Read alongside this later portrait, Woolf's description of what appears to be a made-up research trip for Snowden as "fruitless" seems unkind.

Woolf includes actress and screenwriter Miss Valerie Taylor (1902-1988) in her Preface. Taylor acted with Laurence Olivier and Michael Redgrave in the 1920s and 1930s and perhaps was included by Woolf as a representative of the celebrity and popular culture that was frequently condemned as middlebrow. Providing a concrete reason for including Taylor, Woolf had considered using her for her photograph of Sasha in the novel, before opting for her niece Angelica (*L*3 434). As

[17] Prior to Woolf's conception of *Orlando* in October 1927, in a letter to Vanessa Bell dated 14 April 1927 written in Sicily, Woolf does mention that she has received a letter "from that old lady at Cheltenham, whom Snow has been to see." It's unclear if this has any relationship with the acknowledgment.

Fig. 1. NPG x36509 Valerie Taylor by Bassano whole-plate glass negative, 12 May 1926

Figure 1 suggests, Taylor would have made an admirable Sasha in part due to her close resemblance to Violet Trefusis on whom Sasha is based. Taylor is mentioned as the subject of gossip over and over again in Woolf's correspondence, most often in terms of Clive Bell, with whom she had an affair, in letters to Vanessa Bell or Sackville-West (*L*3 466, 496). Woolf characterizes Clive's relationship with Taylor in her diary as one that makes him seem "second rate," the liaison lacking "imagination, intellect, poetry" (*D*3 148-9). Other letters refer to Taylor's affair with another of Woolf's acknowledgments, Raymond Mortimer (*L*3 496). Like Snowden for Woolf, Taylor was a rival for Vanessa Bell. In her capacity as a close friend of Sackville-West Taylor also represented a rival for Virginia Woolf.

In the same category as Valerie Taylor in terms of weaker ties and greater celebrity is Mary Hutchinson, Hogarth Press author. Like Taylor, Hutchinson had been Clive Bell's lover. According to Lee, Hutchinson was "worldly, elegantly fashionable, ugly-charming, had a wonderful taste in clothes, painting and interior decoration ... [a] lively letter-writer, a hostess and a mother, sexually adventurous and with talent for intimacy, she was not much liked by Vanessa and was a threatening and intriguing figure to Virginia" (382). Hutchinson was a cousin of the Stracheys and Duncan Grant, and was among those who identified herself as an "Ape of God." Among her close friends were the Eliots (Hutchinson collaborated with T. S. Eliot) and Lytton Strachey. Her husband, St. John (Jack) Hutchinson, also listed in the Preface, was a barrister. Mary provided Bloomsbury with access to the fashionable world; at her parties one met people who had appeared in *Vogue* (Lee 470). Under Dorothy Todd's editorship (1922-1926) Bloomsbury made frequent appearances in the magazine; Woolf herself was photographed by Man Ray for the magazine in 1926. When Logan Pearsall Smith criticized this engagement with *Vogue* and the middlebrow marketplace, Woolf responded with a defense of the liberty such outlets provided, asserting that "Duncans argument is that if Bloomsbury has real pearls, they can be scattered anywhere without harm" (*L*3 158). The decision to include Hutchinson and Taylor sends a similar message about the diversity of audiences Bloomsbury desired.

Another society figure and among the less obvious choices on the list is Lord Berners "whose knowledge of Elizabethan music has proved invaluable." Lord Gerald Hugh Tyrwhitt-Wilson Berners, fourteenth Baron, was a diplomat, composer, author, painter and eccentric. Berners' biographer Mark Amory cites Osbert Sitwell's description of him as "'a sort of missionary of the arts'" (74), whose "natural home" was "[t]he agreeable spot in English life where society and the arts met" (71). Harold Nicolson and Sackville-West met Berners in Constantinople in 1911 and they introduced him to Woolf in 1924. Berners knew Stravinsky and Diaghilev; he was tied to the Ballets Russes with which Bloomsbury became enamored after World War One. In terms of a direct connection to *Orlando,* he was, like Woolf's hero[ine], by all accounts a bit of a dilettante. He had an odd sense of humor: according to Amory, "[Berners] valued mockery, originality and experiment," and had had a piano installed in the back of his motorcar (74). Woolf may have included him in his capacity as a friendly rival alongside Osbert Sitwell—with whom, along with Edith and Sacheverell, he had close ties. Suggesting other ties to the networks of the list, Berners was a friend of Sibyl Colefax, and he also knew Violet Trefusis.[18] According to Amory, Berners wanted "smarter society" than Bloomsbury and he found it in the Sitwells (74). The Sitwells were somewhat at odds with the Bloomsbury Group: "the two camps regarded each other with suspicion not untouched by contempt," but Osbert counted Virginia Woolf "among his closer, though not closest, friends" (Ziegler 83-4). Osbert Sitwell's publishing relationship with Woolf's half-brother Gerald Duckworth adds a professional as well as a social aspect to his rivalry; after Duckworth published *The Voyage Out* in 1915 and *Night and Day* in 1919 Woolf, uncomfortable about her relationship with a man who she later revealed had molested her as a child, published all of her novels with the Hogarth Press.

Matching these social antagonisms, a thread of discord weaves its way through the list with the inclusion of several people who were at odds with Bloomsbury or with Woolf on a professional level. Among those in this category are fellow writers and critics, including E. M. Forster, Desmond MacCarthy, Arthur Waley, Raymond Mortimer and Hugh Walpole.

Several literary events contemporaneous with the publication of *Orlando* suggest that dissent reigned in Bloomsbury. Woolf did not like Strachey's biography *Elizabeth and Essex*, which was published alongside *Orlando* in 1928, and Quentin Bell describes the difficulties of the relationship Woolf shared with Forster: they admired each other and at the same time found much in each other's work to deplore (*D*3 234; Bell 2.132-5). In Desmond MacCarthy's review of *Orlando* (October 2, 1928), emphasizing again that Bloomsberries could criticize each other's work, he describes himself as a "backward and almost reluctant admirer of Mrs Woolf's fiction, though *To the Lighthouse* impressed me"—although he feels that in *Orlando* "[Woolf] finds herself more completely than ever before" (Majumdar 222). "Critics," he suggests, reflecting the norms of the marketplace, "are suspect when they praise contemporary work enthusiastically, but ruling out the judgment of the unduly literal, I have no fear in this case that praise will not be corroborated" (226). Despite, or because of these differences, Woolf acknowledged all three men, Strachey, Forster and MacCarthy.

[18] In the early 1930s, Berners published a roman à clef called *The Girls of Radcliff Hall* based on *The Well of Loneliness*, Radclyffe Hall's lesbian novel published just before *Orlando*. Famously, while Hall's novel was banned for its portrayal of a homosexual relationship, *Orlando* escaped the censors.

In 1928, the year of *Orlando*'s publication, MacCarthy became senior literary critic for the *Sunday Times*, replacing Edmund Gosse on whom *Orlando*'s Nick Greene was in part based (Whitworth 598). Prior to this, MacCarthy had been literary editor at the *New Statesman* where he wrote the weekly column "Books in General" using the pseudonym "Affable Hawk." In this regard he is among those on the list who functioned as an arbiter of taste in the literary marketplace. MacCarthy was a member of the Bloomsbury Group and Woolf's diary entries suggest that while his views on women and contemporary literature annoyed her, she admired him (see Hussey 151-2). However, there is dispute over whether MacCarthy welcomed this designation. His son-in-law, David Cecil, quotes MacCarthy as saying "Bloomsbury has never been a spiritual home for me," and he adds "[Bloomsbury's] characteristic attitude to the world was alien to [MacCarthy]; its exclusiveness, its intellectual pride, the inability of its members to feel at ease with anyone but each other" (15).

Supporting the argument that with the inclusion of MacCarthy Woolf brings dissent to the list, MacCarthy appears not only on Woolf's acknowledgment list, but also on a list of those "Against Orlando," compiled by Bloomsbury antagonist Cyril Connolly in his diary *after* the appearance of *Orlando*; the motivation for compiling this list is unclear, but might be read as a response to the Preface (180). Alongside MacCarthy, Connolly includes other names from Woolf's list including Arthur Waley, whom he applauds for calling *Orlando* "tinsel" (180). Waley is acknowledged in the *Orlando* Preface for his "knowledge of Chinese—how great I alone can estimate." Woolf made 20 pounds for her review of Waley's translation of *Tales of Genji* for *Vogue* in 1925, thus the thank you may represent a tongue-in-cheek reference to the financial support he afforded her in a venue which Logan Pearsall Smith thought inappropriate to Bloomsbury, rather than to his expertise which has nothing to do with the novel (*D*3 30-1). Waley was sometimes considered Bloomsbury, sometimes not; he is associated with Connolly's Chelsea set. Further indicating his complicated status, he is targeted by Lewis in *Apes of God*. Several other names appear on both Woolf's and Connolly's lists: Lady Colefax, Raymond Mortimer and Francis Birrell. Woolf identifies Ethel Sands (acknowledged) as Chelsea, but Connolly does not list her as "against *Orlando*" (*L*5 119). Revealing that allegiances were fragile and temporary, on Connolly's list (but *not* on Woolf's) are several Hogarth Press authors, Logan Pearsall Smith (*Stories from the Old Testament*, 1920; *The Prospects of Literature*, 1927), Robert Trevelyan (eight titles between 1925 and 1941, including *Poems and Fables*, 1925; *The Deluge and Other Poems*, 1926), and Hogarth Press author-to-be Peter Quennell (*A Letter to Virginia Woolf*, 1932); also included are the *London Mercury*'s

John Squire, writer Maurice Baring, *Vogue*'s Dorothy Todd and (an unidentified) Jennings (*Journal* 180).[19]

Woolf's antagonism to Chelsea is most evident in her interactions with Logan Pearsall Smith (listed by Connolly, but not Woolf), according to Michael Whitworth, a possible model, along with Gosse, for *Orlando*'s Nick Greene. In a stinging 1932 letter to Pearsall Smith, Woolf provides a key to her motives for the inclusion of antagonists in her Preface. The complexity and the irony of the tone of the letter echoes that of the *Orlando* Preface as Woolf uses what Pearsall Smith has said against him; Pearsall Smith was very fond of aphorisms and he has suggested that he and Woolf are enemies.

> I agree with you that one can admire a set or group and at the same time indulge a malicious desire to laugh at it. Am I not just as guilty as you are? Only of course I laugh at Chelsea whereas you laugh at Bloomsbury. And I feel great admiration and respect for Chelsea as you do for Bloomsbury—indeed I can't see any reason for you to prefer Bloomsbury, as you intimate that you do—but then, alas, so much of what you say is ironical. And I too have often thought and I have often said (to quote you again) to the great annoyance of people like Lady Desborough and Mrs [Alice] Keppell (you know what great ladies are) [who] sometimes sneer at Chelsea—that in my opinion it is full of delightful people and brilliant gatherings. How could it not be? I need only mention, besides yourself, Desmond, Maurice Baring, Ethel Sands, Bob and Hilda Trevelyan, Mr. Connolly, Mrs. Hammersley, and then theres Sibyl Colefax round the corner. How can you, even out of politeness, put us in Bloomsbury above you? I'm sure you dont. Its only your fun. But much though I admire Chelsea, I freely admit that I have mocked at you all because mockery is 'my favorite pastime,' just as it is yours. And I may have made up a story or two about you into the bargain. (*L5* 118-19)

Significantly the holograph manuscript of *Orlando* reveals that the antagonism between Bloomsbury and Chelsea was on Woolf's mind as she wrote the novel. In the margin of the page at the moment when Orlando begins to break with the gypsies in Turkey, Woolf wrote "it is not love of truth but love of conquest that animates the Labour party & the Tory party sets [Bloomsbury?] against [gap] Chelsea and Chelsea against Mayfair: We are all engaged in a war for our [incomplete]" (Clarke 119). While the first comparison made it into the final version, the second did not.

[19] In her diary of July 1926, under the heading "Writing by living people," Woolf writes that while "[she] scarcely ever read[s] it" she is reading "C by M. Baring" because he has given her a copy.

When Hugh Walpole, popular novelist, shameless self-promoter and, as his popularity grew, generous patron of the arts, appears in Woolf's letters and diaries, it is as a figure of mockery, as a prime representation of the "unpardonable snobbery" Leonard Woolf contended Virginia Woolf attacked with her Preface (in his letter to Speaight mentioned above). A review of Walpole's recent acquaintance with Woolf in 1928 confirms that the target of the *Orlando* Preface, in which he oddly appears and then disappears, is the contemporary world of writing and ill-conceived ideas about Bloomsbury's integration into that world.

At their first meeting, at a luncheon organized by Sibyl Colefax in November 1923, Woolf is unsparing in her character assassination of Walpole who represents to her all of the misconceptions and narcissism of the contemporary literary scene. She is "in rather a fritter," too much so to read Euripides:

> Indeed, I've been talking to Hugh Walpole—not an impressive man—a man who protests too much; an uneasy, prosperous vain man, who harbours some grudge against clever intellectuals & yet respects them, would like to be one. He has the look of a kindly solicitor or banker; red cheeks; very small bright eyes; a genial, but not profound or cordial manner. We talked of contemporary fame. He dwelt a good deal on the different sets & critics, & how no book was good in the same parish. Somehow it all referred to him. (*D*2 275)

When Woolf encountered Walpole five years later in May of 1928 he was officiating at the ceremony for the Femina-Vie Heureuse prize awarded to Woolf for *To the Lighthouse*. In her diary Woolf decried the pretensions of the literary event and of Walpole, describing the "function" as "dull stupid horror" and Walpole's speech as one in which he said "how much he disliked my books; rather, how much he feared for his own" (*D*3 183). Subsequent to the award ceremony, Walpole apologized to Woolf for what he characterized in his own diary as "a rotten speech" at "a *frightful* occasion" (*L*3 492 n.1). A Press photo of the event captures the awkwardness both Woolf and Walpole felt (see Lee 515).

Later the same month, Woolf is back to mocking Walpole, having dined with him and Lydia Lopokova, reporting this time the prolific writer's dismay at his success in America and his horror at his popular readership. Walpole produced one to two books per year beginning in 1911:

> But Hugh stayed on til 12.30—pouring out his sorrows, which are that he can never sell less than 20,000 of his books, but nobody of any intelligence can bear them. It cuts him to the heart when his chauffeur praises them—He has 10 letters every day from enthusiastic Americans. But Bloomsbury

> sees that he is a fake, and he now sees it too. It all comes from being the son of a Bishop and so taught to tell lies from his infancy. He gave us a long analysis of his soul and his lies and his popularity which was very amusing—considering I'd only met him at the prize giving. (*L*3 499)

When Walpole subsequently reached out to Woolf with a positive review of *Orlando* in the *Morning Post*, pretentiously titling it "On a Certain New Book" and omitting any mention of either the title or the author of the book with an assertion that neither would need an introduction to future readers, Woolf responded with a teasing letter. The review appeared on October 25, four days after Woolf wrote to Walpole informing him he had made the Preface:

> A certain article on a Certain new book faces me. Dare I add certain letters to your O-? Can I take to myself so much praise? I know I've no right to it, yet I admit I have wrapped myself round it, and refuse to be robbed of it. I wear it like an ermine fleece to protect me from the blast. But (except for Squire) they have been rather nice—the blast, I mean; only not so nice as you. How so rapid and various, and generally gifted and busy and successful a man can yet be so generous on such a large scale, I cant conceive. Seriously I am more than grateful and very proud into the bargain. Dont you, after all, share my passion for Waverley?—and lots of other things. (*L*3 552)

The Woolfs had further fun with Walpole as they took his review out into the marketplace using it in an advertisement for *Orlando* (Figure 2). The *Times* advertisement, which Woolf sent to Vita Sackville-West for her amusement, read "'*Orlando* is 'another masterpiece in English letters,' says Hugh Walpole," followed by a series of "*Orlando* is" and other positive quotes, the last: "*Orlando* is published by THE HOGARTH PRESS" (Sackville-West 293).

In a beautiful closing strike at Walpole's snobbery, Woolf wrote him a last letter about *Orlando* to acknowledge how his review had contributed to her financial situation. She and Leonard, she tells Walpole, are planning an addition to Monk's House:

> This room will be called Orlando, and one window will be dedicated to St Hugh. It is financed by Orlando; and without St Hugh, should I have sold ten copies? But this reminds me of the—well I wont mention names since doubtless they are friends of yours: people of blameless character, good fathers, devoted husbands, who talk about royalties and sales; which in Bloomsbury, as you used to think, we don't. (*L*3 567)

ORLANDO
is "another masterpiece in English letters,"
says HUGH WALPOLE

ORLANDO
is "a poetic masterpiece of the first rank,"
says REBECCA WEST

ORLANDO
is by VIRGINIA WOOLF

ORLANDO
costs nine shillings

ORLANDO
is being reprinted

ORLANDO
is published by THE HOGARTH PRESS

Fig. 2. Orlando *advertisement*
The Times *30 October 1928*

Woolf's mockery of Walpole's snobbery and her playful assertion of her materialism, a challenge to the conception that Bloomsbury is not or should not be concerned with sales, sums up beautifully the purpose of the *Orlando* Preface: that is, to assert a knowledge of how the market functioned and to challenge misconceptions about Bloomsbury insularity.

Adding another curious twist to Walpole's inclusion, while he appears in the British edition (between John Maynard Keynes and Violet Dickinson), he is not included in the American editions. *Orlando* came out first in the United States on October 2, 1928, in a limited edition of 861 copies published by Crosby Gaige. The Hogarth Press edition, in which Walpole is named, appeared on October 11 and the American Harcourt Brace edition on October 18. Perhaps simply an editing error, it is tempting to read his excision as deliberate on Woolf's part, a playful honoring of Walpole's desire not to be quite so famous in America.[20] Walpole's inclusion/exclusion also provides an alternative reading of Woolf's last acknowledgment, to an unidentified "gentleman in America." Woolf closes her Preface by thanking this reader, whose name and address she has mislaid, for correcting "the punctuation, the botany, the entomology, the geography, and the chronology of previous works of mine," a service she hopes he will provide for *Orlando*. This is certainly meant sarcastically and is likely motivated by a not new anti-American sentiment on Woolf's part. However, it also reads as Woolf's exaggerated submission to the American reader and the wealth he promises as a means to show up the hypocrisy of Walpole's embarrassment at his substantial American public.

Lists, Literary History and Modernist Writing

The *Orlando* Preface merits particular attention because it provided Woolf's public in 1928 a rare glimpse of her social circle, her intellectual life and her professional activities—one that would not really come into view until the publication of her letters and diaries in the 1970s. Woolf's acknowledgment list represents one of the most detailed (if occluded) statements she made about the material conditions under which modernism operated. The publication of *Orlando* captures Woolf at a rare moment of self-assurance, one she would never again experience at such a pitch. In none of her later books would she so explicitly identify the machinery

[20] We might also read Walpole's (dis)appearance as a comment about how quickly one can be shut out by one's peers, with a stroke of the pen. In fact Walpole would suffer such a plight at the hands of his friend Somerset Maugham who parodied Walpole in his *roman à clef Cakes and Ale* (1930). Walpole based a character on Woolf in his *Hans Frost* (1929). Walpole's *The Historical Novel* was announced as forthcoming in the Hogarth Lectures on Literature in 1930, but never appeared. In 1932, the Hogarth Press published his *Letter to a Modern Novelist.*

behind her work as a writer. After *Orlando*, Woolf did not dedicate any of her major works, although she did, as mentioned earlier, consider dedicating *The Waves* to brother Thoby; and suggesting an additional dedication, *Three Guineas* (1938) was in many respects meant to commemorate the death of nephew Julian Bell in the Spanish Civil War.

With its focus on the material circumstances of Woolf's life and work, this analysis demonstrates how literary history contributes to an understanding of the development of a key modernist text. Methodologically, it shows the importance of lists and the links and network connections they reveal. It suggests an approach that might usefully be applied to other such lists available to Woolf scholars, both in print and in the archive. The lists of *Three Guineas* correspondents or Hogarth Press early subscribers, for example, have the potential to reveal much more about Woolf's networks of cultural, social, and financial capital and her engagement in the business of modernist writing.

Works Cited

Amory, Mark. *Lord Berners*: *The Last Eccentric.* London: Pimlico, 1999. Print.

Apollinaire, Guillaume. "L'Anti-tradition futuriste." *Oeuvres en prose complètes*, vol.2. Paris: Gallimard, 1991.

Bell, Quentin. *Virginia Woolf: A Biography.* New York: Harcourt Brace Jovanovich, Inc., 1972. Print.

——. and Stephen Chaplin. "Ideal Home Rumpus." In S. P. Rosenbaum, ed. *The Bloomsbury Group: A Collection of Memoirs and Commentary*. London: Toronto UP, 1995. Print.

Carey, John. *The Intellectuals and the Masses*: *Pride and Prejudice Among the Literary Intelligensia 1880-1939.* London: Faber and Faber, 1992. Print.

Cecil, David. "Introduction." *Desmond MacCarthy, the Man and his Writing.* London: Constable, 1984. Print.

Clarke, Stuart.Transcriber/Editor. *Virginia Woolf's* Orlando, *The Holograph Draft.* London: Stuart Clarke, 1993. Print.

Collier, Patrick. "Virginia Woolf in the Pay of Booksellers: Commerce, Privacy, Professionalism, *Orlando*." *Twentieth Century Literature* 48.4 (Winter 2002): 363-92. Print.

Connolly, Cyril. *Journal and Memoir.* Ed. David Pryce-Jones. London: Collins, 1983. Print.

Cucullu, Lois. "Retailing the Female Intellectual." *differences* 9.2 (Summer 1997): 25-68. EBSCO. Web. 13 Jan. 2012.

Daiches, David. *Virginia Woolf.* 1942. New York: New Directions, 1963. Print.

DiBattista, Maria. "Introduction." *Orlando*. New York: Harvest, 2006. Print.

Dick, Susan. "Literary Realism in *Mrs Dalloway, To the Lighthouse, Orlando* and *The Waves*." *Cambridge Companion to Virginia Woolf*. Ed. Sue Roe and Susan Sellers. Cambridge: Cambridge UP, 2000. 50-71. Print.

Dubino, Jeanne, ed. *Virginia Woolf and the Literary Marketplace*. New York: Palgrave, 2010. Print.

Eliot, T. S. *The Letters of T. S. Eliot, Vols.1 & 2*. Ed. Valerie Eliot. London: Faber & Faber, 1988, 2009. Print.

Glass, Loren. *Authors Inc.: Literary Celebrity in the Modern United States 1880-1980*. New York: NYU Press, 2004. Print.

Goldring, Douglas. *South Lodge*. London: Constable and Company, 1943. Print.

Hussey, Mark. *Virginia Woolf A-Z*. New York: Facts on File, 1995. Print.

Jaffe, Aaron. *Modernism and the Culture of Celebrity*. Cambridge: Cambridge UP, 2005. Print.

Latham, Sean. *Am I a Snob? Modernism and the Novel*. Ithaca: Cornell UP, 2003. Print.

Lee, Hermione. *Virginia Woolf*. London: Chatto and Windus, 1996. Print.

Levenson, Michael, ed. (Ed.). *The Cambridge Companion to Modernism*. Cambridge: Cambridge UP, 1999. Print.

Lewis, Percy Wyndham. "Apes of God." *Criterion*, April 1924. Print.

Light, Alison. *Mrs Woolf and the Servants: The Hidden Heart of Domestic Service*. London: Penguin, 2007. Print.

Majumdar, Robin and Allen McLaurin, eds. *Virginia Woolf: The Critical Heritage*. London: Routledge & Kegan Paul, 1975. Print.

Noble, Joan Russell, ed. *Recollections of Virginia Woolf*. New York: W. Morrow, 1972. Print.

North, Michael. *Machine-Age Comedy*. Oxford: Oxford UP, 2009. Print.

Partridge, Frances. *Memories*. London: V. Gollancz, 1981.Print.

Sackville-West, Vita. *Letters of Vita Sackville-West to Virginia Woolf*. Eds. . . . . Louise de Salvo and Mitchell A. Leaska. New York: Morrow, 1985. Print.

Schlack, Beverly Ann. *Continuing Presences: Virginia Woolf's Use of Literary Allusion*. University Park: Pennsylvania State UP, 1979. Print.

Seymour, Miranda. *Ottoline Morrell: Life on a Great Scale*. London: Faber, 2008. Print.

Southworth, Helen, ed. *Leonard and Virginia Woolf, The Hogarth Press and the Networks of Modernism*. Edinburgh: Edinburgh UP, 2010. Print.

Spalding, Frances. *Vanessa Bell*. San Diego: HBJ, 1983. Print.

———. *Roger Fry: Art and Life*. Berkeley: U of California P., 1980. Print.

Spotts, Frederic, ed. *The Letters of Leonard Woolf*. San Diego: Harcourt Brace Jovanovich, 1989. Print.

Sproles, Karyn Z. *Desiring Women: The Partnership of Virginia Woolf and Vita Sackville-West*. Toronto: U of Toronto P, 2006. Print.

Theroux, Paul. "Acknowledgments." *The New Yorker*. September 24, 1979: 34-5. Print.

Webb, Caroline. "Listing to the right: authority and inheritance in 'Orlando' and 'Ulysses.'" *Twentieth-Century Literature* 40.2 (Summer, 1994): 190-204. *JSTOR* Web. 13 Jan. 2012.

Whitworth, Michael. "Logan Pearsall Smith and *Orlando." Review of English Studies* 55, 2004: 598-604. Oxford University Press Journals Current WEB. 14 Jan. 2012.

Williams, Raymond. "The Bloomsbury Fraction (1980)." *The Raymond Williams Reader.* Ed. John Higgins. Oxford: Blackwell, 2001. Print.

Wilson, J. J. "Why is *Orlando* Difficult?" *New Feminist Essays on Virginia Woolf.* Ed. Jane Marcus . Lincoln: U of Nebraska P, 1981.170-84. Print.

Willis, J. H. *Leonard and Virginia Woolf as Publishers.* Charlottesville: U of Virginia P, 1992. Print.

Windsor, Alan. "Wyndham Lewis's 'Blast and Bless.'" *Wyndham Lewis: Letteratura/Pittura.* Ed. Giovanni Cianci. Palermos: Sellerio editore, 1982. Print.

Woolf, Leonard. *Hunting the Highbrow*. The Hogarth Essays, Second Series, No 5, 1927. Print.

Woolf, Virginia. *The Letters of Virginia Woolf, Vols 1-6.* Eds. Nigel Nicolson and Joanne Trautmann. New York: Harcourt Brace Jovanovich, 1975-80. Print.

——.*The Diary of Virginia Woolf, Vols 1-5.* Ed. Anne Olivier Bell. New York: Harcourt Brace Jovanovich, 1977-84. Print.

——.*Orlando.* San Diego: Harcourt Brace & Company, 1956

——."The Patron and the Crocus." *The Common Reader*. New York: Harvest, 1953. Print.

Zwerdling, Alex. *Virginia Woolf and the Real World.* Berkeley: University of California Press, 1986. Print.

Ziegler, Philip. *Osbert Sitwell.* New York: Knopf, 2000. Print.

Virginia Woolf's Marginalia Manuscript

Amanda Golden

Annotation is an ambiguous genre.[1] As a Fulbright Scholar at Newnham College, Cambridge University in 1956, Sylvia Plath loaned her books to a classmate who had the gall to annotate them in pencil. Plath responded in her journal, "evidently she felt that since I'd already underlined them in black, nothing further could harm them; well, I was furious, feeling my children had been raped, or beaten by an alien" (226). Unlike Plath, Virginia Woolf envisioned annotating as an act of violence toward the author of the book, instead of toward its owner or former inscriber. She articulated this view in the following manuscript—entitled "writing in the margin" in the contents of the Monks House Papers microfilm—which she probably composed between 1906 and 1908.[2] Woolf had encountered marginalia in others' books, particularly in the library of her father, Leslie Stephen. In *A Room of One's Own* (1929), Woolf distinguishes her protagonist from the British Museum reader "making the neatest abstracts, headed often with an A or a B or a C" (30). Annotation, like outlining, is a student practice that is taught and used to study texts.[3] Both Woolf herself and her character Edward Pargiter in *The Years* (1937), for instance, annotate their texts while translating Greek (in which Woolf had had formal training).[4] Woolf's "writing in the margin" manuscript sheds light on the ways that her responses to academic institutions shaped her representations of annotation practices throughout her letters, journals, and novels.

Since the publication of Hermione Lee's *Virginia Woolf* (1999), readers have cited her quotations from and summary of the essence of Woolf's "writing in the margin" manuscript in the Monks House Papers at the University of Sussex, which

[1] I am grateful to the Society of Authors and the University of Sussex Library for permissions to publish Woolf's manuscript, SxMs18/2/A/A.23/C. This manuscript is also included as "(Writing in the margin)" in the contents of the Monks House Papers microfilm, Reel 2. A Post-Doctoral Fellowship in Poetics from the Fox Center for Humanistic Inquiry at Emory University also facilitated my research.

[2] Woolf wrote 22nd May at the top of her manuscript. The date on the next manuscript on the Monks House Papers microfilm is 6th July 1908. Subsequent manuscripts from this segment of the microfilm are dated 1906. Lee also notes that in Woolf's sketch on "writing in the margin," the readers whom she describes "are forcing their readings on her" (406).

[3] See H. J. Jackson, *Marginalia: Readers Writing in Books*. New Haven: Yale UP, 2001: 21.

[4] See Golden and Dalgarno. Dalgarno also underscored Woolf's training in Greek in "Translation in and out of the University," and Emily Kopley addressed Woolf's critique of academic institutions in A Room of One's Own in "Improving on 'A Dog's Chance': *A Room of One's Own* as a Reply to Sir Arthur Quiller-Couch's *On the Art of Writing" on the* "Institutional Woolf" panel at the Modern Language Association Convention,Seattle, WA, January 7, 2012.

is shown in facsimile and transcribed below. As Lee has argued, Woolf "hardly ever marked her books, and was satirical about people who did" (406). In the past decade, scholars have also worked with the contents of Virginia and Leonard Woolf's library at Washington State University. Diane Gillespie notes of the books in that library that Virginia inscribed "some of her books [with] . . . light marks in the margins" (xviii). Woolf's "writing in the margin" piece introduces readers to a fuller narrative of her response to the practice and her reluctance to contribute to it.

As a writer herself, Woolf underscores in her manuscript the insistence of "this anonymous commentator [who] must scrawl his . . . Beautiful upon the . . . sheet, as though the author received the man upon his flesh." The reader's desire to point out beauty is so strong that it has the opposite effect. She subsequently describes "old Colonel Talboy"[5] with "a remarkable theory of his own" who may present an early version of Professor von X in *A Room of One's Own*, composing his book, *The Mental, Moral, and Physical Inferiority of the Female Sex*. Instead of assaulting a writer's body, Woolf explains that Professor von X was "labouring under some emotion that made him jab his pen on the paper as if he were killing some noxious insect as he wrote, but even when he had killed it that did not satisfy him; he must go on killing it" (33).

Writers' annotations present one record of their response to language. Woolf's reading notebooks have provided scholars with perhaps more thorough commentary than her underlining and notes in the margin could have included. Had she annotated more of her books, however, we would have additional records to consider. In the decades after Woolf composed "writing in the margin," the practice of annotation changed with modernism. Readers approached the difficulty of modernist texts with pens in hand, annotating their books in an attempt to understand them. The influence of the New Criticism in academic institutions subsequently shaped students' inscriptions in the margins of modernist texts. The contents of Woolf's "writing in the margin" manuscript allow us to see the extent to which early in her career Woolf differentiated her own reading practices from those that readers later adopted to interpret her fiction.

Works Cited

Dalgarno, Emily. *Virginia Woolf and the Migrations of Language.* New York: Cambridge UP, 2012.

[5] Lee transcribes the Colonel's wife's last name as Tallboys (406), but there is only one 'l' in Woolf's first mention of the Colonel's last name in the manuscript. Woolf's reference to the Colonel's wife has two ll's.

Gillespie, Diane. "Introduction." *The Library of Leonard and Virginia Woolf: A Short-Title Catalog*. Eds. Julia King and Laila Miletic-Vejzovic. Pullman: Washington State UP, 2003.

Golden, Amanda. "'A Brief Note in the Margin:' Virginia Woolf and Annotating." *Contradictory Woolf: Selected Papers from the Twenty-First Annual Conference on Virginia Woolf*. Eds. Derek Ryan and Stella Bolaki. Clemson: Clemson UP, 2012.

Lee, Hermione. *Virginia Woolf*. New York: Random House, 1996.

Plath, Sylvia. *The Unabridged Journals of Sylvia Plath 1950-1962: Transcribed from the Original Manuscripts at Smith College*. Ed. Karen V. Kukil. Random House: New York, 2000.

Woolf, Virginia. *A Room of One's Own*. 1929. New York: Harcourt Brace, 1989.

——. *The Years*. 1939. Ed. Eleanor McNees. New York: Harcourt Inc., 2008.

——. "(writing in the margin)." Monks House Papers Reel 2. *The Virginia Woolf Manuscripts from the Monks House Papers at the University of Sussex*. Brighton, Sussex, England: Harvester Microform.

22nd May. 1.

It is not in the big affairs of life after all that we most easily detect a persons character. ~~The very~~ For most of us have only not enough individuality to make us twist the great emotions to our own private likeness. ~~We accept them always~~ Rather they mould us to their form, for the time being. So that you find for instance a great family likeness among all people who are in love. But you cannot in any way forecast the temper in which Brown will meet the loss of his umbrella, or in which Smith will ~~take~~ hear that he has been left a legacy of £50 ~~left him~~.

The student of character then, will keep his attention alert upon all such trivial occasions, & will note their various & Essential ~~most~~ significances. When you see how one man eats & another puts on his coat, you are but a simpleton if you cannot follow up the clues thus given ~~a long few~~ way through all the labyrinths & secret chambers of ~~his~~ the soul.

One of the trifles which is curiously characteristic, & affords good practice for a student to work upon, is the habit, which is so common ~~apparently so common, which so many have~~, of writing ~~brief~~ observations in the margins of books. It is a little spontaneous, anonymous expression of ~~character~~ temperament, valuable precisely because it is evidently not to be restrained, & not to be acknowledged. Indeed, so strong is it that the printed prohibition against any mark or annotation, ~~whatever in green~~ has no power to prevent it: in spite of request, even of fines, this anonymous commentator must scrawl his O. or his Pooh. or his ~~very true~~ Beautiful upon the unresisting sheet, as though the author received the marks upon his flesh. Or, ~~for clearly~~ if this is not his wish, you must take it that the Unknown is

22nd May 1.

It is not in these big affairs of life after all that we most easily
detect a persons character. ~~The very~~ For most of us have ~~onl~~y not –
enough individuality to make us twist the great emotions to
our own private likeness. ~~We accept them acqu~~ Rather they
mould us to their form, for the time being so that you find
among all
for instance a great family likeness ~~in~~ people who are in love.
But you can not in any way forecast the temper in which Brown
will meet the loss of his umbrella, or in which Smith will
been left
~~tak~~e hear that he has ^ a legacy of £50 ~~left him~~ .
The student of character then, will keep his attention alert
upon all such trivial occasions, & will note their various &
cies
essential ~~most~~ significan~~t~~ : When you see how one man eats &
another puts on his coat, you are but a simpleton if you cannot
through
follow up the clues thus given ~~or trace[?] you~~r ~~way~~ all the
the
labyrinths & secret chambers of ~~his~~ soul.
One of the titles which is curiously characteristic, & affords good
which is apparently
practice for a student to work upon is the habit, ~~apparently so~~
so common
~~common, which so many have~~, of writing ~~turis~~[?] observations in
the margins of books. It is a little spotaneous, anonymous
temperament
expression of ~~character~~, valuable precisely because it is evidently
not to be restrained, & not to be acknowledged. Indeed, so
strong is it that the printed prohibition against any mark or
annotation, ~~Perhaps is of no~~ has no power to prevent it: in
spite of request, even of fine, this anonymous commentator must
scrawl his O, or his Pooh, or his ~~very true~~ Beautiful
upon the unresisting sheet, as though the author received this
man [?] upon his flesh. Or, ~~for clearl~~y if this
is not his wish, you must take it that the Unknown is
[end of page one]

communicating with you; wishes to nudge you as it were, to admire this
beauty, or to set you emphatically against believing the lies you are
told in the text. ~~So one characteristic~~ The reader, on his side,
~~if he is one who likes to interpret traces~~ of cursory begins to
speculate who this officious old person may be, to figure his
look, his sudden grasp of the pencil, his ~~eager~~ emphatic jerk of the
hand, at which is expressed aloud, maybe, in some ejaculation of
praise or [disapproval] ~~contempt~~, which startle [the] ~~some~~ peaceful [lady] ~~reader upon~~ in
the seated [in the arm chair] opposite him. 'Ah' 'Really this is too bad' he
exclaims, as he makes his vengeance on the margin. Or, perhaps,
'Ah that is what I have always said' & down goes a score of
approval.

This gentleman, old Colonel Talbot, I think he must be, is a peppery
individual, who has reads a variety of works upon the religions &
mythology of the East, & checks them all by a remarkable theory
of his own, which ~~he~~ he has not yet given to the world. He
is forced sometimes, when a more than usually ~~ole~~ pernicious heresy
comes before him, to lay down the book, ~~&~~ & denounce it to his
wife. 'Now my dear, if a man who says that that must either be a
fool or a rascal. It is as plain as a pikestaff to any rational person
that so & so & so on & so" To all of which, Mrs. Talbot agrees
'Certainly, dear' 'Of course, of course' while her lips mechanically
count the stitches in her knitting, & she wishes the Colonel would
~~report~~ write to the Times, or communicate with the author himself.
But the Colonel is content with his pencil & his violated margin.
This 'annotator' is always very vehement [in] ~~after~~ his likes &
dislikes.

There is another commentator ~~who~~ of a different kind, ~~who feeds~~
~~chiefly upon books of poetry~~ who writes a deliberate cultivated hand,

Communicating with you; wishes to nudge you as it were, to admire this
beauty, or to set you emphatically against believing the lies you are
told in the text. ~~for ever[?] characteristic~~ The reader, on his side,
~~if he is one who likes to interpret thele t[?]~~ ~~cannot~~ begins to
speculate who this officious old person may be; to figure his
look, his sudden grasp of a pencil, his ~~anger~~ emphatic jerk of the
hand, at[?] which is expressed aloud, may be, in some ejaculation of
disapproval the lady
praise or ~~contempt~~, which startles ~~some~~ peaceful ~~reader out[?] on in~~
in the arm chair
the seated ^ opposite him. ~~Its~~ 'Really this is too, bad he
exclaims, as he wreaks his vengeance on the margin. or, perhaps,
"Ah that is what I have always said" & down goes a score of
approval.

This gentleman, old Colonel Talboy, I think he must be, is a peppery
individual, who reads a variety of works upon the religions &
mythology of the East, & checks them all by a remarkable theory
of his own, which ~~ha~~ he has not yet given to the world. He
is forced sometimes, when a more than usually ~~al~~ pernicious heresy
comes before him, to lay down the book, ~~de~~ & denounce it to his
wife. 'Now my dear, ~~is~~[?] a man who says that must either be a
fool or a rascal. It is as plain as a pikestaff to any rational person
that so & so & so on & so" To all of which, Mrs. Tallboy[sic] answers
'Certainly, dear' 'Of Course, of course' while her lips mechanically
count the stitches in her knitting; & she wishes the Colonel would
~~report t~~ write to The Times, or communicate with the author himself.
But the Colonel is content with his pencil & his violated margin.
is in
This ~~annotator~~ always very vehement ~~after~~[?] his likes &
~~dislikes~~,

There is another commentator ~~who~~ of a different kind, ~~who feeds~~
~~chiefly upon books of poetry~~ who writes a deliberate cultured hand,
[end of page 2]

2

& suggests literary problems on p. 29: was not this suggested by Wordsworth? [illegible] Excursion b. 2 [illegible]. or, "Cf Shelley Queen Mab p. 16.. This courteous gentleman is a clergyman, in all probability, & conceives that it is incumbent on him as a Christian to disseminate such pieces of information as those given above. He seldom expresses anything but mild approval, & a little classical erudition.

There is another commentator, who is to be found for the most part in the pages of the major poets, & the lesser novelists. He, or perhaps it is a she, finds [illegible] "How beautiful!" & draws thick lines beside all the stanzas which deal with early death, & hopes of immortality. Certain passages are inscribed with dates, & a whole botanical collection is returned to the library, pressed between the leaves. In this case, however, the motive of the annotator is simply to give expression to some transient emotion; & the note represents a half unconscious sigh of tearful satisfaction. They would be ashamed, later, to own their handiwork; indeed in some case you may trace the action of the india rubber.

There is another person of a public spirited temper, who goes through the volumes, correctly inserts the errata in their proper places, corrects misprints, &, when a sentence is doubtful, makes his note of interrogation, & suggests a more likely reading. He is conscientious & honestly useful, but, we conceive, of a precise & pedantic spirit; the sort of person who accosts a stranger in the underground, & tells him that his collar is turned up.

And when you remember how urgently you are reminded in most cases that it is a serious infringement of the rule to utter protest, or approval, or question or correct or in any way assault the book with a pencil, you must agree that the love of annotating books is one of the most permanent & vigorous instincts in the human mind

3

& suggests literary problems as ~~fs~~ Qy[?]: was not this suggested by
Wordsworth? v. Excursion 1. 2 " &c. or, "Cf Shelley Queen Mab –
p. 16 . . ~~Him we conceive~~ This courteous gentleman is a
clergyman, ~~was~~[?] in all probability & conceives that it is incumbent
on him as a Christian to disseminate such pieces of information
as those given above. He ~~is~~ seldom expresses ~~any but[?] the~~ anything
erudition
but mild approval, & a little classical l~~earnin~~g.
There is another commentator, who is to be found for the most part
minor
~~in the~~ aim in the pages of the ~~for lesser~~ poets, & the lesser novelists
Solace[?]
He, or perhaps it is a She, ~~finds much of hours[?]. Item any~~ "How
lachrymose inside
beautiful!" & draws thick tre~~mulous~~ lines. down all the
stanzas which deal with early deaths, & hopes of immortality.
Certain passages are inscribed with dates, & a whole botanical
collection is returned to the library, pressed between the leaves.
In this case, however, the motive of the annotator is ~~different from~~
simply to give expression, to some transient emotion; & the note
represents a halfconscious sigh of tearful satisfaction. They would
be ashamed, later, to see their ~~work~~ handiwork; indeed in some cases
you may trace the action of the india rubber.
There is another person, of a public spirited temper, who goes through
corr~~ec~~ts marks
the volumes, ~~can~~ int~~en~~ds the errata in their proper places, corrects
misprints, or, when a sentence is ~~doubtful~~, makes his note of interrogation,
& suggests a more likely reading. He is conscientious & possibly useful,
but, we conceive, of a precise & pedantic spirit; the sort of person who
accosts
~~corrects~~ a stranger in the underground, ~~whose tell[?] of thinks that x ant collar is turned up~~. & tells him that his collar is turned up.
reminded
And when you remember how urgently you are requested in most cases to
that it is a serious infringement of the rules to utter protest,
or approval, or question or correct or in any way assault the book with
a pencil, you must agree that the love of annotating books is one of the most
permanent
& vigorous instincts in the human mind.

A Note on "Bloomsbury at Play"

Elizabeth Wright

Virginia Woolf's relationship with her eldest nephew, Julian Bell, was characterized by rivalry as well as love. Even when he was a baby Woolf was jealous of him for stealing her sister's attention, though she immediately realized the comic potential in playing the mad aunt for him in later life. "Can't you imagine how airily he would produce her, on Thursday nights," she asked her sister in 1909 before imagining what he would say to his friends: "'I have an Aunt who copulates in a tree, and thinks herself with child by a grasshopper—charming isn't it? She dresses in green, and my mother sends her nuts from the Stores'" (*L*1 417). When he grew up Woolf became his eccentric, but respected aunt; he a mixture between nephew, friend and antagonist. To Woolf he came to represent the privileged young man whose education was expensive and exclusive; while writing *Three Guineas* she reflected in her diary, "Why should all the splendour, all the luxury of life be lavished on the Julians" (*D*3 200-201) and as his mind developed she often disagreed with him over art and politics. Nevertheless, it was a largely loving and somewhat humorous relationship, only intensified by their critical and political differences.

Unsurprisingly, considering the creative milieu in which he grew up, Julian aspired to be a writer and Cambridge don, though his fellowship dissertation in April 1933 was, according to Maynard Keynes, "uneducated" (*D*5 78) and, though he submitted another, he did not succeed in gaining a position. As a child he had collaborated with his brother on "The Charleston Bulletin" and "The New Bulletin" as well as writing, directing and acting in a number of private dramas, many of which were directly influenced by the irreverence of the adults who involved and encouraged the children in disrespectful impersonations of their elders. In an unpublished 1917 letter to her sister, Vanessa Bell described how "We had great fun last night with the children who acted a play, entirely their own invention. Rachel [MacCarthy] as Ottoline, [?] 'Morrell,' Julian 'Keynes' and Quentin a lunatic. Rachel was amazing, accepting first Morrell and then Keynes. I cant think how they got hold of it all" (Wright 90). None of the adults were safe from the caricaturing, but Virginia Woolf was a favorite target. Though often quite cruel in his representations of his author aunt as he grew up, Julian valued Woolf's criticism, he discussed poetry with her and sent her his own poetry and essays. However, Woolf was guarded in her praise and told Vanessa that she thought him "better as a lawyer than a poet" (Bell 352). Julian's collection of poems entitled *Winter Movement* (1930) was published by Chatto and Windus and, though generally well received, Woolf was pleased that the poems were poor, she reflected in her diary: "for all his admirable good sense & observation & love of country life, he is no poet. People who treat words as he does rather afflict me" (*D3* 328).

Eventually Julian accepted a professorship at Wuhan University in China and left to take it up in August 1935. "I'm very sorry he's to go—" Virginia reflected, "the delightful, honest bubbly yet after all so sympathetic & trusty young man" (*D4* 332). While in China he sent her "A Letter to A" about Roger Fry, which he hoped to have published by the Hogarth Press, but when Woolf explained why they could not publish the essay in June 1936, Julian was hurt and did not respond. Vanessa kindled and defended her son, much to Virginia's interest and annoyance, but his work was still refused. David Garnett suspected Virginia of jealousy and Vanessa passed his opinion on to Julian in a letter:

> I do think there's something odd in the Woolves' attitude – which I discussed with Bunny [...] His theory is that V. lives so precariously (in nerves and brain) that she can't face any other writer of any real merit. The responsibility and strain of accepting them would somehow upset her own balance, he thinks. That is why she always gives absurd praise to obscure females. (Bell 424)

Nevertheless, the Hogarth Press did publish his second volume of poetry, *Work for the Winter* (1936), though Woolf's opinions remained cool. This tumultuous literary relationship between aunt and nephew had been lampooned in some of the comic sketches written by Julian (and Quentin) over the 1920s and 30s. The Epilogue (possibly from the skit "A Quiet Morning in Whistler Studios") quoted in my article "Bloomsbury at Play" is a good example of the type of advice Woolf gave her nephew about writing: "Don't write till you're aged about 60 or so" (Wright 89).

In 2004 when I was scribbling notes in the Sussex University Archives from the Monk's House Papers, I came across a short play script satirizing the relationship between Virginia and Julian. It was marked "JB" at the top of the page and I mistakenly attributed the piece to Julian, a mistake which I carried across into my article "Bloomsbury at Play" many years later (Wright 88).[1] However, the misattribution does not alter the point I was making in the article which centered on the use of private drama as a safe way to communicate difficult critiques of others. The script, possibly written in 1931, read as part of Woolf's output, makes some interesting satirical revelations about her feelings for her nephew's poetry. The scene revolves around Julian's noisy attempt to compose a poem in the manner of

[1] See Rosenbaum where the manuscript is published under the title "JB (1931?)" (33-35). Rosenbaum notes that the title may not have been given by Woolf, and that it is "a typescript revision of pages from a notebook, both of which are at Sussex (A.18, B.2.e)" (241).

Gerard Manley Hopkins about a male siskin and Woolf's desire for quiet so that she can write her novel. It satirizes his youthful need to imitate rather than innovate; his inexperience of the forms and terms of poetry; and his competitiveness with others of his generation, but mostly Woolf laughs at the soullessness of his composition; rather than the poem being a work of art, she represents Julian as a thoughtless and immature blunderer in the world of words. Again, the comedic dramatic frame allowed Woolf to criticize his writing, without causing offence, while the satire of herself as the great author-aunt is winning. How can Julian take offence if she is as happy to laugh at herself as at him? she seems to be saying. The satire is, along with the memoir of Julian that Woolf began shortly after his death, one of the most revealing documents about their relationship.

Even at the end of his life, aunt and nephew did not see eye to eye, not only in a literary sense, but also in a political sense. He abandoned his pacifism and became increasingly interested in the tense political climate of Europe. When the Spanish Civil War broke out, he wanted to fight against the fascists. Both his mother and aunt tried to change his resolution to fight in the International Brigade and eventually persuaded him to drive an ambulance instead; as Vanessa pointed out to him: "you have a better intelligence than most people, and so it should be used, and not destroyed by a chance bullet" (Bell 428). Woolf, on the other hand, saw that her arguments against conflict would fall on deaf ears with Julian. She wrote to Stephen Spender, who had already witnessed the conflict: "I feel that its a mistake his going to Spain, but its no good saying so. I dont suppose he would see my arguments" (*L*6 123). It was partly with this political difference in mind that she continued to write *Three Guineas*, which was meant "as an argument with him [Julian]" (*L*6 159). Woolf pressed him to write something on Spain before he left, thus acknowledging, as she admitted in her memoir of him, that she "had treated his essay on Roger too lightly" (Rosenbaum 20). In many ways Woolf was shown to be right in her advice, both literary and political, to Julian Bell for he died on 18th July 1937 from a shrapnel wound while driving an ambulance in the battle of Brunete—he was 29. Woolf described the loss of Julian in her diary as "a complete break; almost a blank; like a blow on the head: a shrivelling up" (*D*5 104) and wrote how she felt "floored by the complete muddle & waste" (*D*5 108). His death led Woolf to acknowledge that Julian's work had potential when she incorporated some of his reminiscences on Roger Fry in her biography and published selected pieces edited by Quentin Bell in 1938. The critical and competitive relationship between aunt and nephew ended with her memoir of him in which she acknowledged that her negative feelings for his writing were partly motived by jealousy, but, as is demonstrated in the short script marked "JB" among the Monk's House Papers, that he was "careless, not 'an artist', too personal in what he wrote, & 'all over the place'" (Rosenbaum 22). She wrote in her memoir of him that the one "regret in [their] relationship" was "that [she] might have encouraged him more as a writer" (Rosenbaum 22). The skit may have been correct in its assassination of his poetic capabilities, but its tone, though humorous, was critical, almost disparaging and certainly not encouraging.

Works Cited

Bell, Vanessa. *Selected Letters of Vanessa Bell.* Ed. Regina Marler. London: Moyer Bell, 1998. Print.

Woolf, Virginia. *The Platform of Time: Memoirs of Family and Friends.* Ed. S. P. Rosenbaum. Expanded edition. London: Hesperus, 2008. Print.

Wright, Elizabeth. "Bloomsbury at Play." *Woolf Studies Annual* 17 (2011): 77-107. Print.

Guide to Library Special Collections

This guide updates the information in volume 17.

Name of Collection: The Beinecke Rare Book and Manuscript Library

Contact: Kevin Repp, Curator of Modern Books and Manuscripts
Patricia Willis, Curator of American Literature

Address: Yale University Library
P.O. Box 208240
New Haven, CT 06520-8240

URL: www.library.yale.edu/beinecke/brblhome.html

Hours: Mon.–Thu. 8:30 AM–8 PM
Fri. 8:30 AM–5 PM

Access Requirements: Register at the circulation desk on each visit.

Holdings Relevant To Woolf: General Collection includes autograph manuscript of "Notes on Oliver Goldsmith." Comments on Edward Gibbon, William Beckford Collection. Letters from Virginia Woolf in the Bryher Papers, the Louise Morgan and Otto Theis Papers, and the Rebecca West Papers. Related material: 41 letters from Vita Sackville-West to Violet Trefusis; files relating to Robert Manson Myers's *From Beowulf to Virginia Woolf* in the Edmond Pauker Papers.

Yale Collection of American Literature includes typewritten manuscripts of "The Art of Walter Sickert," "Augustine Birrell," "Aurora Leigh," "How Should One Read a Book?" "Letter to a Young Poet," "The Novels of Turgenev," "Street Haunting." Dial/Scofield Thayer Papers: manuscripts of "The Lives of the Obscure," "Miss Ormerod," and "Mrs. Dalloway in Bond Street." Letters from Virginia Woolf in the William Rose Benet Papers, the Benet Family Correspondence, the Henry Seidel Canby Papers, the Seward Collins Papers, the Dial/Scofield Thayer Papers, and the *Yale Review* archive. Material relating to translations of Woolf in the Thornton Wilder papers. Related material: Clive Bell, "Virginia Woolf" (Dial/Scofield Thayer Papers); 43 letters from Leonard Woolf to Helen McAfee (*Yale Review*); 11 letters from Leonard Woolf to Gertrude Stein.

Name of Collection: The Henry W. and Albert A. Berg Collection of English and American Literature

Contact: Isaac Gewirtz, Curator

Address: New York Public Library, Room 320
Fifth Avenue & 42nd Street
New York, NY 10018

Telephone: 212-930-0802
Fax: 212-930-0079
Email: isaacgewirtz@nypl.org

Hours: Tue.–Wed. 11 AM–7 PM
Thu.–Sat. 10 AM–6 PM
Closed Sun., Mon. and legal holidays

Access Requirements: After acquiring Library card in room 315, check outerwear and *all* containers (briefcases, computer cases, handbags, folders, etc.) in Ground Floor cloakroom, and proceed to the Berg Collection. Traceable and photo identification required.Undergraduates working on honors theses need letter from faculty advisor.

Restrictions: Virginia Woolf's bound MSS are now made available on microfilm and CD. URL for Berg finding aid: http://www.nypl.org/research/manuscripts/berg/brgwoolf.xml. N.B. *All the Berg's Woolf MSS are on microfilm and CD published by Research Publications and available at many research libraries.*

Holdings Relevant To Woolf: Manuscripts/typescripts of all of the novels except *Orlando*, including: *Between the Acts, Flush, Jacob's Room, Mrs. Dalloway* (notes and fragments), *Night and Day, To the Lighthouse, The Voyage Out, The Waves, The Years*; 12 notebooks of articles, essays, fiction and reviews, 1924–1940; 36 volumes of diaries; 26 volumes of reading notes; correspondence with Vanessa Bell, Ethel Smyth, Vita Sackville-West and others. Su Hua Ling Chen's Bloomsbury correspondence.

Recent Acquisitions: Proof copy of *A Room of One's Own* (July 1929); ALS Vanessa Bell to Vita Sackville-West, April 29, 1941 [in Marler, *Selected Letters* 478-80]; Frank Dean, *Strike While the Iron's Hot: Frank Dean's Life as a Blacksmith and Farrier in Rodmell*, ed. Susan Rowland (S. Rowland, 1994) [includes map, accounts of search for VW's body and of her funeral]; Vita Sackville-West. *Marian Stranways*, authograph manuscript, [1913].

Name of Collection: The British Library Manuscript Collections

Contact: Manuscripts Enquiries

Address: 96 Euston Road
London NW1 2DB
England

Telephone: 0207-412-7513
Fax: 0207-412-7745
Email: mss@bl.uk

Hours: Mon. 10 AM–5 PM;Tue.–Sat.: 9:30 AM–5 PM

Access Requirements: British Library Reader Pass (signed I.D. required and usually proof of post-graduate academic status, or other demonstrable need to use the collections—see www.bl.uk). In addition, access to most literary autograph material only available with letter of recommendation.

Restrictions: Paper Copies, Microfilms, and Photography of selected items available upon receipt of written authorization for photo duplication from the copyright holder.

Holdings Relevant to Woolf: Diaries 1930–1931 (microfilm); Mrs. Dalloway and other writings (1923–1925) three volumes; letter from Leonard Woolf to H. G. Wells (1941); two letters from Virginia Woolf and three letters from Leonard Woolf to John Lehmann (1941); letter written on behalf of Leonard Woolf to S. S. Koteliansky (1946); notebook in Italian kept by Virginia Woolf; notebook of Virginia Stephen (1906–1909); A sketch of the past revised ts (1940); letters from Virginia Woolf in the correspondence files of Lytton and James Strachey; letter from Virginia Woolf to Mildred Massingberd; letter from Virginia Woolf to Harriet Shaw Weaver (1918); letters from Virginia Woolf to S. S. Koteliansky (1923–1927); letter from Virginia Woolf to Frances Cornford (1929); letter from Virginia Woolf to Ernest Rhys (1930); correspondence of Virginia Woolf in the Society of Authors archive (1934–1937); letter and postcard from Virginia Woolf to Bernard Shaw (1940); three letters (suicide notes) from Virginia Woolf (1941); two letters from Virginia Woolf and three from Leonard Woolf to John Lehmann (1941). "Hyde Park Gate News" 1891–1892, 1895 (add. MSS 70725, 70726). Letters of Virginia and Leonard Woolf to Lady Aberconway, 1927–1941. Letter from Virginia Woolf to Frances Cornford. Letters from Virginia Woolf to Macmillan Co. 1903,

1908. Collection of RPs ("reserved photo copies"–copies of manuscripts exported, some subject to restrictions).

Name of Collection: Harry Ransom Humanities Research Center

Contact: Research Librarian

Address: The University of Texas at Austin
P.O. Box 7219
Austin, TX 78713-7219

Telephone: 512-471-9119
Fax: 512-471-2899
Email: reference@hrc.utexas.edu

Hours: Mon.–Fri. 9 AM–5 PM
Sat. 9 AM–NOON
Closed holidays; intersession Saturdays; one week each in late May and late August.

Access Requirements: Completed manuscript reader's application; current photo identification.

Holdings Relevant To Woolf: The manuscript collection includes the typed manuscript with autograph revisions of *Kew Gardens*, and the typed manuscript and autograph revisions of "Thoughts on Peace in an Air Raid." The Center holds 571 of Woolf's letters, including correspondence to Elizabeth Bowen, Lady Ottoline Morrell, Mary Hutchinson, William Plomer, Hugh Walpole and others. Further mss. relating to Virginia Woolf include letters to her from T. S. Eliot and reviews of her work. A substantial collection of the first British and American editions of Woolf's published works, as well as 130 volumes from Leonard and Virginia Woolf's library and a collection of books published by the Hogarth Press, is also housed. An art collection holds a landscape painting of Virginia's garden and a series of Cockney cartoons in a sketch book, signed "V.W." The center also has extensive holdings of materials related to Leonard Woolf, Ottoline Morrell, Mary Hutchinson, Lytton Strachey, Dora Carrington, E. M. Forster, Clive Bell, Roger Fry, Vanessa Bell, Bertrand Russell, Elizabeth Bowen, William Plomer, Stephen Spender and Hugh Walpole.

Name of Collection: King's College Archive Centre

Contact: Patricia McGuire, Archivist
King's College

Address: Cambridge CB2 1ST

Telephone: 01223-331444
Fax: 01223-331891
Email: archivist@kings.cam.ac.uk

Hours: Mon.–Thu. 9:30 AM–12:30 PM and 1:30 PM–5:15 PM. *Closed during public holidays and the College's annual periods of closure.*

Access Requirements: Proof of ID, letter of introduction, appointment in advance.

Holdings Relevant To Woolf: Woolf MSS and letters: Minute book, written up by Clive Bell, of the meetings of a play-reading society, with cast lists and comments on performances by CB. Dec. 1907–Jan. 1909, Oct. 1914–Feb. 1915. Players included variously Clive and Vanessa Bell, Roger and Margery Fry, Duncan Grant, Walter Lamb, Molly MacCarthy, Adrian and Virginia Stephen, Saxon Sydney-Turner. *Freshwater, A Comedy*—photocopy of editorial typescript prepared from the MSS at Sussex University and Monk's House; photocopy of covering letter from the publisher to "Robert Silvers," Jan. 29, 1976. Papers relating to the Virginia Woolf

Centenary Conference held at Fitzwilliam College, Cambridge, Sept. 20-22, 1982. TS with corrections of "Nurse Lugton's Curtain." Typed transcript of R. Fry's memoir of his schooldays. Correspondence with Clive Bell, Julian Bell, Vanessa Bell, Richard Braithwaite, Rupert Brooke, Mrs. Brooke, Katharine Cox, Julian Fry, Roger Fry, John Davy Hayward, J. M. Keynes, Lydia Keynes, Rosamond Lehmann, Charles Mauron, Raymond Mortimer, Frances and Ralph Partridge, G. H. W. Rylands, J. T. Sheppard, W. J. H. Sprott, Thoby Stephen, Madge Vaughan. Woolf-related archival collections held: Charleston Papers; Rupert Brooke Papers; E. M. Forster Papers; Roger Fry Papers; J. M. Keynes Papers; Frances Partridge Papers; George Humphrey Wolferstan ('Dadie') Rylands Papers; J. T. Sheppard Papers; W. J. H. Sprott Papers. Various works of art by Vanessa Bell, Duncan Grant, and Roger Fry, held in various locations around King's College. Access via Second Bursar's secretary.

Name of Collection: The Lilly Library

Contact: Breon Mitchell, Director
Cherry Williams, Curator of Manuscripts

Address: The Lilly Library, Indiana University
1200 East Seventh Street
Bloomington, IN 47405-5500

Telephone: 812-855-2452
Fax: 812-855-3143
Email: liblilly@indiana.edu, mitchell@indiana.edu
chedwill@indiana.edu

Hours: Mon.–Fri. 9 AM–6 PM; Sat. 9 AM–1 PM;
Closed Sundays and Major Holidays

Access Requirements: Valid photo-identification; brief registration procedure.

Restrictions: Closed stacks; material use confined to reading room; wheelchair-accessible reading room and exhibitions (but no wheelchair-accessible restroom).

Holdings Relevant To Woolf: Corrected page proofs for the American edition of *Mrs. Dalloway*; letters to Woolf from Desmond and Mary (Molly) MacCarthy; 77 letters (published in *Letters*) from Woolf to correspondents including Donald Clifford Brace, Robert Gathorne-Hardy, Barbara (Strachey) Halpern, Richard Arthur Warren Hughes, Desmond MacCarthy and Molly MacCarthy; "Preliminary Scheme for the formation of a Partnership between Mr Leonard Sidney Woolf and Mr John Lehmann to take over The Hogarth Press" (includes contract signed by Lehmann, Leonard Woolf, and Virginia Woolf and receipt for Lehmann's payment to Virginia Woolf to purchase Virginia Woolf's share in the Hogarth Press); photographs of Virginia Woolf, Leonard Woolf, Lytton Strachey, Strachey family, Roger Fry, and Vanessa Bell (Hannah Whitall Smith mss.); (Richard) Kennedy mss. (four hand-colored lithographs of Virginia Woolf: artist's proofs for RK's portfolio, VIRGINIA WOOLF: "AS I KNEW HER"; Sackville-West, V. mss. (10,529 items: includes the correspondence of Vita Sackville-West, and Harold Nicolson); MacCarthy mss. (ca. 10,000 items: papers of Desmond and Molly MacCarthy); correspondence between LW and Mary Gaither regarding publication of *A Checklist of the Hogarth Press* (1976, repr. 1986); Todd Avery, *Close and Affectionate Friends: Desmond and Molly MacCarthy and the Bloomsbury Group* (The Lilly Library / Indiana University Libraries, 1999).

Name of Collection: Culture & Literature, Special Collections, University of Maryland, College Park, Libraries

Contact: Ann Hudak, Culture & Literature, Special Collections Librarian

Address: University of Maryland Libraries
College Park, MD 20742

Telephone: 310-405-9213
Fax: 301-314-2709
Email: ahudak@umd.edu

Hours: Dates and hours of operation subject to change. Contact Ann Hudak or Jason Speck before planning a research visit.

Access Requirements: Photo ID.

Holdings Relevant To Woolf: Papers of Hope Mirrlees contain five autograph letters and postcards (1919–1928) from Virginia Woolf to Mirrlees. Also in the collection are 113 letters from T. S. Eliot to Mirrlees, and three letters from Lady Ottoline Morrell to Mirrlees. A finding aid is available at http://hdl.handle.net/1903.1/1536.

Name of Collection: Monks House Papers/Leonard Woolf Papers/Charleston Papers/Nicolson Papers

Contact: Fiona Courage, Special Collections Manager

Address: University of Sussex Library
Brighton
Sussex BN1 9QL
England

Telephone: 01273-678157
Fax: 01273-678441

Email: Library.Specialcoll@sussex.ac.uk
URL: www.sussex.ac.uk/library/speccoll

Access Requirements: By appointment. Identification to be presented on arrival. Application for access (including contact details of referee) to be completed on arrival.

Restrictions: Photocopying strictly controlled.

Holdings Relevant To Woolf: The University of Sussex holds two large archives relating to Leonard and Virginia Woolf: The Monks House Papers, primarily correspondence and MSS of Virginia Woolf, including the three scrapbooks relating to *Three Guineas*; and The Leonard Woolf Papers, primarily correspondence and other papers of Leonard Woolf. (Monks House Papers are available on microfilm in many research libraries.) The Charleston Papers consist in the main of letters written to or by Clive and Vanessa Bell and Duncan Grant which had accumulated in their home; the library houses Quentin Bell's photocopied set; letters from Roger Fry, Maynard Keynes, Lytton Stachey, Virginia Woolf, Vita Sackville-West, E. M. Forster, T. S. Eliot, Frances Partridge and others. The Maria Jackson letters comprise some 900 letters from Maria Jackson to Julia and Leslie Stephen. The Nicolson Papers complement these three Sussex archives relating to the Bloomsbury Group, and consist of Nigel Nicolson's correspondence relating to his editorial work as principal editor of the six-volume *Letters of Virginia Woolf*, published between 1975 and 1980.

The Bell Papers. A. O. Bell's correspondence relating to her editorial work on Virginia Woolf's diaries, a parallel collection to the Nicolson Papers. Collection level description may be accessed at www.archiveshub.ac.uk

Name of Collection: The Morgan Library & Museum

Contact: Reading Room

Address: 225 Madison Ave.
New York, NY 10016

Telephone: 212-590-0315
Email: readingroom@themorgan.org
URL: www.themorgan.org

Access Requirements: Admission to the Reading Room is by application and by appointment. See http//www.themorgan.org/research/reading.asp for application form.

Holdings Relevant To Woolf: Virginia Woolf. Autograph manuscript notebook, 1931 Sept. 24. 1 item (52 p.) ; 265 x 208 mm. Contains drafts of "A Letter to a Young Poet," a brief letter to the press entitled "The Villa Jones" [ff. 3–5] and a monologue by a working-class woman [ff. 44–46]. MA 3333. Purchased on the Fellows Fund with the special assistance of Anne S. Dayton, Enid A. Haupt, Mrs. James H. Ripley, Mr. and Mrs. August H. Schilling, and John S. Thacher, 1979.

Virginia Woolf. Autograph letters signed (2) and typed letter signed, dated London [etc.], to E. McKnight Kauffer, 1931 Apr. 4–23, and undated.

3 items (4 p.). Concerning a drawing of her and a bibliography of her works. MA 1679. Purchased in 1959.

Vanessa Bell. 84 autograph letters, 3 typed letters, 7 postcards, and 3 telegrams. Most, but not all, are written by Vanessa Bell to John Maynard Keynes. Concerning Duncan Grant, Roger Fry, Clive Bell, the Bell children, Leonard and Virginia Woolf, Lytton Strachey, John Maynard and Lydia

Lopokova Keynes, David Garnett, Ottoline Morrell, and others. MA 3448. Items in this collection are described in 97 individual records (MA 3448.1-97). Purchased on the Fellows Fund, special gift of the Gramercy Park Foundation (Mrs. Michael Tucker), 1980.

Name of Collection: University Museums and Special Collections Service

Contact: University Archivist

Address: University of Reading
Redlands Road
Berkshire RG1 5EX
England

Telephone: 0118-378-8660
Fax: 0118-378-5632
Email: specialcollections@reading.ac.uk

Access Requirements: Appointment needed to consult material. Permission required to consult or copy material in the Hogarth Press and Chatto & Windus collections from Random House, 20 Vauxhall Bridge Road, London SW1V 2SA, UK. (Jean Rose, Library Mgr. JRose@Randomhouse.co.uk)

Holdings Relevant To Woolf: Hogarth Press (MS2750): editorial and production correspondence relating to publications of the Press including Woolf's own titles. Production ledgers 1920s–1950s. Correspondence between Leonard Woolf and Stanley Unwin about progress with his collected edition of the works of Freud. Order books – e.g. lists of booksellers, book clubs and how many books they have ordered for a particular title. Newscuttings – press clippings of advertisements for Hogarth Press books including Virginia Woolf publications.

Chatto & Windus (MS2444): small number of letters 1915–1925; 1929–1931. Various letters and notes by Leonard Woolf; outgoing letters to Leonard Woolf: 22 November 1927 (Letter Book 119); outgoing letters to Virginia Woolf: 29 January 1936 (Letter Book 171), 22 December 1931 (Letter Book 135), 31 December 1931 (Letter Book 135), 15 December 1920 (Letter Book 100), 20 December 1920 (Letter Book 100).

George Bell & Sons (MS1640): 5 letters from Leonard Woolf 1930–1966.

Routledge (MS1489): Reader's report by Leonard Woolf on George Padmore's "Britannia rules the blacks" (1935); "How Britain rules Africa." 1 letter from Leonard Woolf (June 1941) from Miscellaneous publishing correspondence 1941-1942 Wi-Wy RKP 174/15. Draft introduction by Leonard Woolf to *Letters on India* by Mulk Raj (1942) and 1 letter to Leonard Woolf from Mulk Raj Anand 1942-1943 RKP 178/3. Correspondence concerning the publication of *The War for Peace* by Leonard Woolf, 1939-1940 RKP 160/5. 1 letter from Virginia Woolf declining an invitation from Routledge to write a biography of Margaret Bondfield, 25 May 1940 RKP 160/5.

Megroz (MS1979/68): 2 letters from Leonard Woolf, 1926.

Allen & Unwin (MS3282): Correspondence with Leonard Woolf c.1914-1918 (re. his book *International Government*), 1923-1924; 1939-1940; 1943; 1946; 1950-1951; 1953; 1965 (concerning ill-founded rumors about the Hogarth Press); 1967 (concerning a reprint of *Empire and Commerce in Africa*).

Jonathan Cape (MS 2446): All correspondence from file JC A43. Correspondence between Jonathan Cape and Virginia Woolf and Cape and A.C. Gissing concerning Virginia Woolf's introduction to George Gissing's *Ionian Sea* to which A.C. Gissing objects. 1 postcard (1935), 1 letter (1933), 2 letters (1932) from Virginia Woolf. 1 letter (1932) from Virginia Woolf declining to write an introduction to Jane Austen's *Northanger Abbey*. 4 letters (1931) from Virginia Woolf declining to write an introduction to one of Miss Thackeray's books.

Letters from Vanessa Bell:1 letter from Bell CW 152/2;1 letter from Bell CW 171/10; 2 letters from Bell CW 578/1; 1 letter from Bell CW 59/9; 1 letter from Bell (1936) CW 61/10. Artwork by Vanessa Bell for various Virginia Woolf titles

Artwork by Angelica Garnett, Philippa Bramson and others for various books.

Name of Collection: Frances Hooper Collection of Virginia Woolf Books and ManuscriptsElizabeth Power Richardson Bloomsbury Iconography Collection.

Contact: Karen V. Kukil, Associate Curator of Special Collections
Mortimer Rare Book Room

Address: William Allan Neilson Library
Smith College
Northampton, MA 01063

Telephone: 413-585-2906
Fax: 413-585-4486
Email: kkukil@email.smith.edu
URL: www.smith.edu/libraries/libs/rarebook

Hours: Mon.–Fri. 9 AM–5 PM

Access Requirements: Appointment to be made with the Curator.

Holdings Relevant To Woolf: The Hooper Collection emphasizes Woolf as an essayist but also includes many Hogarth Press first editions, limited editions of Woolf's works, and translations. The collection includes page proofs of *Orlando*, *To the Lighthouse,* and T*he Common Reader,* corrected by Woolf for the first American editions, a proof copy of *The Waves* that Woolf inscribed to Hugh Walpole, and the proof copies of *The Years* and of *Flush.* The Collection also has one of the deluxe editions of *Orlando* that was printed on green paper. Other items include twenty-two pages of reading notes from 1926, three pages of notes on D. H. Lawrence's *Sons and Lovers*, thirty-three pages of notes for *Roger Fry*, a six-page ms. "As to criticism," a five-page ms. of "The Searchlight," and a fourteen-page ms. of "The Patron and The Crocus." The Hooper Collection also owns 140 letters between Woolf and Lytton Strachey as well as other correspondence, including a 13 February [1921] letter to Katherine Mansfield and ten letters to Mela and Robert Spira.

The Richardson Collection is a working collection of books and materials used by Richardson in preparing her *Bloomsbury Iconography*. It includes Leslie Stephen's photograph album, ninety-eight original exhibition catalogs dating back to 1929, clippings and photcopies of such items as reviews of early Woolf works, and Bloomsbury material from British *Vogue* of the 1920s. The Collection also has three preliminary pencil drawings by Vanessa Bell for *Flush.*

The Mortimer Rare Book Room also owns Woolf's 1916 Italian ms. notebook and her corrected typescripts of "Reviewing" and "The Searchlight." In addition, there is a 1923 photograph of Woolf at Garsington. Original cover designs for Hogarth Press publications include *The Common Reader, On Being Ill,* and *Duncan Grant*. The Mortimer Rare Book Room also has a Sylvia Plath collection that includes eight of Woolf's books from Plath's library, several of which are underlined and annotated, as well as Plath's notes from her undergraduate English 211 class at Smith (1951–1952) in which she studied *To the Lighthouse.* The collection also includes Woolf's 26 February 1939 letter to Vita Sackville-West, a 1931 bronze bust of Virginia Woolf by Stephen Tomlin, a 1923 Hogarth Press edition of T.S. Eliot's *The Waste Land,* a 1919 Hogarth Press edition of *Paris* by Hope Mirrlees and first editions of Vita Sackville-West publications. Online exhibitions are available on the Mortimer Rare Book Room's web site.

Name of Collection: Woolf/Hogarth Press/Bloomsbury

Contact: Robert C. Brandeis

Address: Victoria University Library
71 Queens Park Crescent E.
Toronto M5S 1K7
Ontario Canada

Email: victoria.library@utoronto.ca
URL: http://library.vicu.utoronto.ca/special/bloomsbury.htm

Hours: Mon.–Fri. 9 AM–5 PM

Access Requirements: Prior notification; identification.

Restrictions: Limited photocopying.

Holdings Relevant To Woolf: This collection, the most comprehensive of its kind with more than 4,600 items, contains all the work of Virginia and Leonard Woolf in various editions, issues, variants and translations; all the books hand-printed by Leonard and Virginia Woolf at the Hogarth Press, including many variant issues and bindings, association copies and page proofs; a nearly comprehensive collection of Hogarth Press machine printed books to 1946 (the year Leonard Woolf and the Press joined Chatto & Windus) including presentation copies, signed limited editions, page proofs, variants as well as substantial amounts of ephemera, such as the *Catalogue of Publications to 1939* with annotations by Leonard Woolf. The collection is also very strong in Bloomsbury Art and Artists, especially the decorative arts, including important examples of Omega Workshops publications and exhibition catalogues. Materials include the catalogue of the second post-impressionist exhibition, 1912; catalogues relating to Vanessa Bell and Duncan Grant exhibitions; bronze medal of Virginia Woolf by Marta Firlet; oil on canvas portrait of Amaryllis Garnett by Vanessa Bell (c.1958); Portrait sketch of Leonard Woolf by Vanessa Bell; Duncan Grant and Vanessa Bell designed Clarice Cliff dinner plates; original Vanessa Bell and Duncan Grant sketches and designs for dust jackets, novels, and other special projects; bronze busts of Lytton Strachey and Virginia Woolf by Stephen Tomlin (1901–1937); as well as the Marcel Gimond bust of Vanessa Bell and the Tomlin bust of Henrietta Bingham. Original correspondence and mss material includes that by Vanessa Bell; Leonard Woolf; Ritchie family re: Anne Thackeray Ritchie/Stephen family; Duncan Grant; Quentin Bell; S. P. Rosenbaum mss. Large Ephemera Collection including items revealing Virginia Woolf's effect on popular culture.

Name of Collection: Library of Leonard and Virginia Woolf (Washington S U)

Contact: Trevor James Bond
Special Collections Librarian

Address: Washington State University Libraries
Pullman, WA 99164-5610
Email: tjbond@wsu.edu
URL: www.wsulibs.wsu.edu/holland/masc/masc.htm

Hours: Mon.–Fri. 8:30 AM–5 PM

Access Requirements: Letter stating nature of research preferred; student or other identification.

Restrictions: Materials must be used in the MASC area under supervision. Photocopying or photographing is permitted only when it will not harm the materials and is permitted by copyright.

Holdings Relevant To Woolf: WSU has the Woolfs' basic working library including many works which belonged to Woolf's father, Sir Leslie Stephen, and other family members. Over 800 titles came from their Sussex home, Monks House, including some works bought at auction soon after Leonard Woolf died in 1969. Later additions include: 1,875 titles from his house in Victoria Square, London; 400 titles from his nephew Cecil Woolf; and over 60 titles from Quentin and Anne Olivier Bell. WSU has been actively collecting: all works in all editions by Virginia Woolf; all titles by Leonard Woolf; works published by the Woolfs at the Hogarth Press through 1946; books by their friends and associates, especially those by Bloomsbury authors and about Bloomsbury artists; relevant correspondence and original works of art. Original artwork by Vanessa Bell; scattered letters by Vanessa Bell, E. M. Forster, Roger Fry, Leslie Stephen, Lytton Strachey, and Leonard Woolf. Original artwork by Richard Kennedy for illustrations in his book *A Boy at the Hogarth Press*; scattered letters by Roger Fry, Leslie Stephen, Ethel Smyth, and Leonard Woolf. Virginia Woolf's initialed copy of *Cornishiana*; Leonard Woolf's annotated copy of *An Anatomy of Poetry* by A. William-Ellis; Leslie Stephen's copy of *Lapsus Calami and Other Verses*, inscribed by James Kenneth Stephen. Several letters from Virginia Woolf, including two written in 1939 to Ronald Heffer, and a letter to Edward McKnight Kauffer. New in the Hogarth Press Collection are a copy of E. M. Forster's *Anonymity, an Enquiry*,bound in cream paper boards, and what Woolmer calls the third label state of Forster's *The Story of the Siren*.

Name of Collection: Yale Center for British Art

Contact: Elisabeth Fairman, Senior Curator of Rare Books and Manuscripts

Address: 1080 Chapel Street
P.O. Box 208280
New Haven, CT 06520-8280

Telephone: 203-432-2814
Fax: 203-432-9613
E-mail: elisabeth.fairman@yale.edu

Hours: Tue.-Fri. 10 AM-4:30 PM

Access Requirements: Permission needed in order to reproduce.

Holdings Relevant To Woolf: Rare Books & Mss Department: 94 letters from Vanessa Bell and Duncan Grant to Sir Kenneth Clark; Prints & Drawings Department: 4 drawings by Vanessa Bell; 4 drawings by Duncan Grant;

6 drawings by Wyndham Lewis; 1 drawing by Frederick Etchells; Paintings Department: 1 painting by Vanessa Bell, 4 paintings by Duncan Grant (including portrait of Vanessa Bell); 3 paintings by Roger Fry.

Recent Acquisitions: 6 letters from Lytton Strachey (to Clive Bell, Siegfried Sassoon, et al.).

Reviews

Celebrating Katherine Mansfield: A Centenary Volume of Essays. Eds. Gerri Kimber and Janet Wilson (Houndmills and New York: Palgrave Macmillan, 2011) xiv +241 pp.

Circulating Genius: John Middleton Murry, Katherine Mansfield and D. H. Lawrence. Sydney Janet Kaplan (Edinburgh: Edinburgh UP, 2010) 228 pp.

A Literary Modernist: Katherine Mansfield and the Art of the Short Story. Gerri Kimber. Foreword by Vincent O'Sullivan (Birkbeck, England: Kakapo Books, 2008) 86 pp.

Katherine Mansfield and Literary Modernism. Eds. Janet Wilson, Gerri Kimber and Susan Reid (London and New York: Continuum, 2011) xii + 216 pp.

Katherine Mansfield and the Modernist Marketplace. Jenny McDonnell (Houndmills and New York: Palgrave Macmillan, 2010) viii + 220 pp.

Katherine Mansfield: The Storyteller. Kathleen Jones (Edinburgh: Edinburgh UP, 2010) viii + 524 pp.

Katherine Mansfield: The View from France. Gerri Kimber (Bern, Switzerland: Peter Lang, 2008) 290 pp.

Modernist Short Fiction by Women: The Liminal in Katherine Mansfield, Dorothy Richardson, May Sinclair and Virginia Woolf. Claire Drewery (Farnham UK and Burlington VT: Ashgate, 2011) vii + 150 pp.

In an introduction to a collection of Katherine Mansfield's stories published in the 1950s, Elizabeth Bowen lamented the way in which Mansfield's untimely death in 1923 had effectively cheated Mansfield of the recognition due her achievements: "Where is she now, our missing contemporary?" Bowen asked (vi). It is a question that has long puzzled Mansfield scholars: despite a steady stream of studies that established Mansfield as a pioneering modernist, as a woman writer deeply engaged with defining the relationship between female artistry, subjectivity, and embodiment, and as an important and influential fellow writer to such friends as Virginia Woolf and D. H. Lawrence, Mansfield has remained oddly marginalized. She has been overlooked in part because her genre of choice has been marginalized within literary studies more generally; she also moved in the more marginal circles of periodicals and little magazines, which are only now garnering sustained critical attention. Yet her reputation has also suffered from other impediments, most notably the management of her posthumous career by her husband and literary executor, John Middleton Murry: while the latter undoubtedly kept her name in front of the public, he also created a sentimentalized view of Mansfield that not only considerably sanitized her literary persona but that deeply alienated friends and acquaintances and that indelibly marked earlier literary assessments. As Frank O'Connor observed in his study of the short story, "It may be that for me and people of my own generation her work has been obscured by her legend" (128). Or, as Woolf more succinctly put it, "there was Murry squirming and oozing a sort of thick motor oil in the background" (*L4* 366).

Yet as the wealth of new scholarship on Mansfield demonstrates, we are witnessing a resurgence of interest in modernism's missing contemporary. A number of new developments have contributed to this resurgence. First, the completion of the five-volume *Collected Letters* in 2008 and the *Complete Edition* of her notebooks in 1997 has provided impetus for a revaluation of Mansfield's life and work. Second, an important conference held at Birkbeck College, University of London in September 2008 to commemorate Mansfield's arrival in London in 1908 to establish herself as a professional writer witnessed the founding of the international Katherine Mansfield Society, the establishment of the peer-reviewed journal *Katherine Mansfield Studies*, and plans for future conferences. Mansfield scholarship has also benefited from new critical trends that have helped to foreground her unique position within British and European modernism. New work on modernism's little magazines, for example, has renewed interest in Mansfield's important role as both contributor to and editor of such periodicals as the *The New Age*, *Rhythm*, and *The Blue Review*. Similarly, interest in the way modernists marketed their writing has paved the way for a new appreciation of how Mansfield reconciled her literary experimentalism with the demands of a popular readership. A new understanding of modernism's transnational aspects—most evident in postcolonial readings of Mansfield—has illuminated Mansfield's doubled position as London insider *and* colonial outsider. As the editors of *Celebrating Katherine Mansfield* observe, Mansfield's colonial status and nomadic adult life speak to "problems of dislocation, estrangement, and displacement" that render her in some ways modernism's "most iconic, most representative writer" (1).

One of the most surprising developments in this critical efflorescence is the emergence of a much more nuanced and sympathetic view of John Middleton Murry. In both Kathleen Jones's new biography and Sydney Janet Kaplan's *Circulating Genius*, Murry figures as far more than the self-serving "motor oil" who failed Mansfield miserably during her life and contaminated her literary reputation after her death. Jones boldly constructs her biography as two parallel stories: one, told in the present tense, begins with Mansfield's death at the Gurdjieff Institute in Fontainebleau in 1923 and circles back in time; the second story, told in the past tense, picks up from her death and follows Mansfield's afterlife in Murry's obsessive dissemination of an angelic version of his late wife. As Jones notes in her introduction, Murry's diary and letters are now held by the Alexander Turnbull Library in Wellington, and for the first time it is possible to read these texts alongside Mansfield's own notebooks and letters; his diary, Jones observes, "is a harrowing record of emotional inadequacy and how his obsession with Katherine destroyed two of his three subsequent marriages and adversely affected the lives of his four children" (20-21). Jones's biography is essential reading for anyone who wishes to understand the creation of the "Mansfield myth" and how Murry's marketing of Mansfield obscured and undermined her reputation as a modernist writer. The effect of splitting the narrative into two stories with different tenses glosses Jones's point: the past tense "afterlife" of Mansfield bears witness to Mansfield's *function* for others after her death. While Jones's handling of the Murry material is by far the most innovative aspect of her biography, she also adds considerably to our understanding of other vexed aspects of Mansfield's life, including the disastrous early love affair and pregnancy that ensued soon after her arrival in London in 1908; her lifelong relationship with Ida Baker, who also emerges here as a more nuanced and complex personality than has been hitherto recognized; and Mansfield's enigmatic medical history, which Jones reads more carefully and fully than other commentators.

Sydney Janet Kaplan's *Circulating Genius* brings a different light to bear on Murry's connection with Mansfield. Drawing on Murry's unpublished diaries and long-forgotten novels, Kaplan foregrounds how "modernist literary history looks different when Murry is at its centre" (9): she examines in particular how Murry's critical and fictional efforts took shape in a tumultuous emotional terrain that encompassed relationships with D. H. Lawrence *and* Mansfield. Kaplan teases out the intertextual strands linking Murry's novel *Still Life*, Lawrence's *Women in Love*, and Mansfield's "Bliss" and "Je ne parle pas français"; her close reading of the tangled erotic triangles and quartets of these texts illuminates their indebtedness to one another even as it confirms Kaplan's thesis that literature develops out of a "conjunction of outward circumstance and inward necessity" (11). Kaplan weaves this analysis into an examination of the interpersonal dynamics of the literary and artistic circles of Garsington and Bloomsbury. Of particular interest to readers of this journal is her chapter on Murry's assumption of the editorship of the *Athenaeum* in 1919, a position that would enable him to consolidate his and Mansfield's position in the literary establishment (105). As

Lawrence became more peripheral to Murry's personal and professional life, T. S. Eliot and Virginia Woolf became more central, and Kaplan devotes much of this chapter to detailing Woolf's personal and professional friendship and rivalry with Mansfield. "If Woolf was initially flattered to be included among the contributors ... she discovered quickly how deeply her involvement in it affected her tentative yet blossoming relationship with Mansfield, a friendship already vexed by the complexities of Bloomsbury gossip and the competitive pursuit of literary dominance," Kaplan writes. "Yet the period of Murry's editorship culminated for both Woolf and Mansfield in a higher level of awareness of the possibilities and complexities of the prose medium" (109). Murry's role in fostering the competitiveness between the two women, Kaplan argues, heightened Woolf's anxiety about female "genius," an anxiety that would eventually culminate in Woolf's formulation of genius as the function of an historical process in *A Room of One's Own* (112).

Later chapters of *Circulating Genius* trace how Murry continued to "circulate" his versions of Mansfield and Lawrence after their deaths; Murry's professed spiritual awakening after witnessing Mansfield's death at Fontainebleau coincided with his increasing antagonism to modernist experimentation, and in his new publishing venture, the *Adelphi*, Murry published confessional accounts of these "revelations" as well as Mansfield's unpublished and mostly unfinished work. "In each subsequent issue ... Murry would publish work by Mansfield: poems, drawings, sketches, fragments of stories and, most controversially, extracts from her notebooks, often prefaced with his own self-conscious 'introductions,'" Kaplan writes (171). The publication of this material damaged Mansfield's literary reputation, while his hagiographic portrayal of Mansfield as a "child withouten stain" puzzled and alienated friends such as Woolf, who valued her friendship with Mansfield not only because of their intensely shared sense of writing, but because Mansfield, as Woolf wrote Vita Sackville-West, "had a quality I adored, and needed; I think her sharpness and reality—her having knocked about with prostitutes and so on, whereas I had always been respectable" (*L*4 366). But if Murry's shaping of Mansfield's persona played an important part in creating a dismissive critical reaction against her in the English-speaking world, it played a very different role in France, a subject Gerri Kimber takes up in *Katherine Mansfield: The View from France*. There, Murry's hagiographic portrait resonated with reactionary and conservative Catholic critics who saw in Mansfield an antidote to more controversial women writers such as Colette and Rachilde: "her saint-like persona has been set in stone since it was invented in a few short years after her death and the critics who have attempted to oust this popular perception have seen their viewpoints submerged by the huge tidal wave of French critical opinion, determined to uphold this falsely created persona at whatever cost to historical accuracy," Kimber observes (181). Kimber meticulously traces the development of the Mansfield cult in France, not only by chronologically mapping the publication of reviews and articles devoted to Mansfield, but by analyzing the ways in which translation of her work adversely impacted her experimental modes of narration. The French Mansfield, as Kimber shows, developed mostly out of the biographical materials, the *Journal* and *Letters*, which were heavily shaped and edited by Murry, but the hagiographic process worked the other way as well: Kimber argues that "her writing was edited, manipulated and mistranslated in order to aid the creation of the 'French' Katherine Mansfield" (126). In particular, Kimber laments the way in which Mansfield's biting and sarcastic humor disappears: "The ethereal spirituality and general 'otherworldliness' perceived by the French critics ... ignores the constant echoes of darkness, bitterness and ... humour, which inform all her work," Kimber writes. "Their vision of a Mansfieldian prelapsarian world of fairies, parties, songs and dolls' houses, is far removed from the world Mansfield actually wrote about, which included the gassing of soldiers at the Front, the orgasm experienced by a school girl in a French class, together with compelling depictions of women's struggles for various kinds of liberty" (228). This misperception and misreading is even more disheartening given Mansfield's actual indebtedness to French literature, which Kimber establishes in earlier chapters of her study.

Murry's prominent role in shaping critical reaction to Mansfield's life and work takes a back seat in Jenny McDonnell's outstanding examination of Mansfield's *own* role in promoting her writing. In *Katherine Mansfield and the Modernist Marketplace: At the Mercy of the Public*, McDonnell follows the critical lead of Lawrence Rainey and Mark S. Morrison in taking up the ways in which Mansfield conceived of herself as a professional writer and deliberately worked to find ways of reconciling her experimental modernist narration with the demands of a popular readership. Citing Frank O'Connor's well-known characterization of Mansfield as "the brassy little shopgirl of literature who turned herself into a great writer," McDonnell challenges the binary, either/or logic evident in this remark, whereby the "great writer" is somehow impervious to the material demands of publishing and reader reception. Indeed, McDonnell observes that Mansfield's restoration to the modernist canon has taken place without adequately accounting for what were once termed her "suspiciously popular tendencies," tendencies that McDonnell contends went "hand-in-hand with her literary experimentation with prose forms and techniques ... it was precisely Mansfield's ability to occupy another marginal space—between 'literary' and 'popular'—that made her writing possible" (11). McDonnell focuses on the periodical and book publishing worlds with which Mansfield interacted between 1910 and 1922, analyzing the changing nature of her literary communities, as Mansfield moved from small coterie publications to more commercial venues. Along the way Mansfield shed her youthful and naïve notion of the artist as "an isolated figure attempting to preach to an indifferent mass/audience from his elevated position," a notion she came to view as "an artistic pose" and that she later lampooned in "Je ne parle pas français"(71, 137). McDonnell's focus on Mansfield's pragmatic and hard-headed business decisions constitutes a welcome antidote to the many critical studies that attribute Mansfield's actions to personal and emotional motivations. To cite just one example, McDonnell takes issue with the accepted view that Mansfield's decision to leave her position as book reviewer at the *Athenaeum* and dismiss Murry as her literary agent was prompted by her jealousy over Murry's romantic involvement with another woman; instead, McDonnell convincingly argues that Mansfield's decision derived from her dislike of Murry's handling of the publication and marketing of *Bliss and Other Stories*.

McDonnell's study also foregrounds another little-studied aspect of Mansfield's literary modernism, her choice of the short story as her favored form. That choice itself contributed to Mansfield's need to negotiate between literary value and mass culture, McDonnell argues: "she eventually turned its combination of popular appeal and experimental attributes to her advantage as she sought to carve out a position for herself that could be marked by both commercial viability and literary credibility" (11). McDonnell reads Mansfield's book reviews for the *Athenaeum* in 1919 and 1920 as particularly crucial in determining the shape of the final phase of Mansfield's career. Her reviews motivated her to reappraise fictional forms and literary conventions and question the relationship between author, text and reader (119, 125). Perhaps most crucially, Mansfield used the reviews as a sounding board for considering the pros and cons of her chosen form: "'Wanted, a New Word' provides a blueprint for the kind of fiction that Mansfield now aimed to promote, and its discussion of the short story form is in keeping with a recurring feature of her review column: an endorsement of the short story rather than the novel as the genre most adaptable to literary experimentation in the post-War world" (123).

A focus on the short story in its specifically modernist manifestations is the subject of Claire Drewery's *Modernist Short Fiction by Women: The Liminal in Katherine Mansfield, Dorothy Richardson, May Sinclair and Virginia Woolf*. As Drewery notes in her introduction, the short fiction of Sinclair, Richardson and, to a lesser extent, Woolf has suffered from neglect, a reflection of the genre's marginalized status (7). Further, no comparative study of the short fiction of modernist women writers predates her own, despite the fact that the short story functioned as an ideal space for modernist experimentation, a potential recognized by Woolf when she termed her shorter pieces "wild outbursts of freedom" (cited in Drewery 13). Drewery proposes reading the work of these four writers through the theoretical lens of the liminal, a concept she adapts from the anthropological theories of Arnold van Gennen and Victor Turner. Citing Victor Turner's description of the liminal as "an instant of pure potentiality when everything … trembles in the balance" (1), Drewery identifies major sites of liminality that link these writers' work: "mourning, the literal or metaphorical journey, the uncanny, and the transient moment, as well as rites of passage involving the transition into speaking subject, adolescence, old age and death" (3). Both liberating and restrictive, liminal experiences challenge the limits of language, subjectivity, and social structure and offer glimpses of other social and personal possibilities, albeit possibilities that entail marginality, exclusion, or even psychosis (120-121). Significantly, these glimpses are ephemeral and fleeting: "Liminal experience makes it possible to envisage a space of subjective and cultural possibility; not to inhabit it," Drewery comments (121). Drewery's thesis is an intriguing one, and the critical and creative dialogue she engenders between these four women modernists a distinctly original and welcome contribution that lays the groundwork for further studies of women modernists and the short story.

Two volumes of essays on Mansfield also stake out new paths for further inquiry. *Celebrating Katherine Mansfield* and *Katherine Mansfield and Literary Modernism* read Mansfield's work through diverse theoretical lenses and in tandem with a range of contemporaneous movements; both feature essays that make good use of the life writings recently made available to critics. Essays by Elleke Boehmer and Janet Wilson in *Celebrating Katherine Mansfield* argue for a more transnational understanding of modernism that would encompass both Mansfield's Anglo-European and colonial identities: Boehmer draws upon Homi Bhabha to show how Mansfield encodes colonial otherness in a number of her stories, thereby situating otherness "within the metropolis, even within the metropolitan self" (58). Wilson notes the overlap in Mansfield's work between practices traditionally defined as modernist and those defined as postcolonial: "the internal ventriloquism, discontinuous narrative structures, and alienated states of being … can be associated with the interstitial positioning of the colonial as well as with modernist practice," she asserts (186). Several essays in the same volume read Mansfield's literary practices against other contemporaneous artistic practices, such as cinema (Sarah Sandley) and music (Delia da Sousa Correa). Others expand our understanding of Mansfield's literary modernism: Angela Smith shows how Mansfield championed Charles Dickens, in contrast to her fellow writers E. M. Forster and Virginia Woolf, while Clare Hanson reads a number of Mansfield's stories against Freud's essay on the uncanny. In *Katherine Mansfield and Literary Modernism*, Susan Reid compares Mansfield's and Lawrence's writings on gender and relationships, finding a surprising correspondence in their shared need "to recognize the other as the basis of relationship" (159), a recognition of otherness which anticipates Irigaray's theorization of the ethics of sexual difference. In the same volume, Gerardo Rodriguez Salas and Isabel Maria Andrés Cuevas compare Mansfield's and Woolf's representations of maternity, arguing that the grotesque nature of such representations was a means of subverting the "conventionally sacred vision of maternity" (146). Two essays in *Katherine Mansfield and Literary Modernism* expand our knowledge of *Rhythm*, one of the earliest and most significant modernist magazines. Gerri Kimber analyzes Mansfield's contributions to *Rhythm* as both writer and editor, demonstrating Mansfield's early commitment to modernist literature, music, and art within a distinctly international framework. Eiko Nakano's essay nicely complements Kimber's in its focus on the Bergsonian philosophy underpinning *Rhythm* and the impact that philosophy had on Mansfield's approach to fiction-writing.

Gerri Kimber emerges here as one of the driving forces of the new Mansfield scholarship, and her short monograph *A Literary Modernist: Katherine Mansfield and the Art of the Short Story* is an indispensable introduction to Mansfield's work. Kimber usefully summarizes some of the reasons underpinning Mansfield's marginalization—her colonial status, her choice of genre, and Murry's involvement in her posthumous reputation—and she reminds us of how revolutionary Mansfield's short stories were, "unlike anything the English story previously had been" (2). Kimber provides an overview of significant themes and symbols in Mansfield's work and contextualizes her narrative techniques (e.g. epiphanies, cinematic devices, literary impressionism) within literary modernism more generally. This volume in particular would be an excellent classroom resource for those teaching Mansfield to readers new to modernist literature.

When Mansfield died in 1923, Woolf recorded her feelings of loss and depression in several diary entries, admitting that she was jealous of Mansfield's writing—"the only writing I have ever been jealous of" (*D*2 227)—and lamenting the loss of Mansfield's support and example: "Go on writing of course: but into emptiness. There's no competitor. I'm cock—a lonely cock whose crowing nothing breaks—of my walk. For our friendship had so much that was writing in it" (*D*2 228). Scholars have finally caught up with Woolf's prescient evaluation of Mansfield's talent and her contributions to modernist literature: Mansfield is modernism's "missing contemporary" no longer.

—Patricia Moran, *University of Limerick*

Works Cited

Bowen, Elizabeth. Introduction. *Stories*. By Katherine Mansfield. New York: Vintage, 1956. Print.

O'Connor, Frank. *The Lonely Voice: A Study of the Short Story*. Cleveland, OH: World, 1963. Print.

Leonard & Virginia Woolf, The Hogarth Press and the Networks of Modernism Ed. Helen Southworth (Edinburgh: Edinburgh UP, 2010) ix + 276 pp. 13 b&w ill.

Although children are admonished *never* to judge a book by its cover, if they are lucky enough to be bitten (or smitten) by the book historian's bug at an early age, they have scholarly sanction to ignore such well-meaning but misguided parental advice. The cover of Helen Southworth's engaging, readable, and timely essay collection, *Leonard & Virginia Woolf: The Hogarth Press and the Networks of Modernism*, telegraphs a similarly transgressive message, even as its contents declare Woolf's welcome arrival within those hotly contested areas of the new modernist studies being transformed by book historians, sociologists, material modernists and, more recently, digital humanists.

Woolfians will recognize the cover image. With its striking Japanoiserie, art-deco pattern, its geometry of white nodal circles and red triangles generating a web of horizontal and diagonal white lines, it replicates the cover of *Two Stories*, the inaugural Hogarth Press booklet handprinted in 1917 that coupled Virginia's story "The Mark on the Wall" with Leonard's "Three Jews." Its mesmerizing interconnections of line and circle, triangle and edge in seemingly infinite repetition conjure a visual starburst evoking energy, innovation, and connectivity. Kudos to Edinburgh University Press's production team for designing such a clever dust jacket. You can almost feel the auratic soft-weave texture of the original (*pace* Walter Benjamin). Perhaps only the too-perfectly positioned title label and glassine cover paper hint otherwise (*touché* retorts Benjamin). But this tension between "old" book and new critical context is precisely the point. It positions Southworth's edition as both interventionist and differently iconoclastic. Instead of the expected picture of Woolf's face fronting a new book about Woolf's career, we confront a material signifier of the Press itself: a multiform icon that not only foregrounds the Press's institutional significance in Woolf's writing life, but one that also declares it high time critics re-cover new associations between the Hogarth Press, modernism, print culture, and textual criticism.

D. F. McKenzie, the influential bibliographer and pioneering theorist of the "sociology of texts" reminds us that the word 'text' derives from the Latin, *texere*, "to weave" (13). The strikingly tactile cover of *Two Stories* even in reproduction encodes multiple material signs about an interweave of narrative, marriage, and business whose ethos of experimentation, alterity, and diversity would become, as Southworth's book freshly reminds us, the non-accidental hallmark of the Hogarth Press as a modernist publishing enterprise. Southworth's wide-ranging introduction skillfully contextualizes the Woolfs' adventures in the book trade within broader pressures affecting the contemporary publishing industry—mapping the tensions and creative possibilities of the intermarriage of art and commerce, private and public ownership, coterie and mass readership, literature and politics—while the nine essays duly support her thesis that "experiment, idiosyncrasy, hybridity and 'heterogeneity'...were keywords for the Press ..." and that "[c]ollaboration and reciprocity were also indispensable to [its] unique personality" (15).

Southworth's book itself might be said to stake a claim to a "two stories" critical imprimatur: it is only the second monograph publication on the Press, a companion piece of sorts to J. H. Willis's *Leonard and Virginia Woolf as Publishers: The Hogarth Press 1917-1941* (1992), which similarly foregrounds the colophon of double-ownership. But Southworth's is no secondary text. Rather, as she points out, the diachronic survey in Willis's book "mostly leaves out the complex and fascinating histories of the diverse network of authors, artists and workers involved with the Woolfs and the work they produced" (15). Her collection showcases a few of these network relationships, demonstrating just how significant a change in the literary critical landscape the intervening twenty years has effected on this growth-area within Woolf studies. Without the "material turn" in modernist studies, no less the broader impact of new historicism and cultural studies, many of these dynamic essays would struggle to find fair hearing. No longer need materialism be straitjacketed into a static economic model but can legitimately refract the people and friendships, tools and trade practices of a broad cultural circuitry where books and people intermingle in complex "biobibliographical" ways that demand fresh critical frameworks (Greetham).

Southworth cites the creative admixture of once sidelined critical and material sources as influencing her selection criteria, crediting the rise in periodical studies with providing an applicable model for analysis of the modernist small press movement. The heterogeneity of the Hogarth Press's activities invites comparison with multi-sized periodical ventures which were "social forums for writers from different genders, backgrounds, races and nationalities" providing "loci of identification and difference" where we might "recover lines of connection, influence, conflict and resistance that entangle the many strands of modernism"

(14 quoting Churchill and McKible). Given that one of Virginia Woolf's earliest unrealized speculations about their newfound press was that it might (fashionably perhaps) produce an in-house periodical, this seems a compelling way to open up the Press to analysis beyond its more famous associations with Woolf herself, the Freud publications, or other now canonical modernist productions.

The collection straddles three broad categories: Part One "Class and Culture"; Part Two "Global Bloomsbury"; Part Three "Marketing Other Modernisms." This tripartite structure has the implicit effect of encouraging us to make comparisons not only within discrete sections, but also across the banner headings. So, for instance, Melissa Sullivan's study in Part One of the Hogarth's courtship of middlebrow women writers resonates with Helen Southworth's essay in Part Three on the Press's solicitation and cultivation of male working class writers. Anna Snaith's essay in Part Two on the South Asian and Caribbean writers championed by the Press bridges race with gender and class as diversifying features of the Press catalogues. In Part One, Mark Hussey excavates the overlooked child-poet Joan Adeney Easdale. His assertion that Woolf didn't publish Easdale simply *because* she was a woman finds proof in Woolf's kindly rejection of the poetry of Ann Kauffer, sister of the prominent graphic designer E. McKnight Kauffer whose role as in-house artist Elizabeth Willson Gordon excavates in Part Three. The production, reception, and circulation case studies within this volume fruitfully proliferate. Their dialogic interactions excite new network theories about how the Hogarth Press operated as a conduit for the circulation of modernist aesthetics, no less the politics of modernity, thereby helping to undermine the once-traditional *cordon sanitaire* between the business of making books and the cultural impact of the stories told between the covers.

Within each of the three sections there are more obvious if equally slantwise interconnections. "Class and Culture" features essays by Hussey on Easdale, Sullivan on middlebrow women writers, and Diane Gillespie on the Hogarth Press and religion. Hussey takes Easdale out of the shadows of the "Auden generation" making a persuasive case both for Easdale's poetic distinction and the Press's investment in the development of an unorthodox writer. Easdale's long and mystical narrative poem, *Amber Innocent*, showcased how, under Virginia's co-editorship, the Press took a chance on a work far less socially engagé than that advocated by the thirties (male) poets. *Amber Innocent*, in which Hussey detects Easdale "drawing on an image-world mapped out by Virginia Woolf" (44), emphasizes less a female tradition than the cultivation of a distinctive poetic style that chimes unexpectedly against the background of the workaday life and production methods at the Press. Notably, Hussey's resurrection of John Lehmann's voice in unpublished journals and letters gives vernacular immediacy to the tensions between Woolf and Lehmann in the late 1930s not just about the development of poetry, but also the gender politics of publication choice (Lehmann had objected to Easdale).

While Easdale had the social connections to get her noticed by the Woolfs, the more middlebrow women writers, Rose Macaulay and E. M. Delafield, came to the Press, as Sullivan argues, dissimilarly. If Macaulay had the class standing and academic background to meet with the Woolfs on an (almost) equal footing, Delafield, the popular journalist and chronicler of the *Provincial Lady* series, had no such "in." But like Macaulay she proved an adept writer for the "academic" wing of the Press's catalogue. Indeed, an arguably underplayed strength of this new lens Sullivan offers into the oft-cited "battle of the brows" is to situate how the Press groomed these kinds of writers as accessible academic voices—Macaulay for her contributions to language theory; Delafield on Victorian fiction—during an era when the perception of English studies was undergoing seismic changes within both the university system and the culture at large. Cultural changes were also in the wind with respect to religion, and Diane Gillespie gives a similarly compelling study of what today's critics might be surprised to learn was the "Religion" category in the Press's 1934 catalogue. Macaulay's work on *Religious Elements in English Literature* was part of this list, which included R. B. Braithwaite's *The State of Religious Belief*, but so too were many other disparate texts. In tracing the evolution of Braithwaite's pamphlet from its genesis as a questionnaire in *The Nation* that Leonard Woolf, as literary editor, had helped prepare, Gillespie demonstrates how hybridized publication venues helped the Press expand "its professional engagement with the larger world of letters and serious public debate" (84).

"Global Bloomsbury" highlights another troika of essays that variously situate the Hogarth Press within networks of transnational modernisms drawing lines of influence and confluence to the far corners of empire—South Africa (John Young on William Plomer), India and the Caribbean (Anna Snaith on, respectively, Mulk Raj Anand and C. L. R. James)—and the continental politics of post-revolutionary Russia (Jean Mills on D. S. Mirsky, Jane Harrison, and Virginia Woolf). Snaith makes a strong case for identifying the Press as "a key disseminator of anti-colonial thought in the interwar period" (104), foregrounding its role as cultural, geographic, and institutional crossroads for a heated exchange of ideas between colonial and metropolitan intellectuals at a time when a faltering colonialist discourse and an emergent postcolonial politics were in tense transitional dialogue. Snaith nimbly reads both Anand's and James's writings *for* a Bloomsbury Press and *about* the Bloomsbury circle as emblematic of an ambiguously admired British ideal. Particularly bracing in its close textual analysis of the voices of these radical colonial thinkers (no less for *how* their contacts with the Woolfs helped radicalize them), her arguments offer an evenhanded contribution to Woolf-centric readings of the perspicacity as well as the intransigent blind spots of Virginia Woolf's own political aesthetics. From a different vantage point (nationally, racially, imperially), but with the same keen attention to close textual critique leavened with book history, John Young's analysis of the biographical, narratological, and transnational routes by which William Plomer became a Press author who challenged racial, gendered, cultural, and heterosexualist norms shines new light on equally bold publication choices by both Woolfs, providing new archival evidence for the extent of their joint editorship. Jean Mills examines the back-story of how the Press's last Russian translation, *The Life of the Archbishop Avvakum, by Himself*—"the first English translation of the earliest autobiography ever written in the Russian language" (151)—brought its preface writer, the Russian historian and literary critic D. S. Mirsky, into the orbit of the Woolfs through its translator Jane Harrison. For Mills, this overlooked publication exposes "the Hogarth Press' key role in the networks of the European intellectual left" (154) following the Bolshevik revolution, but it is her more inventive reading of Harrison's translation as it demystified the too-facile romanticization of the "Slav soul" then in vogue that will most resonate with critics rethinking connections between translation, modernism, and book history; it obliquely reminds us that *all* the essays in this section deal at some level with the politics and problematics of translation across borders in cartographic or geopolitical flux.

Finally, "Marketing Other Modernisms" focuses on the Press's evolution from coterie to commercial publishing house in the late-twenties and early-thirties. Elizabeth Willson Gordon identifies 1928 as a tipping point when the Press hired E. McKnight Kauffer to recraft the Press's wolf's head logo and various book jackets (here attractively reproduced). Kauffer was the then well-known American graphic designer, painter, and, most famously, poster artist for the London Underground whose mediation of the high and commercial art worlds Gordon deftly maps onto the sometimes conflicting but never implacable oppositions between the coterie creative and public professional worlds the Press increasingly sought to navigate. Gordon's conflation of biography and cultural theory is picked up by Southworth in her rich analysis of the numerous now almost forgotten male working class writers the Press began to nurture at this time, mainly for their social theory, but also for their creative fiction. Edwin Muir, Ben Bowker, Thomas Sharp, R. M. Fox, John Hampson and Huw Menai were all either northern or so-called "provincial" writers or those with experiences of life beyond the London-Oxford-Cambridge axis. Choosing to cultivate these voices highlights both Woolfs' commitments to non-privileged viewpoints, Southworth argues, and shows a canny awareness that they would have to vie with trendier left-wing presses with more established working class backlists. Competing to sign the decidedly non-working-class writer Vita Sackville-West, who already had an established publisher, was one of their smartest economic moves. Stephen Barkway crafts an intimate portrait from published and unpublished letters of a business relationship between friends and erstwhile lovers that, almost miraculously, never foundered until very late in the day (after Virginia's death) but which enriched the Hogarth's coffers almost beyond measure (Barkway does the math and it is eye-popping).

As we near the hundredth anniversary of the founding of the Hogarth Press, this collection reminds us what a bold, iconoclastic, time-consuming, but always adventurous enterprise it was for the Woolfs personally, professionally, and intellectually. If they sometimes lamented the strains of running a book-publishing firm out of their basement, it remained a labor of love (in the many complicated senses of the phrase). This collection proves just how broadly integrated its operations were with political, cultural, and social movements of the interwar years and just how much the Woolfs' business model intersected developments within the wider book trades, the cultivation of emergent readerships, and the evolution of modernism in all its literary and political dimensions. If developments in Woolf studies over the last thirty years have thoroughly eradicated the ethereal Woolf of long-ago imaginings, these essays catalyze a vital critical dialogue about how the "real" world of publishing and book production reflexively shaped the Woolfs' aesthetic and political worldviews. Some of its studied gaps—the de-emphasis on the more famous publications; the Press and Woolf's writings; the internally coherent or incoherent generic differences between novels, poetry, essays and pamphlet series—help us return with new eyes to how future work in this area must necessarily come to terms with the dense cultural networks behind the literary as well as extra-literary creative output from the Press, even as they put pressure on whether those distinctions remain germane theoretically or, more problematically, historically. 2010 witnessed a number of positive movements on these fronts (see related essays by Marcus, Shannon, and McTaggart) with Southworth's book a distinct—and distinctive—bellwether of a renaissance in this field. It marks important reading not just for Woolf critics, but also for those more generally interested in the history of the book, modernist publishing, network theory, and cultural studies. And when its own dust jacket has long ago been discarded by those devourers of time (aka library shelving practices), these essays will remind us that what has been materially lost or hidden from view is well worth digging up, re-presenting, and crafting into new narratives that challenge the orthodox view.

—Alice Staveley, *Stanford University*

Works Cited

Churchill, Suzanne W. and Adam McKible, eds. *Little Magazines and Modernism: New Approaches*. Aldershot, England: Ashgate Publishing, 2007. Print.

Greetham, David. *Textual Transgressions: Essays Toward the Construction of a Biobibliography*. New York and London: Garland Publishing, 1998. Print.

Marcus, Laura. "Virginia Woolf as Publisher and Editor." *The Edinburgh Companion to Virginia Woolf and the Arts*, ed. Maggie Humm. Edinburgh: Edinburgh UP, 2010: 263-79. Print.

McKenzie, D.F. *Bibliography and the Sociology of Texts*. Cambridge: Cambridge UP, 1999. Print.

McTaggart, Ursula. "'Opening the Door': The Hogarth Press as Virginia Woolf's Outsiders' Society." *Tulsa Studies in Women's Literature* 29.1 (Spring 2010): 63-82. Print.

Shannon, Drew Patrick. "'The Book is Still Warm': The Hogarth Press in the Age of Mechanical Reproduction." *Virginia Woolf's Bloomsbury: International Influence and Politics*, Volume 2, eds. Lisa Shahiari and Gina Potts. New York: Palgrave Macmillan, 2010. Print.

Virginia Woolf and the Russian Point of View. Roberta Rubenstein (NY: Palgrave, 2009) xvi +265

Rare are the scholarly studies that combine timeliness, impressive originality, and acutely precise and detailed analysis with a gently reassuring sense that we are not so much engaged in "criticism" as being invited to read over a writer's shoulder and catch the very passions and wonder that they might have felt as they read. What a delight then to come at last upon Roberta Rubenstein's *Virginia Woolf and the Russian Point of View.* Why "at last"? The answer is simply that no matter how poisedly and confidently critics have affirmed the close bond between Russian literature in translation and English modernism, or referred authoritatively to the particular significance that reading the Russians had for Virginia Woolf, no book-length study had yet been devoted to the question. The gap was indeed intriguing: Neil Cornwell's *James Joyce and the Russians*, after all, dates back to 1992. Our critical insights for Woolf relied on analogies, intimate convictions, Rubenstein's own unpublished thesis, a growing number of articles (such as the valuable work by Laura Marcus, Darya Protopopova, Emily Dalgarno and Natalya Reinhold to name but a few) or biographical accounts. Our impressions are at last challenged, explored and borne out, in a superb account that does not just range with impressive ease over the entire Woolf œuvre, but also anchors Woolf's Russian point of view in a sense of history and chronology as her interests dawned, matured, waned and evolved.

In so doing, Rubenstein charts Woolf's Russian readings from the honeymoon *Crime and Punishment* to Tolstoy in the bleakness of the Second World War; she examines very precisely the force and repercussions of the four Russian "greats" on various facets of Woolf's own creative processes, and also offers a profound understanding of Woolf's richly comparative approach to reading, as the Russians were not just read *per se,* but explored via the complementary tangents of re-reading and reading alongside English fiction. And while Rubenstein's approach focuses on Woolf's individual reception of the writers, rather than on a more broadly construed cultural reception, it does sketch the posterity of Woolf's vision, tracing her intuitions through to contemporary Russian scholars' works: George R. Clay, Orlando Figes, Joseph Frank, Lucia Aiello. Such interdisciplinary dialogues and overtures make Rubenstein's book not just a significant contribution to Woolf studies, but to comparative Slavonic studies too.

Each chapter of the book is devoted to one author in turn, thus eschewing those cultural commonplaces that abound when one speaks too glibly of "The Russians" and "their literature" as some homogeneous entity in time and space. Looking at Dostoevsky, Rubenstein explores the very tangible impact of his dialogic poetics feeding into Woolf's own representations of random consciousness and passing "trains of thought" whereby she sought to open up the world within. The potential interweaving of Dostoevsky's and Woolf's intensely personal experiences of "mental extremity and a wish for self-annihilation" (47) is also tackled with immense skill and sensitivity. In this chapter, as throughout the study, what makes Rubenstein's approach so very successful is that she interweaves essays and reading notes (cited in full in the rich appendices here that have been transcribed for the first time from the Berg Collection at the New York Public Library) so that we follow the notes Woolf made as she interrupted her readings to record her own impressions. Another very welcome editorial strategy adopted by Rubenstein is to refer the reader back to the very page references in the Russian text itself, so that we see Woolf's thoughts emerging in perfect dialogue with the novel's own fabric. This is particularly striking when, without Rubenstein's guidance, we may have read these notes without perceiving whose voice we were hearing, Woolf's, or the Russian author's.

The chapter devoted to Chekhov focuses on the importance of his formal method and artistry in terms of Woolf's own aesthetic experiments and innovations: a heightened sense of the trivial, the transitory and the fragmented which, almost out-Chekhoving Chekhov, Woolf would work not only into stories but into *Jacob's Room* and *To the Lighthouse* too. We also see Woolf as theatre-goer, writing her impressions of *The Cherry Orchard* into what Rubenstein sees as a "riff" on Chekhov, thus blending stage, page and ear into a cross-cultural and inter-semiotic dialogue. Similarly, our understanding of Woolf's comparative literary dynamics expands immeasurably thanks to Rubenstein's reading of the previously unpublished essay fragment "Tchekov on Pope," conceived as an idiosyncratic encounter between the "British Augustan poet and the Russian storyteller" (83), between the mirror and the magnifying glass. And again, by comparing polished texts to random notes and drafts, Rubenstein charts out the very processes by which Woolf worked through her readerly intuitions before fashioning them into a personal framework for her poetics. One lingers, for example, captivated, by the passing annotation in the essay draft, "A collision of brittle particles which falling, lend the air a rainbow brilliance" (180), and its endless, random echoes and resonances.

The third chapter explores the lifelong significance of Tolstoy as "critical benchmark" for Woolf. It takes us from what Lytton Strachey recognized as the Tolstoyan overtones of *The Voyage Out* to a revealing note in 1940 detailing the exquisite shock of rereading Tolstoy and marking *War and Peace* as "the greatest novel in the world" as Woolf prepared for an essay that poignantly remained unwritten. We see Woolf weighing up biography and poetics from a feminist angle, as she tackles Tolstoy's ambivalence in terms of his domestic life, and his moralizing perspectives on women, in comparison to his intensely sensitive handling of female characters. What Rubenstein brings to the fore in this chapter are the visual dynamics, thus embracing not only those telescopic details that pierce through Tolstoy's narratives, but also Woolf's own encounters with cinematographic narrative via *Anna Karenina*. And second, it is the intense suggestive power of Tolstoy's aesthetics that Rubenstein highlights, thanks to a superb linking up of that recurring Woolfian image of the globe turning on the fingertips of protagonists and minor characters alike across the years.

And finally to Turgenev, whom Woolf grew into gently rather than discovered with passion, and indeed at a moment when her British contemporaries were tending to move away from the Russian master of melody and formal artistry. In a very different mode from earlier Dostoevskian dialogism, we see Woolf engaging with multiple points of view, poised feeling and the understated hum of life. And here too Rubenstein opens up our reading of *The Years*, very convincingly relating the East European figure Pomjalovsky commonly known as Brown to that other Woolfian character who shines out from the margins, Mrs. Brown, and her embodiment of novelistic aesthetics to come.

Rubenstein's work achieves admirable depth, resituating as it does so many key moments and factors in Woolf's poetics, from craftsmanship, heightened consciousness and time sequence to personality, characterization and critical stance, to show how "inestimably decisive, transformative and enduring" (162) Woolf's readings of the Russians were over the years. She also leaves certain avenues as yet unexplored or only partially illuminated: the importance of the translations from Russian, the encounters with minor Russian writers and how they fit into the troika, or quartet, of "greats," and a broader understanding of how Woolf's personal reception was feeding into, contrasting and overlapping with contemporary cultural debates. But how much better to have done so. For now, equipped with such a rich, readable and amply documented study, new Woolf scholars can follow up these paths, weaving a very dominant Russian thread into the tapestry of trans-European modernism.

—Claire Davison-Pegon, *Université de Provence*

Encountering Choran Community: Literary Modernism, Visual Culture, and Political Aesthetics in the Interwar Years. Emily M. Hinnov (Selinsgrove: Susquehanna UP, 2009) 246 pp.

How did modernist authors and photographers seek interconnectivity—in their works as well as between their works and readers/viewers? What were their visions of utopian community in a time of poverty, racism, and impending world war? How might we as scholars and teachers seek interconnectivity with our colleagues, students, and the larger world around us? Emily M. Hinnov raises such questions in *Encountering Choran Community: Literary Modernism, Visual Culture, and Political Aesthetics in the Interwar Years*.

Hinnov introduces her thesis by noting that studies of modernism often emphasize canonical male writers, whose literature of fragmentation, isolation, and ennui, along with the denigration or romanticization of the social or racial Other, too often holds sway in literary criticism and in the classroom. Hinnov instead focuses on modernist literature by women that she sees enacting a "key counternarrative to Modernism's engagement with early twentieth-century master narratives" (14). Vital to such counternarratives is the choran community arising from the choran moment, terms drawn from Julia Kristeva's concept of the semiotic *chora*, "a prelinguistic state of consciousness and connection with the maternal body that leads to an integrated understanding of self and, by extension, other" (Hinnov 19). It is a place of wholeness and bliss as yet untouched by the symbolic—the realm of structured language and social order we enter into the moment we are born. Throughout our lives, however, the semiotic might pulse through the symbolic as a counter-language, such as poetry or whisperings, murmurs, humming, and song—anti-patriarchal rhythms and sounds capable of disrupting the status quo. Choran community occurs "when characters and/ or readers (re)cognize their connection with a larger, inherently unified whole," Hinnov writes (14).

Hinnov prefaces Chapter 1, "The Phantasmic Mother: Virginia Woolf's Fiction, Gertrude Käsebier's Photography, and Utopian Maternal Longing," with the 1884 photograph of two-year old Virginia Stephen sitting on her mother's lap, gazing at the camera while her mother looks down, and a stylized photograph by Käsebier called *The Manger, or Ideal Motherhood* (1899), in which a woman in a white dress and long diaphanous veil holds a swaddled baby to her breast. Hinnov presents these images of the photographic choran moment to show that both Woolf and Käsebier "made use of maternal longing in envisioning wholeness through their art" (60), and she proposes that readers and viewers of such scenes might recall "their own maternally-bonded self," prompting "a tiny freedom, a sense of life inherent in the intertextuality between our own memory of a similar cohering moment and the image at hand" (61).

Acknowledging that Käsebier comes under criticism for privileging "a visual code of whiteness as ideal" (65), Hinnov nevertheless regards her as "particularly modern" for seeking wholeness "through deeper understandings of early states of consciousness" (65). *The Manger* depicts "unity with the lost maternal body" while *Mother and Child (Decorative Panel)* (1899) shows a woman bending towards a baby girl who has already begun to break the maternal bond, turning away from her mother, like the toddler Virginia looks away from Julia Stephen—a painful rupture but necessary for the child to achieve individuation. In *Blessed Art Thou Among Women* (1899), a mother guides her school-age daughter out the door, "benevolently shepherd[ing] her daughter from one stage of consciousness to the next" (67). While Käsebier might be seen as "replicating the Angel of the House ideology of her day" (68), Hinnov urges us to read these photographs "both aesthetically and politically" (68), for such choran moments between mothers and daughters counteract master/male pictorial narratives with "a phantasmic maternal presence [that] becomes the catalyst for self-revelation" (68).

Hinnov turns to similar choran moments in Woolf, citing examples from the novels after recalling diary entries in which Woolf expresses a desire to create connections between her characters; those connections, Hinnov writes, are "often represented by children's voices in her novels, which in turn emulate the lost fusion with the maternal body in the symbolic order" (73). Discussing the opening of *Jacob's Room* (1922), Hinnov finds Archer's voice calling out to his brother on the beach evoking the solitary wanderer cut off from the maternal core, while Mrs. Flanders and Rebecca, softly crooning over and caring for the children at night, provide a womb-like enclosure for them while a storm rages outside. Thus Hinnov explores harmonious as well as discordant sounds in Woolf, such as the children's song at the conclusion of *The Years* that so unsettles the adult listeners. With such jarring noises, Woolf expresses the "sorrow of that fundamental disconnect between the maternal body and our inevitable wrenching into the social order" (74)—a sorrow that moments of wholeness in Woolf counteract. Hinnov closes the chapter with a discussion of Lily Briscoe, likening the rhythm of Lily's art to the rhythms of the womb and stating that reflections on her childhood summers on St. Ives led Woolf to conclude, "it is those memories of pure, ecstatic maternal unions that hold us together" (85). "In giving us moments of wholeness in her work," Woolf offers readers "a plurality of pleasure" (86).

Hinnov's book includes two chapters on African-American women writers of the Harlem Renaissance, helping to bridge the chasm that still exists between Anglo and African-American modernism and explicating narrative and social concerns unique to women writers of color. Rather than depict choran moments, Nella Larsen's 1928 novel, *Quicksand*, displays the "limitations and ultimate breakdown of this maternal ideal . . . and its sometimes shattered hope for choran community" (89), for its heroine, Helga Crane, daughter of a white Danish mother and black West Indian father, neither of whom acknowledge her, struggles and fails to achieve selfhood in the rural South, the urban North, and Europe. Would-be moments of choran community become acts of manipulation and exploitation as Helga's Danish relatives trot her out as an exotic specimen, as sophisticated Harlemites fault her for being insufficiently race-conscious, and as her husband and female neighbors in the deep South accept her only when she succumbs to a string of physically and emotionally debilitating births. Hinnov's attention to modernist primitivism explains how "white" and "black" writers incorporated notions of race and ethnicity into their narrative aesthetics. Presenting readers with thwarted choran moments, Larsen compels audiences to bring Helga to voice through "an affective kind of reading"; *Quicksand*, then, constitutes "a complication of modernist narratives of gender, race, and community and a vital call for social justice" (92).

The discussion of modernist primitivism continues in a chapter on Sylvia Townsend Warner's *Mr. Fortune's Maggot* (1927). While the main character, the Reverend Timothy Fortune, is a South Seas missionary intent on spreading Christianity to the "heathens," the novel in fact "rewrites notions of racist ideology by employing choran moments of interconnectivity to undercut the hegemony of empire" (110), for an important developing relationship in the novel is that between Fortune and one of the island's young male inhabitants, Lueli, who initially seemed the most ripe for conversion. In fact it is Fortune who converts—to one no longer desirous of forcing Anglo-Christian beliefs onto others, a conversion ironically made possible by his initial missionary zeal. Intense physical and emotional moments of contact—choran moments—between Fortune and Lueli spur Fortune towards this change of heart that he carries into the future. Rather than reaffirming colonial tenets, Hinnov sees Warner gently mocking and satirizing them, writing an anti-colonial narrative counteracting imperialism. In this work and others by Warner, "readers of the present and future can catch a glimpse at the possibly redemptive choran moment and thereby begin building bridges to interconnective community" (122).

The chapter on *Mr. Fortune's Maggot* creates a bridge between that on Larsen's *Quicksand* and Zora Neale Hurston's *Their Eyes Were Watching God* (1937), whose African-American heroine, Janie Crawford, ultimately achieves a strong sense of self. Janie's transformative experiences deny notions of an "essential" self, while the novel's opening scene suggests how we might be more open "to the larger world beyond the view of the horizon" (125). On the road to self-actualization, Janie experiences problematic relationships, not least with her third husband, Tea Cake, whom many readers view as her soul-mate, yet as Hinnov points out, Hurston imbues their relationship with "false moment[s] of utopian intersubjectivity, or, an ironic choran moment" (131). Scenes with Tea Cake, along with the court scene toward the novel's end when Janie is on trial for his murder, demonstrate "the constant cultural mediation of intersubjectivity. There is no such thing as a free social space," Hinnov writes, explicating Janie's confounding silence throughout the court proceedings—"only a negotiation of the social order (which Janie ultimately succeeds in transcending by virtue of the fact that she is always aware of the ever-presence of cultural hegemony)" (132).

According to Hinnov, Janie also expresses a "strong desire to converge with her community" (133), something of which I was not convinced in my own reading of the novel, for as Janie returns to the town she had left to follow Tea Cake into the muck, she ignores the townspeople and sits alone on her porch until the arrival of her friend, Phoebe. While she tells her story to Phoebe and encourages her to share it with the community, she declines to speak to them herself and retreats to her bedroom. It would seem that achieving choran community is not only unlikely for Janie but also not even something she desires. Discussing the split among critics concerning the issue of whether Janie is or is not integrated into community, Hinnov explains convincingly Janie's recognition of the racism and sexism proscribing her experience as an African-American woman, yet like Hurston herself she can "see beyond [the social order] and create a counternarrative to constrictive ideologies" (137). In fact, "this novel enacts the call of choran community itself" (139).

This call may be heard in Woolf's late work, the subject of Hinnov's last chapter. In *The Waves* (1931), *Three Guineas* (1938), and *Between the Acts*

(1941), Woolf "opens up the possibility for illuminated moments of communal awareness based upon convergence in spite of difference—choran community" (140). Fragments lead to wholeness, the isolated individual achieves unity with others, and counterhistorical writing "advocates for more personal, creative, and eventually communal narratives rather than authorized versions of history as told by fascist and/or patriarchal institutions of power" (141). Hinnov clearly and compellingly illustrates how Woolf "invites collaborative meaning-making" as we consider, in reading these later works, how to resist the hegemonic historical record, how to create a society of outsiders working towards community, how to respond to reports and photographs of carnage, and how to become socially active through art. From such works emerge communities of readers effecting choran community, because "[f]or Woolf, art transforms our behavior in the world by reconfiguring our relations to both the artwork and its audience" (154).

In her conclusion, Hinnov examines the phototext *Let Us Now Praise Famous Men* (1941), with writing by James Agee and pictures by Walker Evans of sharecroppers in 1930s Depression-era America—a work similar to *Three Guineas* in "creating an art both politically and aesthetically engaged" on the brink of world war (163). Hinnov explains the ways in which Walker and Agee sought ethical encounters with the families they wrote about and photographed. While they resolved to demonstrate the interconnectedness of all human beings, however, their experience revealed the impassible bridge between them and their subjects, for "their phototext remains vexed with artistic ego, class privilege, and wishful bias" (170). In fact each of the modernists she discusses, Hinnov states, struggled mightily with their desire for wholeness and the virtual impossibility of achieving it. Nevertheless the struggle alone is imperative for demonstrating "that there is no singular, total truth, but instead the complex and poetic eloquence associated with the problem of capturing reality" (173), that "the ethical value lies in the attempt to connect" (176), and that acknowledging our connections to one another "is a political act in itself" (177)—a phrase recalling Woolf's pronouncement in 1940, "Thinking is my fighting" (*D5* 285).

Hinnov's work is valuable and enlightening on many accounts, namely its unlikely yet harmonious joining of diverse figures for a more expansive and inclusive concept of modernism and its steadfast attention to how we might carry the knowledge gleaned from such works into "real life" and into the future. *Encountering Choran Community* will surely stimulate our reading, research, and teaching about these and other modernist works.

—Kristin Czarnecki, *Georgetown College*

The Edinburgh Companion to Virginia Woolf and the Arts. Ed. Maggie Humm (Edinburgh: Edinburgh UP, 2010) xii + 500pp.

At nearly five hundred pages, this generous collection of twenty-six essays on Woolf's relation to every conceivable aspect of the arts from philosophies of aesthetics to photography, film, and dance to entertaining, gardening, and scrapbooking looks like a useful reference text to have on one's shelf and/or recommend for purchase by the local academic library. Further perusal, however, additionally reveals a lively series of conversations on the cutting edge of ongoing debates in Woolf scholarship whose relevance to many of the larger issues at play in the profession makes for entertaining and enlightening reading.

A study of Woolf's relation to the arts with particular notice given to the social and political contexts accompanying the major shifts which mark the onset and development of Modernism, this collection is especially marked by the thoroughness with which historical contexts are integrated with archival research, inquiry into the genesis of Woolf's writing through access to a variety of "pre-texts" and drafts, and new theoretical perspectives to produce invigorating readings of particular texts. The authors of the essays are well-chosen; readers will recognize many voices: Diane Gillespie on Woolf's relation to her sister's arts, Jane Goldman on the complex valence of Woolf's versionings of Modernism, Patrick Collier on journalism, Leslie Hankins on film, Victoria Rosner on Monk's House, Jane Garrity on fashion. But these essays are not mere rehashes of previous work. Instead, they consistently identify current areas of debate, correcting and augmenting previous scholarship and presenting provocative new interpretive insights. The authors' expertise provides scrupulous bibliographies, in most cases adumbrated by helpful lists of additional readings, so that one is made aware of the whole history of controversy on each topic. Theoretical contexts are evoked only sparingly; aside from nods to Adorno, Heiddegger, DeCerteau, and Slavoj Žižek, Walter Benjamin seems to be the genius loci of current criticism on Woolf and the arts.

The *Companion* is divided into six parts. The first, Aesthetics, contains the expected treatments of Woolf's engagements with her Victorian heritage and with the contemporary contested arenas of Modernism, Bloomsbury aesthetics, and the issue of realism. Two additional essays—Gretchen Gerzina on "Performing Race" and Vara Neverow on Woolf and "City Aesthetics"—extend the usual purviews into the arenas of space/place, race, performativity, and popular culture, usefully expanding the notion of what constitutes "aesthetics." Jane Goldman's essay, one of the longest in the collection, sets up a number of the themes and issues which weave throughout subsequent essays, knitting the volume into a much more coherent whole than might be anticipated: the nature of Woolf's relation to her Victorian past; the special characteristics of Woolf's brand of Modernism; the tension between mimetic representation of the so-called "real" and what we would now call a postmodern awareness of language's ability to create reality; Woolf's oscillation between discursive and performative definitions of the self and between a self in the process of becoming and one which is already unified; the central importance of reclaiming subjectivity for the feminine. Freeing Woolf from dependence upon Roger Fry as perpetual interlocutor, Anthony Uhlmann's essay on Woolf and Bloomsbury Aesthetics offers a helpful look at how Cézanne's ideas of rhythm and sensation were adapted by Woolf to verbal contexts. Finally, Linden Peach rescues *Night and Day* from consignment to the rubbish heap of conventional realism, pointing out how the novel's complex tension between feelings and reality reveals the "real" to be "a symbolic order in which particular prejudices, assumptions, and discourses were legitimized," in the process explicating some important similarities between the works of Woolf and Walter Sickert.

Part II, on Paintings, takes up many of the themes sounded in the section on Aesthetics, intensifying their visual context. Diane Gillespie's piece extends her ground-breaking work on the sororal cross-influencing of Virginia and Vanessa, like Uhlmann's essay continuing to disentangle Woolf's visual aesthetics from those of Fry, while providing a useful summary of scholarship on the sisters' relationship. Her essay picks up the thread of the importance of Virginia's reading of Walter Sickert's paintings and starts two new lines of inquiry: the centrality of parties and portraiture as occasions for exploring crucial ambivalences about women's social roles. Ben Harvey's long discussion of how Woolf's writing reveals her museum and gallery-going habits is one of a couple of essays that deal with her critique of the National Portrait Gallery. Beginning and ending with Boris Anrep's inclusion of Woolf as Clio, the Muse of History, in his mosaic for the National Gallery (handsomely illustrated in a color plate), Harvey gathers together many neglected essays in which Woolf reacted to various exhibitions, looking both at how she deals with galleries as spaces in the world and how she makes sections of her texts into galleries. Elizabeth Hirsh's treatment of portraiture in Woolf—she reminds us that every one of Woolf's books has some reference to portraits—gracefully incorporates new theoretical perspectives on the public function of portraiture, linking the private photo album and the country house gallery to biography and history. Showing how Woolf's own "autobiographical myth of modernization" is filtered through a critique of the portraiture of Watts and of her great-aunt Julia Margaret Cameron, Hirsh goes on to present a reading of the alternative (queer) history offered in *Orlando.*

The five essays housed in the middle section on Domestic Arts explicate the centrality of some hitherto overlooked or underestimated spheres of activity such as interior design, fashion, entertaining, and gardening. Arguing that Woolf (like her sister) went to the country not to relax but to work, Victoria Rosner usefully outlines the sixteen remodeling projects undertaken to modernize Monk's House, reducing the need for servants and increasing the time that could be devoted to reading and writing. Her investigation of the importance of private space in chronicling the shifting locations of Woolf's writing lodge as well as the inscription of creative spaces for women in her fiction substantiates her important claim that Woolf needed both a secure sense of spatial privacy and the ability to roam freely in order to be fully creative. Jane Garrity explores a similar paradoxical formulation in Woolf's attitude towards clothing, noting how her pleasure in fashion—her awareness that clothing can be used as a way of performing both autonomy and modernity—is always shadowed by a sense of psychic shame and an awareness of the ways that fashion commodifies and dictates the rules of feminine appearance. Liz and Peter Brooker's essay, a rather indecisive discussion of whether Woolf was or was not a bohemian, is one of the weaker efforts in the collection, failing to cite Virginia Nicholson's *Among the Bohemians* and other relevant sources. Echoing some of the same themes as Garrity's essay on fashion, Makiko Minow-Pinkney's analysis of Woolf's ambivalence towards "party-consciousness" is perhaps a bit schematic in its juxtaposition of modernist "inner depth" with conventional superficiality, but her synopsis usefully includes Woolf's writing on parties in her early journals and her use of the hostess metaphor in "Mr. Bennett and Mrs. Brown" along with the treatments of the hostess roles played by Clarissa Dalloway and Mrs. Ramsay (one could wish she had tried to extend her thesis to include the party scenes in later novels such as *The Waves* and *The Years*, where the hostess role is not so central). Also welcome is the clear photographic reproduction of Woolf dressed as the March Hare for Angelica Bell's eleventh birthday party in 1930. A happily satisfying essay (for me at least) is Nina Hancock's treatment of how the gardens of Woolf's life are transformed into the gardens of her work. While, once again, I see the identification of Woolf's mother with the rural garden at Talland House and Woolf's father with the urban vistas of Kensington Gardens as a bit too schematic, Hancock's account of the associations between walking, chanting, and writing, her brief discussions of Vanessa and Vita's garden-making, and her emphasis on the importance of Woolf's immersion in the organic rhythms of the garden at Monk's House lay the foundations for future work in this area.

Part IV, on Publishing, Broadcasting and Technology, covers a good deal of familiar territory, but does so with efficiency and acumen. Laura Marcus's concise summary of Woolf's activities as a publisher and editor concentrates on the impact of the activities of the Hogarth Press on Woolf's own writing, providing insight into the effects of hand-printing on Woolf's own use of type and spacing and commenting on Woolf's reaction to the Russian writers championed by the press. No one is better equipped to discuss Woolf and Book Design than Tony Bradshaw, and his essay on the topic provides a practical chronicle of how her early experiences with book-binding folded into the Hogarth Press's later interest in innovative cover designs. Aside from a slight digression on Locke's method for keeping a commonplace book, Merry Pawlowski's piece on scrapbooking is exclusively devoted to her area of expertise: the notebooks Woolf kept for *Three Guineas*. Her account of the organizational strategies by which Woolf arranged the pictures in the notebooks is a handy digest of previous work that identifies many of the main themes of Woolf's treatise. Another comprehensive treatment of a topic by the most qualified expert is Patrick Collier's synopsis of Woolf's complicated relation to journalism. Reviewing Woolf's balancing act between preserving the uniqueness of her own vision and appealing to as wide an audience as possible, Collier shows how Woolf adapted to Victorian attitudes towards journalism as a "cultural narrative of literary decline" by publishing in relatively prestigious journals with fairly large circulations. Pamela Caughie's compendium of criticism on broadcasting in Woolf also takes up the issue of Woolf's coming to terms with the emergence of mass culture created by new technologies. Her particularly thorough review of the critical background on this topic (especially work done on *Between the Acts*) extends beyond traditional studies of the representation of sound technology in Woolf's work to ask some provocative questions about how we can learn to listen to Woolf's works as aural entities, challenging scholars to develop a new vocabulary for describing the use of sound and silence in her work.

Opening Part V, on Visual Media, Leslie Hankins's article on Woolf and cinema is an exemplar of the most outstanding qualities of this collection. Witty, deft, and systematic, the essay provides a comprehensive guide to previous scholarship, a number of intriguing readings of particular texts, and a constant fountain of suggested topics for further research. A summary of her own research on the pre-texts of Woolf's "The Cinema" is followed by a chronological survey of the friends, publications, and viewing experiences that shaped and changed Woolf's ideas about the new art form, and the whole is capped by five pages of Works Cited and Suggestions for Further Reading that provide a generous and definitive guide to scholarship. Colin Dickey's essay on photography in Woolf is a workmanlike effort that takes up some of the same issues about mass culture voiced by Collins and Caughie and weaves them into the thread tracing Woolf's relationship to the Victorians. Distinguishing between the unified portrait and the fragmented snapshot, he counters the idea that Woolf saw photography only as an index of superficial realism and charts her developing use of photographic terminology to describe new ways of seeing the invisible. A significant updating of her definitive work on Woolf as a visual and conceptual icon, Brenda Silver's piece reviews the highlights of her previous explications of the fear and anxiety often associated with Woolf's image (linked to her madness and suicide and/ or to her representative status as a female intellectual and activist) in popular culture artifacts of the 1960's-80's such as Albee's play *Who's Afraid of Virginia Woolf* and the 1987 British film *Sammy and Rosie Get Laid.* Silver is able to end, however, with some more current and marginally more positive appearances of Woolf in representations of *The Waves*, and especially in Patti Smith's evocation of her as a warrior using her words to fight against death.

Similar to previous treatments of broadcasting, photography, and film, the essays in Part VI about Woolf and the Performing Arts go beyond recording Woolf's presentation of music, theater, and dance in her works to explore how she embodies them in her writing strategies. Joyce Kelley does a thoroughly competent job of outlining the evolution of Woolf's taste and understanding of music's ability to represent subjectivity from early works such as *The Voyage Out* and "A String Quartet" to her use of music as a structural model for narrative in *The Waves* and *Between the Acts.* Steven Putzel's comprehensive digest of Woolf's experiences as both a spectator and a participant in drama not only traces the increasingly performative aspects of her later novels but also offers a summary of adaptations of Woolf's works and life on stage (including a helpful table). The last article in the collection, Evelyn Haller's reverie on dance, presents a fascinating series of disassociated tidbits which never quite coalesce. The connections she makes, while wonderfully suggestive, can seldom be substantiated; not all feathers evoke the Russian Ballet, and like Elizabeth Steele, who has also written about possible parallels between Woolf's work and Noh drama, she can only offer some provocative coincidences of structure in her analysis of Noh influence on *The Waves.*

Organized with Maggie Humm's usual comprehensive sagacity, meticulous care for detail of fact, and elegance of presentation, this collection of essays clearly sets a new benchmark in interdisciplinary scholarship about Virginia Woolf. The easy commerce between American and British Woolf critics, shown both in the choice of contributors and in their generous citations of previous scholarship, testifies to the increasing de-Balkanization of Woolf Studies. Judiciously illustrated with sixteen well-reproduced color plates and numerous black and white illustrations, the volume's only flaw is its high price. I have summarized its contents in such detail in hopes of making its utility, even necessity, clear to fellow Woolf scholars. One hopes that Edinburgh University Press will bring out a more affordable paperback edition. Until then, urge your library to buy it.

—Elisa Kay Sparks, *Clemson University*

The Nets of Modernism: Henry James, Virginia Woolf, James Joyce, and Sigmund Freud. Maud Ellman (New York: Cambridge UP, 2010) xii + 238 pages.

Maud Ellmann's *The Nets of Modernism* tracks psychoanalytically the proliferation of rat imagery and the development of modern technological networks such as railways, gas lines, telephones and telegraphy as these are represented by Bram Stoker, Henry James, Sigmund Freud, James Joyce, Virginia Woolf, *et al.* Ellmann's linking of Stoker's 1897 *Dracula*, in which the vampire invades Britain in the form of a swarm of rats, to Freud's 1909 "Notes upon a Case of Obsessional Neurosis" (Strachey Vol. X), also known as "Rat Man," yields some clever connections, but overall her free associational readings border on and sometimes cross into the far-fetched or perhaps the too-clever-by-half.

Following the French analysts Gilles Deleuze and Felix Guattari, Ellman calls her reading method "rhizomatic," another name for associational or primary process—human thought freed from the constraints of rationality. Deleuze and Guattari say that rhizomatic thinking, like the associative properties of language *per se*, grows, like weeds or grass, between other things, and has no beginning or end, but provides a milieu from which it spills over. It is labyrinthine.

Ellmann thinks James Joyce's character Stephen Daedalus has a rhizomatic vision of matrilineal nets of navel cords—nationality, language, religion—that oppose the arboreal structure of the family tree, governed by the name of the father. These Joycean navel nets, writes Ellmann (following V. Mahaffey's 1998 *States of Desire*), correspond to Freud's idea of the navel of the unknown at the center of every dream as a "mycelium" or creeping fungus (Ellmann 10).

In Freud's conception, the navel of a dream, writes Ellmann, "marks the point at which the nets of meaning dissolve of their own density, leaving a black hole in the center of the dreamwork," so "the Freudian dream-navel encompasses the contradictory ideas of not and net, absence and entanglement, embodied in the hollow netted omphalos-stone at Delphi" (9). This Delphic claim puts Ellmann's book into the domain explored by Elisabeth Bronfen's 1998 *The Knotted Subject,* which, with learned and imaginative analogies that offer a model for Ellmann's style of reading, traces human subjectivities as particular knots subtended by a fundamental, central absence or nothingness marked on the body at birth by the cut umbilical cord. Our knots of subjectivity are illusory and multifarious, threaded with our genetic codes, histories of our nations, cultures, languages, and the people around us. Ellmann's knot of subjectivity is Lacanian.

An inspiration for Ellmann's interpretation of Virginia Woolf is found in Nicholas Abraham and Maria Torok's 1978 *The Shell and the Kernel*, in particular in their analysis of the cryptonomy of Serge Pankejeff's magical words, a rereading of Freud's [1914] 1918 case "The History of an Infantile Neurosis" (Strachey Vol. XVII), also known as "Wolf Man," whose symptoms, Freud discerned, derived from a repressed memory of having observed his parents in sexual intercourse. This primal scene received disguised expression in Pankejeff's dream of seven wolves staring at him from outside a window, hence the appellation "Wolf Man." This name catalyzes Ellmann's connection of Pankejeff's primal scene to the primal scene of the Ramsays in intercourse that informs James's resentment of his father and Lily Briscoe's final painting in *To the Lighthouse*. In order to build up to her investigation of convergences between Woolf's novel and the Wolf Man case history, Ellmann presents fanciful accounts of Woolf's wish to be a dog and her fear of being an animal. Ellmann quotes Quentin Bell to the effect that Woolf wrote *Flush*, her joke biography of Elizabeth Barrett Browning's spaniel, "'not so much as a book by a dog lover as a book by someone who would love to be a dog'" (Ellmann 68). Ellmann goes on to link this to the famous passage in Woolf's "A Sketch of the Past" where Woolf describes her "looking-glass shame" and its connection with her dreadful experience of Gerald Duckworth's molestations of her when she was very small. Woolf says, "I dreamt that I was looking in a glass when a horrible face—the face of an animal—suddenly showed over my shoulder" (*MOB* 69). To Ellmann, this animal face suggests Lycanthropia, for to Ellmann, the "animal" must be a wolf, to chime with Virginia's married name, a fanciful reading to go with the idea of Woolf as a dog.

Woolf specifies in "A Sketch of the Past" that "the shock-receiving capacity is what makes [her] a writer" (72), suggesting that putting the severed parts together, making a scene come right, and a character come together can resolve into art what has been traumatic. Serge Pankejeff's trauma was the raunchy scenario of parental intercourse from behind, combined with the loss of an artistically superior sister who committed suicide. Deploying Freud's 1917 essay "Mourning and Melancholia," which explains that a bereaved subject "incorporates" the lost loved one, Abraham and Torok argue that the melancholic survivor hollows out a crypt within the psyche where the lost loved one is preserved as if alive. "In the case of the Wolf Man, this incorporated object consists of the incestuous dyad of his father and sister" (Ellmann 78). In Virginia Woolf's case, it is Julia Stephen who is encrypted, for the writer was haunted by her mother, who died when Virginia was thirteen years old. Woolf recalls in her diary how writing *To the Lighthouse* laid her parents to rest; but despite this exorcism, "Woolf's mental illness, whose onset coincided with her mother's death in 1895, persisted throughout her life, the worst attacks triggered by the completion of her novels." These recurrences, says Ellmann, "indicate that writing, despite its power to exorcise the dead, also creates a further object to be mourned—the book itself" as it becomes accessible to critics (63). None of these observations about Woolf are new.

Ellmann concludes her discourse on *To the Lighthouse* by pointing out that the "to" in the title hints that the novel is a gift, "dedicated 'to' its central image," which Ellmann, following Woolf, says means "nothing." This promising observation about the novel being dedicated to nothingness as a loved one or a muse devolves into a discussion of Pankejeff's gambling habits and about how patients in psychoanalysis submit themselves to "'penetrating interpretations coming from behind,'" as Patrick Mahony has observed. This anal analysis recalls the Rat Man fantasy of being tortured by being seated shackled to an open bottom chair above a heated pot of live rats who bore into the victim. Having drawn on psychoanalytic tools throughout her interpretation of Woolf, Ellmann then remarks that psychoanalytic "patients squander money, words, and time, to be rewarded with the gift of silence—which is the only gift one can be certain to receive from God" (90).

It is difficult to say whether Maud Ellmann's rhizomic burrowings are boring or just off the wall. To quote T. S. Eliot's 1922 *Waste Land*, "I think we are in rats' alley."

—Dianne M. Hunter, *Trinity College, Hartford, Connecticut*

Works Cited

Eliot, T. S. *The Complete Poems and Plays, 1909-1950*. New York: Harcourt, Brace & World, Inc., 1952. Print.

Strachey, James. Ed. and Trans. *The Complete Psychological Works of Sigmund Freud.* London: Hogarth Press, 1955. Print.

Woolf, Virginia. *Moments of Being: Unpublished Autobiographical Writings*. Ed. Jeanne Schulkind. New York: Harcourt Brace Jovanovich, 1976. Print.

A Specially Tender Piece of Eternity: Virginia Woolf and the Experience of Time
Teresa Prudente. (Lanham: Lexington Books, 2009) xiv + 193 pp.

Those of us who work on and teach Woolf often find ourselves making statements to the effect that Woolf's work is characterized by a productive tension or internal contradiction between active and passive, internal and external, mystical and political, cyclical and linear, and so on. Of particular relevance here, we will often say that innovations in the representation of temporality are among her texts' most significant qualities, asserting that, in various different ways, her work challenges the notion of linear, chronological time as the guiding temporality of narrative fiction. But precisely because we often say these things, they sometimes risk taking on the status of truisms; we may lose a sense of the specific features of the narratives on which such assertions are based. One of the significant qualities of Teresa Prudente's book is its careful and sustained grounding in Woolf's statements about time and fiction in her essays, and, more significantly, in close attention to the content, style and structure of her novels. Particularly when the discussion becomes—as perhaps is inevitable when the topic is so slippery and complex as time itself—fairly dense, it is reassuring to the reader that the analysis frequently returns to and locates itself in specific and close textual readings.

This admirably nuanced and well-structured monograph "aims at shedding light on the stratified temporality characterising Woolf's novels" (ix): the a-linear temporalities of Woolf's texts (following Ricoeur), and in particular temporalities of eternity and the ecstatic. But in doing so it necessarily touches on many of the internal contradictions which make Woolf's work so enduringly intriguing —indeed, in many ways the coexistence of apparently mutually exclusive, or at the very least contrasting, facets within Woolf's narratives is Prudente's central critical concern. The first part of the book reads *To the Lighthouse* and *Orlando* with special reference to "moments of being," in which, Prudente argues, "the coexistence and interdependence of the two feelings of ecstasy and emptiness ... appear as the climax of Woolf's insistence on the modern subject's divided perception" (63). Moments of being are in fact offered throughout the book as exemplary, particularly condensed instances of the kind of temporality Prudente is exploring; the temporality of the "moment of being" resonates throughout Woolf's oeuvre.

Some signal examples of Prudente's highly productive close readings can be found where, for example, Prudente attends to two of Mrs. Ramsay's "moment[s] of ecstasy" (16). One, comprising all of section XI of the first part of *To the Lighthouse*, demonstrates Mrs. Ramsay's need for solitude, freed from the demands of communication and the gaze of others, and enables her to reach a "vision of eternity." In the other, during the famous "boeuf en daube" scene, Mrs. Ramsay "seems to have reached a balanced co-existence between external and internal reality … the external movements of the character, her gestures and thoughts, are harmonically in accord with her thoughts and sensations" (17). This is "underlined," Prudente suggests, "by the use of a parenthetic sentence: 'It partook, she felt, carefully helping Mr. Bankes to a specially tender piece, of eternity'" (17). Thus not only is the source of Prudente's evocative title revealed, but we also discover that it has been chosen not just for its poetic qualities. While the title might seem to imply a reading of Woolfian temporality as ultimately transcendent, its relocation in its original context demonstrates that, in fact, it aims to embody the flowing together of dualities—of internal and external perception, of mystical and material—which Prudente argues is crucial to Woolf's attempts to capture the full and complex temporality of the modern subject.

A similar instance of the novel's grounding in the details of everyday reality comes where, later in this first section, Prudente turns back to section XVII to observe Mrs. Ramsay experiencing "a moment of revelation in communion with the other characters," which consists in "the sense of opposition between ephemeral and eternal, and the subject's attempt to crystallize an instant in the flowing of time" (62). Here the word "opposition" perhaps overstates the contrast between "moments" and "what endures" in the passage cited; Mrs. Ramsay states, rather, that the latter is made out of the former. Indeed, just earlier, Prudente has argued, in a clear and elegant articulation of a central point, that "the coexistence of two simultaneous and opposite temporal perceptions is undeniably one of the essential features in Woolf's portrayal of the subject's experience of time" (59)—it is this coexistence to which Prudente's analysis returns again and again, each time with increased conviction and complexity. But, again, the material is the context for these excursions deep into internal temporality: "'Here she felt, *putting the spoon down*, was the still space that lies about the heart of things'" (quoted in Prudente 62, my emphasis).

The second part of the book moves to "a specific inquiry into the relationship between ecstasy and writing" (xi) focusing on the ineffability of the ecstatic moment. Prudente carefully expresses how the ineffable engages a foundational problematic of artistic representation: "The un-representability of ecstasy thus seems to function also as an allegory which suggests the less specific discrepancy between experience and expression" (71). That the reconstruction and artistic representation of the moment of being, in Prudente's analysis, can never hope to achieve more than "temporary coherence and significance," itself prompts what is, after all, the only possible aim of the artist; namely in Prudente's attractively Beckettian phrase, "achieving a less and less imprecise act of re-creation" (86).

Here as elsewhere Prudente carefully couches her arguments so that they fall just short of the claim that Woolf's work can actually overcome "the limits of ordinary communication" (87) or express "what can not be entirely grasped by language" (130).

Of particular interest is Prudente's attention to metaphor. Drawing on Ricoeur's analysis of metaphor as "a powerful expressive instrument which releases the potentialities of language" (81), she explains that "metaphor succeeds in incorporating the simultaneity of different and contrasting elements in one single expression"—a capacity clearly significant to her argument here—and in particular that it "allows the subject to embrace in one single enunciation two different and temporally distinct points of view and in this sense the dualism inherent in experience, different from what happens in ordinary language, is preserved and expressed" (82).

The third part of the book, in many ways the most effective, looks at Woolf's novels in relation to Gide's *Les Faux-Monnayeurs*, moving toward a discussion of the novel genre's capacity to handle time. (It is worth noting that quotations from Gide are given in the original French, with no translations; while in most cases Prudente's subsequent analyses make the main thrust of their significance clear, it obviously means that readers who do not have French might miss some of their nuances.) Here the comparison between the two novelists brings into sharp focus their particular characteristics, facilitated by Prudente's exquisitely systematic approach. Noting, for example, their comparable admiration for the narrative innovations of Dostoevsky, in particular his "de-construction of the monologic form of the novel in favour of polyphonic narration" (146), Prudente shows how this manifests itself in very different ways in these two writers: while in Woolf ("starting from *Mrs. Dalloway*," says Prudente) the narrator's voice dematerializes, in Gide the narrator becomes more and more "human" (148); while Woolf's interest is in "pre-linguistic states of consciousness," Gide focuses on "the attempt to convey the subject as a *speaking* consciousness" (151). In her final chapter, Prudente brings these discussions back round to focus on temporality, noting that in both novelists "the experience of an exit from linear time and the crystallisation of time in an a-temporal dimension … are to be understood not as opposite to the notion of time, but rather as complementary and interacting with it" and, returning to her key concept, that "*moments of being* are inscribed within a temporal frame in which the *passage of time* proves fundamental" (171). This insistence on the location in, and interaction with, linear time, of the ecstatic temporalities revealed in the moment of being, are crucial to understanding the dialectical nature of Prudente's analysis.

While the book is clearly grounded in relevant scholarship (in particular Ricoeur and Banfield) Prudente's book eschews the opening familiar in many scholarly monographs, namely a version of the literature review situating the book in relation to recent work in Woolf studies. Whether this absence of what might be seen by some as automatic name-checking, by others as necessary acknowledgement of the current field, is welcome, will depend on the individual reader's point of view—I simply note it here. A more substantive point to which objections might be raised is the use of the male third person pronoun in discussions of "the subject." On the one hand, one might instruct oneself to read this as neutral (in the absence of a manageable neutral alternative), understanding that in these cases Prudente is making a point applicable beyond the specific character recently discussed. On the other hand, where analyses of, for example, the experiences or interiority of Mrs. Ramsay or Lily, are immediately followed by a somewhat jarring discussion of their implications using "he/his," the question of the significance of gender appears unavoidable. Prudente does notice differences of gender—for example in her discussions of Septimus in chapter 6—but she does little more than this; there is no significant discussion of the relationship between the states of temporal experience she describes and the gender of the characters describing them (Septimus's difference from the "female characters" is associated primarily with his state of mental health, 118-19). And yet no monograph—not even one as capacious and resonant as this—can cover all theoretical approaches. It is perhaps indicative of the potential of this work that it prompts the reader to explore its assertions in those of Woolf's texts it does not discuss, and to take them down those critical avenues it does not pursue.

—Bryony Randall, *University of Glasgow*

True Confessions: Feminist Professors Tell Stories Out of School.
Ed. Susan Gubar (New York: Norton, 2011) xviii + 327

As graduate students in the early 1990s, we participated in "mock interviews" in preparation for going on the job market. After my interview, during which I felt a little glamorous, sitting at a monumental table in an Ivy League seminar room like a potential colleague, I was given feedback so that I could proceed more confidently into the real interviews. The first professor offered his critique. "You weren't bubbly enough." I have a vague recollection that someone else caught a glimpse of my utter mortification at this remark, and muttered something about "being yourself." Practically hallucinatory in my shock, I exited the room into the dazzling Connecticut autumn, wandered along the border between Ivy League fortress and retail strip on Chapel Street, ran into a fellow female graduate student, and delivered a long, livid rant on a street corner to her, vastly relieved to have encountered a sympathetic, outraged female ear.

Hearing from a senior male professor of the humanities that I needed to be "bubbly" in a job interview was like being slapped in the face and told by a modeling agency that I was fat. Here was my great epiphany: once at the job interview, I would be perceived as a woman, and expected to act like an unthreatening one: i.e. I would be expected to act like a girl. And I would complain about it to commiserating female friends standing on street corners, feeling outside an institution whose walls loomed large, forbidding, and exclusive: I would be livid. *Plus ça change, plus c'est la même chose.*

Woolfians who read *True Confessions: Feminist Professors Tell Stories Out of School* may be struck by the endurance of women feeling that they are outsiders to a rarefied, exclusive male educational establishment, and the persistence of the spatial metaphor that governs Woolf's *A Room of One's Own.* This collection of essays by prominent female academics who represent the "first generation" of women breaking into post-WWII American higher education resonates with many of Woolf's texts. Being told to keep off the turf at Oxbridge, being told that women aren't allowed in the library: these foundational moments are echoed by Ann Douglas, who, as a professor at Princeton, "was kept constantly aware of my status as an interloper" (175). Douglas recounts her experience as an undergraduate at Harvard in the 1960s, when "Radcliffe students...were prohibited from entering Lamont, one of Harvard's two main libraries" and were excluded from Harvard's "prestigious honor societies, traveling fellowships, or, presumably, most of its professorships" (173). The theme of spatial exclusion persists in Martha Nussbaum's indignation as a graduate student, also at Harvard, "learning that women could eat lunch at the Harvard Faculty Club only if they used the side dining room" (160). The sense of marginalization by an all-male establishment even appears in an older woman's experience of a new generation of scholars, when Jill Dolan, a professor at Princeton, participates in a queer studies conference and feels that feminism and lesbianism are "effectively eras[ed]... from the stage" by an all-male plenary panel (315). Dolan's history is "swept back into the dustbin," and the cycle begins anew: women keep fighting to get (back) onto the stage.

When women are told to keep off the grass or out of the library, and they are given second-class citizen status at meals, the foes are most often men. *AROO*'s Nick Greene has his twentieth-century counterpart in the womanizing classicist who teaches at both Harvard and Cambridge, as passionately described by Nussbaum, who delivers a rousing list of "Men's ways of being infantile" (161). Nussbaum also recounts the story of a female academic committing suicide, but one is not to assume her progenitor is Shakespeare's sister; the guilty party and oppressor, in that episode, is actually the stringent, rule-bound Society of Women in Philosophy (159). Although there may be other female foes in *True Confessions*, such as the vicious female colleagues in Annette Kolodny's contribution, many readers may find the dominant enemy to remain the patriarch. The collection opens with several particularly grueling reminiscences by daughters of emotionally abusive fathers who wield cruel power over their children. Woolfians will be cast into reflections on key moments in *To the Lighthouse*. Rage is a powerful creative catalyst, and while Woolf wrote in *AROO* of its power to distort, she also used it to articulate an inspiringly defiant stance: "I refuse to allow you, Beadle though you are, to turn me off the grass. Lock up your libraries if you like; but there is no gate, no lock, no bolt that you can set upon the freedom of my mind" (75-6). Similarly, Ann Douglas: "For me, it's worth fighting. I still believe with all my heart in what my great Harvard teacher Perry Miller called 'the life of the mind,' the gold-rush kingdom of first strikes and second chances. Its sole prerequisite is freedom, its only law, democracy" (180). It is not the case, of course, that men are always the enemy. To find favor with a male mentor, as Douglas does, is not unheard of in *True Confessions*; Nussbaum mentions an avuncular scholar offering her sage advice at Cambridge; Sandra Gilbert pays tribute to all the men in her life who have fed and nurtured her; Linda Nochlin's grandfather steers her to reading the great Russian novelists. Still, the prevailing tone of *True Confessions* is frustration and rage, often at male-dominated institutions, often at the multiple burdens of being marginalized, misunderstood, or silenced on account of not only gender, but race, sexuality, or class.

Generally absent from *True Confessions*—and their absence may also give Woolfians food for thought—are sustained, repeated descriptions of a female academic's adoration for another woman who can play the role of mentor, tormentor, or muse. Where are the images of Lily Briscoes worshipping at the feet of goddesses like Mrs. Ramsay? We do find some examples of older women inspiring younger ones: Rosemary Radford Reuther, for example, writes in appreciation of her intellectual, polylingual, and spiritually formidable great-aunt (267). Lillian Faderman cites nearly the same female tradition of great writers that Woolf does in *AROO*, adding Emily Dickinson, Willa Cather, and Woolf herself (183). But the point is generally to underscore the absence of women, whether mentors or tormentors, in the male-dominated bastions whose doors these women are knocking down. Thus, *True Confessions* stands in stark contrast, in this and other ways, to another recent work of female academic confessional writing, Terry Castle's *The Professor* (2010). The eponymous essay of that volume ends by describing a monstrous Australian female crocodile whose terrifying jaws could easily devour her quavering admirers with a single chomp. The crocodile is a stand-in for the female professor who drove Castle to the brink of suicide with her seductiveness and endless appetite for emotional control. Castle *twice* writes the story of one woman infatuated with another: in "The Professor," the female graduate student adoring the female professor, and in "Desperately Seeking Susan," the female academic adoring the iconic female intellectual (Sontag). Perhaps the professor in the first instance is an allegory for the Profession, in which case we are left with an image of academia as a monstrous female crocodile who will eat you alive. In the second case, we are left with a rumination on the greatness of a "troubled and brilliant American" without whom it is impossible to imagine the "history of modern feminism…as it evolved in the United States in the 1970s," for, according to Castle, Sontag occupied for modern feminism "the absolutely central, catalytic role" (103-4). Sontag is absent from the pages of *True Confessions*, but the spirit of adulation may be discerned in Nochlin's excursions to New York's art museums. Whether of Sontag or Kandinsky, the point of these adorations is that they are arguably outside the academy: like Woolf herself.

After reading *True Confessions*, one may find oneself re-reading *Three Guineas*' fundamental inquiry into "how we can enter the professions and yet remain civilized human beings" (75) having been taught, as outsiders, by such teachers as "poverty, chastity, derision, and freedom from unreal loyalties" (78). Has the word "feminist" lost its meaning because "the right to earn a living has been won," as *TG* declares (101)? In her contribution, Douglas asks us to think about those who are outside, now: the "multiplication of ill-paid and often benefits-free part-time" academic employees (176). The word "feminist" has currency.

—Rishona Zimring, *Lewis & Clark College*

Works Cited

Castle, Terry. *The Professor*. New York: HarperCollins, 2010. Print.

Woolf, Virginia. *A Room of One's Own*. New York: Harcourt, 1981. Print.

——. *Three Guineas*. New York: Harcourt, 1966. Print.

Intermodernism: Literary Culture in Mid-Twentieth-Century Britain. Ed. Kristin Bluemel (Edinburgh: Edinburgh UP, 2011) viii + 254 pp.

This ambitious volume counters recent critical attempts to broaden the chronology and the objects of modernist studies, as Kristin Bluemel moves modernism back toward the chronological and canonical boundaries of previous critical decades and advances intermodernism to claim the vacated ground. Two major recent movements in modernist studies are important for Bluemel as she situates *Intermodernism* within the larger critical field. The first is the growing body of criticism examining "late modernism"—exemplified by scholars like Tyrus Miller, Jed Esty, and Marina MacKay—which has traced the persistence of modernist style into the midcentury (3-5). While Bluemel is sympathetic to this project, since her intermodernism is a largely midcentury phenomenon, she argues that late modernist scholarship is too intertwined with the second recent critical movement against which she writes, the New Modernist Studies, whose "apparent colonisation of virtually all areas of study of twentieth-century literary cultural activity" (2) means that modernism as a critical term has become so overextended that it has lost some of its explanatory value (3). Bluemel proposes that the concept of intermodernism better describes the "diverse literary forms" and "more populist genres" particularly evident in the midcentury (4).

Beyond serving as a practical term to communicate the many points of liminality (stylistic, chronological, geographic) that are potentially obscured by an overextended modernism, "intermodernism," Bluemel emphasizes, "is an ideology" (5). That ideological component is evident in the "three defining features" that Bluemel attributes to intermodernism: "cultural features (intermodernists typically represent working-class and working middle-class cultures); political features (intermodernists are politically radical, 'radically eccentric'); and literary features (intermodernists are committed to non-canonical, even 'middlebrow' or 'mass' genres)" (1). Intermodernism is a period and a style, but it is also "a *social formation*" and "an expression of *shared values*" (5).

Part of this focus on community entails an effort to define a body of intermodern authors, as the extensive appendix cataloguing both well-known and little-known intermodern authors reveals. Yet this volume is every bit as much about defining a community of intermodern *critics*, for intermodernism is a "postmodern invention," a "retroactive, after the fact intervention." Accordingly, "Twenty-first century scholars of intermodernism are the 'real' intermodernists" (6), and to establish this community, Bluemel emphasizes the common purpose shared by the contributors (1-2) and closes her introduction with a call for other scholars to join in this critical effort (14).

The essays are organized into four thematic subsections—“work, community, war and documents”—identified as central to intermodern texts (2). Some seem to fit the assigned theme only loosely, and many address multiple themes, but that looseness of classification may be intentional, for Bluemel asserts that the thematic groupings are merely precursory to the “more subtle or complex frames of analysis” that will arise when scholars have had time to theorize this new field (2). Because Bluemel herself sees the thematic organization as provisional, I will discuss the essays out of order.

The volume’s emphasis on productive community—whether of intermodern authors or of intermodern critics—informs contributors’ analyses of individual texts, as they frequently identify intermodern writers’ exploration of new ways of forming community in the wake of the perceived modernist focus on individual subjectivity over sociality. Such is the case in Elizabeth Maslen’s analysis of Storm Jameson’s involvement in European politics through her work with “refugee writers” as part of the P.E.N. Club (24). That experience would grant her a concern with “contemporary communities” and an insight into fascism’s dangers, which would in turn inform her formal choices (25). According to Maslen, many of the period’s critics, conditioned by modernist aesthetic autonomy, “could not cope with matter…which privileged community in all its complex intricacy” (25). Lisa Colletta attributes to J. B. Priestley a similarly acute social vision by demonstrating that Priestley’s unconventional travel narratives centered on the opportunity for a “classless democracy” to emerge after the Second World War (98), as opposed to Hollywood culture’s “standardisation of a people without building a real sense of identity or creating a real political agency based on communal experiences and shared values” (103). The notion that intermodern writing had the potential to empower an entire body of citizens carries over into Nick Hubble’s painstaking analysis of poet and critic William Empson’s influence on Charles Madge, founder of Mass Observation, a movement that was at one time going to be called “‘Popular Poetry’” (183) and was intent on “allowing the masses to become writers” (172) and “conscious of their own desires” in the service of pushing for a “liberated heterodox society” (179).

This emphasis on collectivity without uniformity informs Janet Montefiore’s examination of Sylvia Townsend Warner and T. H. White, “eccentric writers whose habitats, political allegiances and sexual preferences differed from the norm” and who are consequently often overlooked in criticism on historical fiction (39). White’s fiction, influenced by psychoanalysis, and Warner’s fiction, influenced by Marxism, “put into question the patriotic fantasy of an ideally unchanging England through their unconventionally fictionalised histories” (39); Montefiore describes White’s work as a “playfully modernist historicism” in the style of T. S. Eliot that might even be viewed as a “proleptic post-modernism” (43). This pairing of an author's rewritten national history with the contributor's retelling of modernist history to highlight intermodernism's deft handling of transition reappears in John Fordham's meditation on how proletarian literature borrowed "the new modernist techniques" (56). For Fordham, Harold Heslop exemplifies the paired historical and aesthetic transition as Heslop's description of mining —a regional enterprise then embroiled in national "industrial struggle" (64)— draws from modernism's "metaphors of distance and separation" (60) while foreshadowing what Fredric Jameson would call postmodernism's "'spatial turn'" (56). Faye Hammill too employs space to think through literary history as she examines Stella Gibbons's use of suburban space to position herself "in a literary no-man's land between urban high modernism and pure pastoral, between the experimental and the realist" (91).

Though Bluemel stresses that intermodernism is more than a period, and "all efforts of periodisation are open to critique for being arbitrary" (5), much of the most complex work in the collection emerges around the question of intermodernism's historical emergence. Such is the case with Phyllis Lassner's essay on detective and spy fiction of the Second World War, where she identifies its intermodernism as a response to "modernism's political risks," most notably the correlation between the mythic method and "fascist aesthetics" (121). Allan Hepburn likewise lays a firm historical foundation, as the new relationships between individuals and communities identified by contributors like Hubble as key to intermodernism gain added force in Hepburn's essay with Elizabeth Bowen's exposure to war trials and the tension they introduced between individual and national culpability (133). Laura Marcus also seeks a political basis to intermodern aesthetics, turning to the documentary film in order to examine the 1930s exchanges "between literature (often allied to inward, subjective forms) and film (conceived in terms of externality)" (195). Documentary's "intertwining of a modernist aesthetic and a realist imperative, a poetics and a politics," she argues, elucidates intermodernism's political and aesthetic shifts (205). That recognition of intermodernism's politicization of form also enters Debra Rae Cohen's discussion of Rebecca West's "distinctive multigeneric or intergeneric voice" (151). Cohen argues that West, through combining genres and breaking their rules, challenges the political and social content traditionally associated with those genres.

Together these accounts present an invitingly flexible picture of intermodernism, even if the very broadness of intermodernism's definition— seen, for instance, in the varying attitudes toward realism contributors attribute to intermodernism—means that the term at times risks the same looseness as Bluemel finds in "modernism." Bluemel emphasizes intermodernism's independence from modernist studies by stating that "*Intermodernism*...is not especially concerned with the critical vocabulary of high modernism or with tracing the relations between intermodern and modernist texts" (5). Without drawing from this vocabulary, however, modernism can sometimes serve too rigidly as intermodernism's elitist and subjectivist other. What, for example, are we to do with the high modernist Woolf's *Jacob's Room*, with its depiction of female community formed in the liminal space of the moors? And how does intermodernism relate to the decisive turn towards collectivity that Esty has influentially identified in the later work of modernists like Woolf and Eliot? Evidence from within these essays indicates that intermodernist criticism *can* present a rounded picture of modernism while maintaining its own distinctiveness. Prominent instances include Lassner's account of intermodernists' reaction against modernist myth and fragmentation, newly treacherous in light of midcentury European political developments (121), and Marcus's examination of Hugh MacDiarmid, "whose 'experimental' poetics were inseparable from his far-left politics" (196-97) such that, for MacDiarmid, "the 'difficulty' of modernist writing...should not be seen as exclusionary or elitist" and the sound qualities of modernist writing could potentially contribute to the seemingly more populist form of cinema (196), a crossing of aims that for Marcus characterizes intermodernism. Bluemel attributes to intermodernism the capacity to transgress boundaries, and the greatest critical promise may in fact lie where modernism and intermodernism meet.

—Ashley Maher, *Washington University in St. Louis*

Glamour in Six Dimensions: Modernism and the Radiance of Form.
Judith Brown (Ithaca: Cornell UP, 2009) xiv + 199pp.

Glamour may not be a quality readers associate with Virginia Woolf specifically or modernism generally. Some writers, like F. Scott Fitzgerald, are imbued with glamour by our cultural memory, but scholars tend to value Woolf, in contrast, for her luminous prose, intellectual ferocity, and moving plots and characters. Judith Brown's study, which defines glamour as a form as well as a quality, as "a formal category and an experimental site of consumer desire, fantasy, sexuality, class, and racial identity" (1), uncovers previously unanticipated locales for modernist glamour and links together writers and figures one would not otherwise think to compare. Its creativity, persuasive local readings of material objects and modernist texts, and well-crafted prose make *Glamour in Six*

Dimensions a valuable example of the new modernist studies. Although Brown's comparisons occasionally overreach, this is a book that Woolf scholars will want to add to their shelves.

Brown's study first addresses the problem of how to define glamour, which might be read as an emotional affect, a specific quality, or (less flatteringly) marketing technique. Her study variously positions glamour as: an abstraction (5); a "negative aesthetic" that is "cold, indifferent, and deathly" (5); and as resisting the subject (7). As the argument develops, Brown also argues that glamour inheres in the past (89) and in absence (117), rendering glamour a temporal quality in that it is most readily perceived in an individual's history (such as in a photograph) or collective "fantasy of what is irrevocably past" (141). In its footing in such times and qualities, glamour almost becomes an aesthetic without or apart from the human. While Brown acknowledges commodity culture arguments in which glamour would only serve as a mystification (11), she persuasively argues that we need to consider glamour "beyond good and evil" in order to fully understand an aesthetic that "is not entirely subsumed by any political or moral ideology" (13).

The chapters in *Glamour in Six Dimensions* are generally organized around a glamorous quality that comes into view through reading a product or object alongside a modernist writer. Chapter 1, on "Perception" reads Chanel #5 and the poetry of Wallace Stevens; Chapter 2, on "Violence," examines *The Great Gatsby* and Katherine Mansfield's "Je ne parle pas français" in light of the pervasive violence of the 1920s. Subsequent chapters take on "Photography" (snapshots and *Mrs. Dalloway*), "Celebrity" (Greta Garbo, Woolf's "Mr. Bennett and Mrs. Brown," and T. S. Eliot's "Tradition and the Individual Talent"), "Primitivism" (Josephine Baker, Wallace Thurman's *Infants of the Spring*, and Nella Larsen's *Quicksand*) and "Cellophane" (plastics and Gertrude Stein's *Four Saints in Three Acts*). As this list indicates, Brown's project is transatlantic and bridges cultural and literary studies to tease out glamour's power, pleasure and dangers.

Brown's most striking and persuasive chapters begin with a specific object and demonstrate how its glamorous operation parallels modernist texts and form. Her first chapter, for example, starts with a brief history of Chanel #5, a scent that did not aim to mimic a single, natural note (21) and the first perfume "to rely on a mixture of synthetic and organic scents" (20). Wallace Stevens seems to have little in common with this glamorous fragrance, and yet Brown pairs the two in an exploration of the "transformation from mere object . . . to aesthetic effect" (23). She argues that this transformation is precisely where glamour emerges, and what she calls "the aldehydic effects of Stevens's poetry" surface as he "pursues the shift from mere sensory object to magical emanation through the force of the invisible, ordering structure" (23). As she advances readings of many of Stevens's most canonical poems, Brown demonstrates that Chanel's perfume offers both a metaphor for "the cool synthetic effect of Stevens's poetry, and points to a particular historic moment" the product shared with *Harmonium*, "thus situating their shared aesthetic within a specific cultural, and modernist, context" (41). This chapter and "Cellophane," which offers equally creative and generative comparisons, are the stars of Brown's study in that she turns what might have been gimmicky comparisons in the hands of a less talented critic into searching analyses that will satisfy even the most dubious of readers.

WSA readers will, however, be most interested in chapters 3 and 4, where Woolf's fiction and essays receive sustained attention. Given the extensive work Maggie Humm, Diane Gillespie, Emily Dalgarno, and others have published on Woolf and photography, this chapter's approach may initially seem less inspired than those that precede it. Brown carves out a unique niche, however, in arguing that *Mrs. Dalloway* employs a "grammar shared with photography." This grammar includes "the effects of stasis, the excision of time, and the role of fantasy in photography" (71), and Brown argues that *Mrs. Dalloway*, like photographs, attempts to capture moments of memory and desire (72). Reading the Woolfian "moment" alongside still photographs and the lyric (and in contrast to ordinary time, film, and narrative), Brown positions the glamour in and of Woolf's work as a "reformulated sublime": the terror and ecstasy of arrested time (73). Despite the power of such moments, in Woolf's novel the sublime is also belated, an effect of regarding the past, like an image, from the present (89). This approach enriches an understanding of the novel and particularly illuminates Peter's final thoughts, which close the book: "It is Clarissa, he said. For there she was" (*MD* 194). Brown calls this passage a "photographic gesture" (96), and while her framework works somewhat less well as an approach to Septimus Warren Smith, the grammar of photography helps to unpack some of Clarissa's most significant actions and thoughts.

While Chapter 4 focuses most of its attention on the glamorous Greta Garbo, Brown forges parallels between the aesthetic ideals of the film star and those of "Mr. Bennett and Mrs. Brown" and Eliot's "Tradition and the Individual Talent." These seemingly disparate personalities and texts are brought together around a date (as Brown notes, 1910 was not only the date "human character changed" but also the first year an actress emerged as a celebrity) and, more importantly, by a formal sense: "Woolf's view of character, Eliot's call for impersonality, and the birth of the media-age personality share some fundamental features, including the evacuation of detail in order to convey luminous (or radiant) form" (100). Brown's examination of parallels between her main texts is suggestive, and she is also attentive to differences among the three. For example, she notes that in Garbo's case, "The celebrity did not offer life, in the sense of Woolf's Mrs. Brown; rather her superhuman image conveyed something more closely associated with static perfection and therefore death. Yet the power of her image, like that of Woolf's ideal character, lifted her away from the dulling aspects of everyday life and produced an intoxicating image that would enthrall those who encountered it" (102). Such comparisons suggest that our understanding of Woolf might be enriched by comparing her to popular phenomena with which she has no literal connection. At the same time, this kind of passage can revive a reader's suspicion of "bad glamour" and generate niggling questions: is not this "thrall" of different kinds? If the intoxication of Mrs. Brown inspires the writer to creative heights, makes her "begin almost automatically to write a novel" (*CE*1 324), what does Garbo's thrall produce? As Judith Brown notes, her celebrity "may be understood as a negative space, a space that absorbs but does not produce meaning" (103), which is precisely the opposite impact of Mrs. Brown's fascination. Similarly, Garbo's glamour was based not in emoting but in indifference (116), a distancing strategy foreign to Woolf's Mrs. Brown (albeit similar to the power that glamorizes Jacob Flanders). At such times, the labor of getting beyond the great divide—of thinking of high modernism with and through popular culture, which Brown elsewhere accomplishes—seems still unfinished.

In the final chapter of *Glamour in Six Dimensions*, as Brown dazzlingly reconstructs the history of cellophane, and plastics more generally, she prompts readers to recognize how alien we are from the modernist cultural moment. As her reading of Stein's play and the Fred Astaire-Eleanor Powell musical *Broadway Melody of 1940* demonstrates, we need to reacquaint ourselves with what now seem to be the most abject of materials in order to understand the aesthetic form of period fiction, poetry, drama and film. In her concluding summary, Brown reminds readers of glamour's power and the scope of its radiance. While the modernist aesthetic is no longer our own—even the most committed scholar would be hard pressed to feign an enthusiasm for the plastics, violence, and primitivism that fascinated Woolf's contemporaries—Brown's study helps us rediscover the period's intangible, deathly, and always retrospective-looking glamour.

—Celia Marshik, *SUNY Stony Brook*

"I'd Make It Penal": The Rural Preservation Movement in Virginia Woolf's Between the Acts. Mark Hussey. Bloomsbury Heirtage Series 62 (London: Cecil Woolf, 2011) 15pp.

Reading the Skies in Virginia Woolf: Woolf on Weather in Her Essays, Diaries, and Three of Her Novels. Paula Maggio. Bloomsbury Heritage Series 54 (London: Cecil Woolf, 2009) 48pp.

Virginia Woolf and "Dress Mania": "the eternal and insoluble question of clothes." Catherine Gregg. Bloomsbury Heritage Series 57 (London: Cecil Woolf, 2010) 52pp.

Leslie Stephen as Mountaineer: "Where does Mont Blanc end, and where do I begin?"Catherine W. Hollis. Bloomsbury Heritage Series 56 (London: Cecil Woolf, 2010) 60pp.

Bloomsbury Heritage, a series of monograph pamphlets published by Cecil Woolf, nephew of Leonard and Virginia, offers a wide range of brief studies of the Bloomsbury group. While general readers interested in Bloomsbury are likely to find the essays approachable, they are written by scholars attuned to the background of other Bloomsbury scholars. The real virtue of the monographs is in the brief format, which gives the reader a quick introduction to a topic with which he or she is not familiar. This brevity, of course, is also a downside of the series: one must acquire the essays separately, and without an anthology or other collection, it may seem difficult to choose from among the sixty titles and counting in the series. Fortunately most can peruse the titles to find something of interest, and for the Woolfian, there is an abundance of lively approaches worth a look.

The topics of the essays in this series can be quite narrowly focused: Mark Hussey devotes his slender volume to the question of rural preservation in a single novel, *Between the Acts.* He proposes to explain the context of, in his words, "chance remarks" in the novel that today's reader is likely to overlook or discount as a representation of idle conversation. The piece does an admirable job of connecting those few remarks in the novel to questions of country and city in the period, which in turn brings an unexpected dimension of the text into relief. It is not a wholly new interpretation of the novel, but a concise revision of its place in the literature of the English countryside.

Paula Maggio's *Reading the Skies in Virginia Woolf* also asks us to rethink ostensibly minor details in the author's fiction. Maggio surveys Woolf's writing about weather from her diaries as well as the novels *Mrs. Dalloway, To the Lighthouse,* and *Orlando*; her central claim is that the importance of Woolf's engagement with weather has been overlooked by scholars. She is most persuasive when she presents Woolf's observations on climate side-by-side, so we can witness the abundance and range of Woolf's thinking about the weather. As Maggio observes, Woolf recorded notes about weather on a daily basis and sought to employ weather as an active force in her fiction. A section drawn from the diaries abounds with Woolf's fascinating variety of description, from "yeasty frowsty August" weather to "cold, dark, inhuman, primeval weather" (13). Maggio has evidently spent considerable time studying the history of English preoccupation with weather, but her analysis of Woolf's actual language is at times unsatisfying. While discussing a passage from the diary that describes "ink black, octopus pouring" storms, Maggio seems to miss the obviousness of the image; she lauds the "creative connection" of black ink and an octopus, as if it is an unusual pairing, going on to say that the image "connects the human and the natural realm by linking a manmade product, ink, with a creature of nature, the octopus" (14). A quick bit of research might have convinced the author that nothing could be more *natural* than to associate an octopus and black ink; too often, unfortunately, her analysis follows the same pattern of hasty connections. This is a shame, because her choice of novels is perfect for the topic, especially *Orlando*, in which Woolf defines entire eras of English literary history through weather (The Great Frost, the cloud and gales that begin the nineteenth century). A longer, more in-depth study would likely remedy the issues with analysis, but the reader of this essay will surely gain a greater appreciation of the importance of weather in Woolf's work. In that respect, the essay hits its mark.

The longer Bloomsbury Heritage monographs sit somewhere between a long journal article and a few book chapters. The essays of this type fulfill the promise of the series, as they are in-depth enough for detailed scholarship without exhausting their small-scale topics.

Catherine Gregg's *Virginia Woolf and "Dress Mania"* offers a concise biography of Woolf entirely through her relationship to clothes, the act of dressing, and her image of her own body. Readers eager to learn more about clothes in Woolf's fiction will find Gregg's essay useful, particularly the author's insight into the psychology of Woolf's "clothes complex." The study moves from Virginia Stephen's early memories of her mother's dress to traumatic episodes with her half-brothers, which Gregg persuasively casts as central to Virginia's anxieties about dressing and undressing. Leonard Woolf presents a turning point in the sense of his "shabbiness," allowing Virginia a measure of relief from her self-consciousness about fashion. Further short chapters on Woolf's relationship to Vanessa Bell and the influence of Vita Sackville-West—both personal and as a model for *Orlando*—round out Gregg's portrait of Virginia Woolf, a woman continually vexed by the "question of clothes."

One will have to look elsewhere for a critical study on, say, the dresses of *Mrs. Dalloway*. Gregg primarily draws on Woolf's diaries, and pays little attention to her fiction. It is to Gregg's credit that her story of Woolf's lifelong concern about clothes, about being both beautiful and "being above the superficialities of appearance" (24) is so engrossing; those who have not delved into Woolf's "frock consciousness" will find this essay a strong introduction to scholarship on fashion in Woolf, with the caveat that this essay sensibly restricts itself to biography.

Good scholarship has the useful and pleasurable function of revelation, as Gregg shows us in dimensions of dress we may have overlooked. Catherine W. Hollis, in *Leslie Stephen as Mountaineer*, may be able to make Woolf's readers see Stephen from a fresh new perspective, particularly if their primary image of the man derives from the difficult moodiness of Mr. Ramsay in *To the Lighthouse.* It may surprise those who know her father from Woolf's world that he was and is, in the world of mountaineering, an accomplished and celebrated climber who played a major role in the early years of the sport. A Venn diagram of Woolf scholars and alpine climbers with an appreciation for the sport's history may not overlap at many points, but Hollis sits right at that intersection. She admirably brings Leslie Stephen into full relief, demonstrating his deep and complex engagement with the mountains he loved as well as the effect his alpine experiences had on his writing. Stephen emerges, in this portrait, as humane, humorous, and at the same time fully committed to both his mountains and his marriages.

Hollis's study manages a striking thoroughness within a concise format: in fifty-one pages plus notes and appendix, she manages to delve into a detailed account of Stephen's prodigious climbing resume. The volume is also generously illustrated with rare photographs, maps, and a painting by one of Stephen's guides. For readers not versed in the minutiae of alpine climbing, Hollis explains the more arcane terminology and puts his accomplishments in their proper perspective. Stephen was no mere Victorian dabbler in the Alps; he was an exceptional athlete in his time, known to walk forty miles in a day, or, as Hollis notes, run a mile in under six minutes. He made the first ascent of a significant number of peaks in the Alps, and here again Hollis puts these accomplishments into an accessible perspective. Alongside her account of Stephen's mountaineering exploits, Hollis explains how his experiences in the mountains influenced other aspects of his life, notably his relationships with his first and second wives. Hollis shows us that mountains and marriage were at times in a complementary, but more often competing, relationship for Stephen, yet he remained committed to both. The mountains offered Stephen solace and rejuvenation after his first wife's death, and continued to be a place of renewal as career and family demanded more of his time and energy.

Hollis's key insight concerns the role mountaineering played in Stephen's materialist philosophy. She manages to trace a line from writings on, in one key example, "Sunset on Mont Blanc" (1873) to his "What is Materialism?" (1886), written after his climbing summit was behind him. Hollis develops a persuasively argued account of how vital the idea of perspective was for his philosophy, and how the perspective afforded by climbing—especially climbing a peak for the first time, and finding a new viewpoint previously uninhabited by a human observer—is a key component of this philosophical system. Hollis draws comparisons between Stephen and John Muir, but notes that where Muir sees God's grandeur in the landscape of the Sierras, Stephen instead sees an "empirical sublime" (42) that revises the Romantic conception of the connection of self and landscape.

The thread that ties the entire study together is Stephen's emphasis on experience, and, fittingly, Hollis writes a couple of delightful asides in which she herself follows in his footsteps. She recounts summiting Mont Blanc (and, fittingly again, talks about her guide, just as Stephen would) and ends the essay by stepping into the shadow of the Shreckhorn, site of one of Stephen's most important first ascents. These episodes do not intrude on her portrait of Stephen, but work instead to demonstrate his principled connection between knowledge and experience, as well as Hollis's willingness to pursue scholarship as adventure. This characterizes the best of the Bloomsbury Heritage series as a whole: original scholarship that takes risks and shows us a new perspective on otherwise well-traveled territory.

—Ted Wayland, *Olympic College*

Virginia Woolf: A Musical Life. Emilie Crapoulet. Bloomsbury Heritage Series 50. (London: Cecil Woolf, 2009) 36pp.

Beyond the Icon: Virginia Woolf in Contemporary Fiction. Alice Lowe. Bloomsbury Heritage Series 58. (London: Cecil Woolf, 2010) 32pp.

Desmond and Molly MacCarthy: Bloomsberries. Todd Avery. Bloomsbury Heritage Series 59. (London: Cecil Woolf, 2010) 32pp.

Virginia Woolf and the Thirties Poets. Emily Kopley. Bloomsbury Heritage Series 60. (London: Cecil Woolf, 2011) 76pp.

How Vita Matters. Mary Ann Caws. Bloomsbury Heritage Series 61. (London: Cecil Woolf, 2011) 24pp.

The Bloomsbury Heritage Series, published by Cecil Woolf Publishers and available by request to the publisher, is the project of Cecil Woolf (Leonard Woolf's nephew) and his wife, Jean Moorcroft Wilson, who serves as general editor of the series. The stated goal of the series, subtitled "The Life, Works, and Times of the Bloomsbury Group," is to "provide concise, original, and authoritative introductions to a wide range of approaches to the Bloomsbury group." Purporting to be written for an audience ranging from general readers to academics, Bloomsbury Heritage offers sixty-two volumes as of the latest catalog, which was distributed in June 2011. Though the series offers a wide range of perspectives on and contexts for the members of Bloomsbury and their descendants, its monographs are introduced in conjunction with the Annual Conference on Virginia Woolf, thus the centrality of Woolf to Bloomsbury is often invoked within these pamphlets as a way of justifying the relationship of a more obscure artist or text to the Bloomsbury group.

The five monographs that are the subject of this review represent a wide range of approaches, and provide a striking example of the inconsistent offerings of a series striving to be accessible to all types of readership. While monographs such as Todd Avery's and Emily Kopley's studies of figures and texts represent a more traditionally academic end of the spectrum, some of these booklets seem to have grown out of—and enjoy an ongoing lifespan as—entries on the *Blogging Woolf* website (bloggingwoolf.wordpress.com), which is comprised of blog entries by a group of writers who maintain an exhaustive catalog of Woolf "sightings" in contemporary media, news, and events, and post elsewhere on the web under the collective title, "Woolfwriter." Thus, a particular author's "expertise" seems often to refer to a particular author's "Woolfophilia," as opposed to a more rigorous standard of research-based expertise, since the authors of the Bloomsbury Heritage series titles range from freelance writers to musicians to academics. That being said, the fact that this series is a generic anomaly within the arena of academic journals is also what marks it as a refreshing and enthusiastic contributor to a wide range of fields, including but not limited to Woolf studies and modernism.

Emilie Crapoulet's *Virginia Woolf: A Musical Life* takes as its starting point the fact that biographical studies of Woolf frequently overlook the influence of music on both her life and writing. Though Crapoulet writes that her perspective is "deliberately biographical," she hedges when establishing whether Woolf has "technical" knowledge of music or not. This biographical focus quickly becomes conflated with technique in her readings of Woolf's fiction, and it is not clear what she hopes to accomplish by invoking this debate about Woolf's musical proficiency, particularly in terms of interpreting Woolf's novels (4). Crapoulet's central argument that Woolf looked to music for inspiration "as she sought to transcend the boundaries of her own art" is an important one, and one that could (and should) be extended to other modernist authors (3). There is more to be said, for instance, about Huxley's concept of the "musicalization of fiction" as it applies to Woolf's novels. Instead, Crapoulet moves quickly through a lengthy list of examples of music and musicians in Woolf's writing, including her diaries, letters, and novels. This cataloguing of musical references—broadly and loosely defined—in Woolf's writings soon reads like a concordance entry on Woolf and music, and falls back on tired metaphorical language. What, exactly, does it mean for a novel to rely on "sonata-form" (6)? More importantly, why is such a term necessary for understanding what Crapoulet calls the "musicality" of Woolf's novels (7)? Unfortunately, Crapoulet's volume misses an important opportunity to push beyond the music-as-metaphor approach to discussions of literature and music that persists in modernist studies, despite the valuable contributions of scholars such as Daniel Albright and Brad Bucknell.

Crapoulet's most important contribution to the frustratingly scant study of music and modernist literature is the point she makes regarding Woolf's attraction to the simultaneity of musical lines and the possibility for simultaneous sounding of multiple notes as an inspiration for Woolf's boundary-pushing literary endeavors. She makes a compelling case for music as inspirational to Woolf, as the proliferation of references she collects here convincingly demonstrate, particularly the many references to music that occur in Woolf's daily writings. However, her conclusion that the "musicality of Woolf's ... novels is undeniable and is underpinned by her knowledge and experience of music" does not do much to advance scholarly discussions of Woolf's novels as musically significant. I found myself waiting for at least one concrete example from one of Woolf's works that would display Woolf's "musicality" in practice. Instead, Crapoulet leaves that work to the reader; luckily, the juxtaposition holds much promise.

In her overview of Woolfian literary allusions, *Beyond the Icon: Virginia Woolf in Contemporary Fiction*, Alice Lowe uses much the same method as Crapoulet—tracing instances of a particular subject within a larger body of work—to expand on what she sees as the "perpetual longevity" of Woolf's work, particularly since the 1960s (4). Lowe notes that scholars analyzing the phenomenon of Woolf's popularity have tended to focus on her presence in Anglo-American popular culture, in particular "visual and verbal images" such as theatre, film, television and fashion (4). In this contribution, Lowe moves beyond studies of the commercialization of Woolf-as-icon in order to explore allusions to Woolf in the arena of contemporary literature and popular fiction (though she makes little distinction between the two), particularly fiction from the 1970s to the present. Lowe begins her task by defining the concept of a literary allusion at length, which seems unnecessarily simplistic. This basic definition is followed by a list of works of fiction that are organized by the type of allusion used: Woolf's physical likeness, Woolf as reading material, Woolf as cultural reference, and Woolf as muse. As a whole, it seems these allusions typically signify a character's feminist or intellectual leanings. Though she gestures toward an argument about allusions to Woolf serving "specific literary goals," Lowe never progresses much beyond a few examples of these various types, and the necessary vagueness that arises when attempting to cover more than thirty novels in as many pages results in numerous reductive or obvious statements, such as "the fact that [a character] was reading *A Room of One's Own* suggests that she had been questioning her choices and values, resulting in her move towards independence" (12). Like Crapoulet, Lowe ultimately traces the existence of various examples of Woolf in contemporary fiction without a clear purpose other than noting the existence of a pattern. While useful for outlining in broad strokes the pervasiveness of Woolf as an allusive figure within contemporary fiction, Lowe resists making an argument about what these allusions accomplish, other than that "the authors were adamant that Woolf was essential to what they were attempting to say" (25). By declining to offer any sort of conclusion about the proliferation of references to Woolf, Lowe does not do much to distinguish her collection of references from those analyses of Woolf's celebrity and growing commercialization that she so purposefully distances herself from in her focus on fiction.

In *Desmond and Molly MacCarthy: Bloomsberries*, Todd Avery takes us away (but never too far) from Woolf to address the "broad critical and popular neglect" suffered by the figures of Desmond and Molly MacCarthy, whom he argues are more central to Bloomsbury than previously perceived (8). Avery provides evidence for his claim about the centrality of the MacCarthys primarily by surveying what their fellow Bloomsbury friends had to say about them, and what has been said about them over the course of the past century. While acknowledging that Desmond MacCarthy was (and is still) often considered primarily a "literary journalist" (MacCarthy's own term), thus a lesser artist than his Bloomsbury contemporaries, Avery makes the case for MacCarthy's critical value by aligning his aesthetics with Woolf's in terms of their critical approach to literature. Drawing from his 2006 study, *Radio Modernism: Literature, Ethics, and the BBC, 1922–1938*, Avery makes the case that MacCarthy's 1932-1933 radio broadcasts on "The Art of Reading" not only resemble Woolf's approach to the issue of "how to read and why reading is important," but "compose a manifesto of Bloomsbury values" that can be traced back to G. E. Moore's emphasis on the individual in *Principia Ethica* (19). Overall, Avery aligns MacCarthy's conviction that the enjoyment of art is ultimately personal with Woolf's explanation of reading as involving "self-work"; both views, which insist on reading as a pleasurable experience, "express a fundamental Bloomsbury conviction" (18, 20). Ultimately, Avery reads MacCarthy's broadcasts as a concerted effort to promote the Moorean values which had shaped those of Bloomsbury from its inception.

As with his account of Desmond MacCarthy, Avery makes the case that Molly MacCarthy, about whom there is a dearth of information, played a pivotal role in the process of defining Bloomsbury. In Avery's telling, Molly is central to the making of Bloomsbury for two reasons: she coined the term "Bloomsberries," and she founded the Memoir Club, which was significant to the process of Bloomsbury self-definition. Thus, Avery argues, while Desmond expressed fundamental Bloomsburian attitudes in his writing and radio broadcasts, Molly was "instrumental in shaping the Group's identity during its middle and later years" (9). Further, she made contributions through her own writings, which have been unfortunately dismissed. Avery offers a reading of Molly's only novel, *A Pier and a Band* (1918), as both a Bloomsbury novel and a feminist novel in terms of theme, while acknowledging that, formally and stylistically, the novel is more problematic in terms of reading it as modernist fiction, for it falls squarely within the category of the "materialist fiction" Woolf so famously problematized. Nonetheless, Avery repeatedly aligns Molly MacCarthy's writing with Woolf's in order to establish the value of her work. While her novel might be what Woolf condemned as "materialist" in style, Avery posits that its theme addresses the everyday and "what is commonly thought small"—goals Woolf set for modern writers in her oft-quoted "Modern Fiction" (1925).

In this piece, Avery broadens the range of talents typically considered critically valuable by addressing Desmond's prolific literary criticism, and Molly's modest writerly output. Yet beyond the recuperation of individual reputations, Avery's refusal to align a lack of attention with critical merit allows him to make a compelling case for the MacCarthys' contributions to the establishment of

Bloomsbury itself. His emphasis on such seemingly minor figures allows him "to recalibrate, however slightly, what exactly we mean when we say Bloomsbury" (29). Avery both questions and confirms what constitutes "core" membership of Bloomsbury, using the example of the MacCarthys to illustrate how Bloomsbury's members somewhat contradictorily resisted attempts to fix their group identity even as they worked to define it.

Emily Kopley's *Virginia Woolf and the Thirties Poets* is the clear standout in this (admittedly limited) selection of volumes. In her meticulously researched monograph, Kopley presents a sustained study of the often mischaracterized relationship between Woolf and the generation of male poets (those whom Samuel Hynes termed "the Auden generation") who emerged in Britain in the 1930s. These poets include W. H. Auden, Julian Bell, Cecil Day-Lewis, John Lehmann, Louis MacNeice, Peter Quennell, and Stephen Spender. Kopley draws primarily from two of Woolf's essays, *A Letter to a Young Poet* (1932) and "The Leaning Tower" (1940), in order to advance the argument that Woolf's relationship to both the poetry of the 1930s and the young poets producing this poetry is much more complex and nuanced than previously understood. As Kopley convincingly shows, both of Woolf's essays addressed to these younger poets advance the argument that poetry—particularly of the lyric variety—no longer accurately represents modern life and that the novel was a more promising form.

Kopley devotes the bulk of the volume to carefully nuanced and textually nimble analyses of these essays, as well as utterly persuasive readings of contextual materials that shed light on Woolf's perceived audience, inspiration, and motivations for writing them. A key point for Kopley is what she terms Woolf's "ambiguous sincerity," which she repeatedly illustrates by highlighting Woolf's contradictions and ambivalence regarding the young poets' project (27). Woolf's *Letter*, she argues, was meant to be encouraging to the young poets while demanding that they "[sharpen] their ambition to create new forms," albeit with a "slippery tone" that complicates Woolf's purported goal of supporting the production of poetry suitable for the age (27). Kopley also relies on a great deal of archival research in order to trace the reactions and responses of the young poets to Woolf's *Letter*, including the full text of a letter from Spender to Woolf in which he engages some of her concerns by sharing that her books "seem to [him] to be poetry" (34). These various examples of private correspondence allow Kopley to discuss the responses of Lehmann, Spender, MacNeice, and Auden. As she traces this complex matrix of intellectual exchange, she also argues that some of the poets' responses to Woolf were made publicly, using the vehicle of the poetry about which Woolf had voiced objections. She contends, for example, that MacNiece's poem "Snow" is a response to Woolf, and that Auden alludes to Woolf twice in 1935: an allusion to *A Room of One's Own* in *The Dog Beneath the Skin* and to her short story "A Mark on the Wall" in his introduction to the anthology *The Poet's Tongue*. Throughout her discussion of Woolf's *Letter*, Kopley makes a compelling case for these poets' attention to Woolf's criticism of their art as well as her mastery of fiction. Their deep engagement with her work, and their description of it as "poetry" attest to their "high esteem" (45). Kopley demonstrates that the young poets consistently claim Woolf's fiction as belonging to their own form, and she goes so far as to suggest that Auden's composition of verse dramas is attributable to Woolf's advice that the young poets "revive past poetic forms" (44).

In the penultimate section, Kopley addresses Woolf's second essay on the young poets, "The Leaning Tower," within the context of the aesthetic and political debates taking place within their circle, as represented by Day-Lewis's *A Hope for Poetry* and Bell's "The Proletariat and Poetry." Terming it a "bookend," Kopley places this essay within the context of the proliferation of literary attempts to reflect on the importance of the 1930s immediately after the decade's close. In this essay, Woolf returns again to Day-Lewis, Auden, Spender, and MacNeice, while adding Christopher Isherwood to the list of celebrated literary men of the 1930s, this time arguing that their elitist and socialist leanings keep them at a dangerous remove from the general population. As in her *Letter*, Woolf maintains her argument in "The Leaning Tower" that poetry is outdated and outmoded, and soon to be subsumed by the novel. But what is presented in her *Letter* as an issue of form becomes for Woolf "an issue of class"; Woolf conflates poets with the educated elite, linking herself "with the working classes in order to promote the novel" (49, 50). Kopley reads "The Leaning Tower" as "the class-focused counterpart to the gender-focused *A Room of One's Own*," and uses a particularly lovely reading of what she believes to be an intentional misquotation of Wordsworth on Woolf's part to explain the contradiction between Woolf's condemnation of homosociality and her advocacy of frank discussion of one's own physical experiences by equating this "male cult" with other patriarchal plots to limit women's education and contributions to the literary tradition, of which the 1930s poets considered themselves a part (50, 54). Thus we return in the end to Kopley's argument that Woolf viewed the contest between poetry and prose as inherently gendered, and herself as a champion for the disadvantaged, whether women or the working class.

Kopley closes her study with a survey of the 1930s poets' reception of Woolf after her death in order to show how Lehmann, Spender, and Auden continued to celebrate her fiction after her death, describing her as a poet who wrote in prose. It is through this emphasis on continuity that Kopley seeks to shift our understanding of what has elsewhere been presented as a purely antagonistic relationship between generations of writers, and between genres. Though they may not have understood the stakes of Woolf's defense of her gender through defense of her form, by praising her novels for their poetic qualities, the 1930s poets recognized in Woolf's unsettled use of the words "novel" and "poetry" a project similar to their own, and one which they greatly respected.

The final selection in this group, Mary Ann Caws's *How Vita Matters*, returns again to the recuperative model and highlights selections from Vita Sackville-West's writings beyond her poetry, which has garnered the most attention. Championing Sackville-West's work with "an admitted bias" due to her previous role as editor of 2002's *Vita Sackville-West: Selected Writings*, Caws approaches Sackville-West's oeuvre by breaking it into three categories: her "most modernist" fictional work, *Seducers in Ecuador* (1924); her book of dreams; and her extensive travel writing juxtaposed with her notes on gardening and country life (5). Caws is clearly intimately familiar with Sackville-West, as evidenced by the proliferation of affectionate asides throughout. However, the overwhelmingly chatty tone and frequent typos wear thin even in such a short volume. Perhaps it would be more suitable for a public lecture on the character of Sackville-West, but as a contribution to the Bloomsbury Heritage series, I found myself wanting more critical attention paid to Sackville-West's work. That is, readers interested in her novel should have more to recommend it than that it is Caws's favorite. Caws emphasizes throughout that Sackville-West's writing places stock in the concept of a personal truth that is often impossible to communicate, and it is perhaps this theme of personal enjoyment that inspires her frequent interjections about how she engages with Sackville-West. Indeed, Caws's insights into how Sackville-West's other writings influenced her better known poetry are useful, particularly the overview of Sackville-West's travel writings and their emphasis on finding freedom "from place and self" (16). Like Avery, Caws follows the pattern of aligning Sackville-West's literary achievements to those of Woolf whenever possible, but what emerges from these ruminations on a woman commonly viewed as a sexual footnote to Woolf's career is that she held her own in the expression of what Caws terms "the consistency of style and vision" across the span of her work. For Caws, overlooking Sackville-West is a failure on our part, and one that we will come to regret once we familiarize ourselves with her writings beyond what is commonly considered to have literary cachet.

Ultimately, the idiosyncrasies that mar Caws's monograph are indicative of the Bloomsbury Heritage series as a whole: the inconsistency of its offerings is as frustrating as it is useful. Though there are the occasional volumes—such as those by Avery or Kopley—that are indeed addressed to both general and academic audiences, too often a volume is targeted toward one or the other. This discrepancy between well-researched argument and broad observation is a necessary side effect of a series with such a far-reaching scope, yet it is this scope that makes this series most valuable to both academics and Woolfophiles alike. Though a reader might be left wanting more in terms of each volume's larger contribution to Woolf studies, or to modernist studies, these monographs offer access to ongoing and emerging approaches to both Bloomsbury's socio-political context and its present reputation.

—Sarah Terry, *Oglethorpe University*

Works Cited

Albright, Daniel. *Untwisting the Serpent: Modernism in Music, Literature, and Other Arts*. Chicago: U of Chicago P, 2000.

Avery, Todd. *Radio Modernism: Literature, Ethics, and the BBC, 1922–1938*. Burlington: Ashgate, 2006.

Bucknell, Brad. *Literary Modernism and Musical Aesthetics: Pater, Pound, Joyce, and Stein*. Cambridge: Cambridge UP, 2001.

——. "The Sounds of Silence in Two of Jacob's Rooms." *Modernism/modernity* 15.4 (2008): 761-82.

Huxley, Aldous. *Point Counter Point*. Toronto: Dalkey, 2004.

Hellenism and Loss in the Work of Virginia Woolf. Theodore Koulouris (Farnham, UK: Ashgate, 2011) x + 242pp.

Hellenism and Loss in the Work of Virginia Woolf is the first book-length study of Woolf's "Greekness" by a scholar who is a native speaker as well as a student of ancient Greek. The argument is focused on Woolf's holograph "Greek Notebook" (1907-09), which contains notes on her reading of Homer, Plato, Sophocles, Euripides, Aristophanes, Juvenal and Virgil. Koulouris chooses the term "Greekness" as a way to distinguish Woolf's response from the idealized Greece suggested by "Hellenism," and to suggest the originality and complexity of the question he investigates: the "distillation of her own understanding of canonical Greek texts, filtered through an intricate network of *gendered* socio-cultural and political structures, into what I shall be referring to as 'the poetics of loss'" (8). While acknowledging the history of Greek studies in Victorian Britain, and the association of loss with psychoanalysis, he chooses to concentrate on the complexity of Woolf's position as a modernist and an intellectual at the turn of the twentieth century. Her Greek studies fostered a language in which she mourned not only the death of family members but the loss of educational opportunities and the carnage of two world wars, so that mourning became part of her identity as a woman of letters. Koulouris acknowledges theories of the modernist subject in the notes, while concentrating the body of his argument on a reading of Woolf's work in an historical context. The book studies what might be called Woolf's subject position, that he prefers to call an aesthetic of Greekness "somewhere between her life and text" (17).

The argument proceeds on several fronts. In Part I, "Loss in the Making," Koulouris examines Woolf's relationship to her parents and to Thoby, and notes that her Greek studies began after the deaths of her mother and of Stella. After several years of study her knowledge of Greek made her social position problematic. He makes good use of the anecdote from *Moments of Being* in which Woolf recalls being escorted by George Duckworth to a dinner with Lady Carnarvon, where her discourse on Plato and the emotions brought the conversation and the evening to a halt. Koulouris writes of "her justified impatience to express herself in a discipline with which she had been occupying herself for five years" (167). As a result she was neither the properly silent Victorian young woman, nor did she have the credentials to enter a profession. The hegemony of British Hellenism in the church as well as the university diffused it throughout British culture, where it often served as a kind of congratulatory self-recognition. Although Woolf's position was not unlike that of several of her female characters, in that she endured the loss of educational opportunities justified by the use of Greek to refuse women admission to the university, as an artist she transformed that position. "Woolf's informal study of Greek was a constitutive factor in the crystallization of a poetics of 'loss,' a poetics in which Greek is both, and at the same time, an agent of (sociocultural) exclusion and an instrument of textual and intellectual fulfillment" (99). This is the thesis of Koulouris' book.

Part II, Chapter three, "The Greekness between Life and Text," addresses the question, how was Woolf able to transform nineteenth-century Hellenism into the poetics of "Greekness" ? He first explores Woolf's problematic relationship to members of the Bloomsbury group, and identifies the tension that underlay her relationship with the men who had been trained at Cambridge as epistemological. That is, although Koulouris sides with Roger Poole in defending Woolf's powers of mind, he sees her occasional display of elitism (her refusal on occasion to translate) as acceptance of Victorian patterns of thought at the same time as she worked to subvert them. Her portrait of Edward Pargiter in *The Years*, while not hostile, images the Hellenism of the Apostles and of Bloomsbury, a position against which she developed her sense of "Greekness."

Chapter four reorients the discussion towards Woolf's language, in particular the meaning of *love* and *truth* in Greek texts and in Woolf's fiction. Here the focus of the book on "both a biographical and textual examination of 'love' in Woolf's intellectual development…" (99) has the effect of channeling the discussion of Woolf's language towards characterization. Antigone is a heroic figure associated with social injustice. While it is true that *love* for her brother is a facet of her character, the word/sign that generates disputes like those about her speech to Creon that is echoed in *The Years*, also leads to a recognition of the history of *love* in language, so that Greek becomes "a rich repository of literary paradigms" (117).

Chapter five reinterprets Woolf's intellectual relationship to Jane Harrison. Koulouris asks why if Jane Harrison is a significant figure in Woolf's development, the reference to J—H—in *AROO* is virtually the only time Woolf refers, other than in her letters, to Harrison's work. He interprets Harrison's career less as a story of a female scholar's struggle against odds than of her recognition of the shift in the cultural status of Greek studies during her life, which vacillated between an emphasis on philological accuracy and the introduction of archeology, myth, and ritualism. Unlike Woolf, Harrison created for herself a new British Hellenism. Her "intellectual route, vacillating between adherence to, and denunciation of, classical Hellenism and rationalism, is paradigmatic of her rare intellectual fervour, and gives evidence of her confident as well as astute awareness of what was happening around her not only in academia, but also in broader cultural scenarios" (148). The disparity between her attitude and Woolf's may be that whereas Harrison associated *logos*, thought, with male Hellenism, it was "paradoxically enough the only intellectual weapon at her [Woolf's] disposal" (165).

Chapter six, entitled a synthesis, sets out to explain "Woolf's vacillation between 'masculine' and 'feminine' codifications of British Hellenism" (177). Woolf's study of Greek, carried on for years in solitude, partly explains her lifelong distrust of academic institutions. Yet her mistrust of British Hellenism also made her more open to the upheavals of Greek society when she visited in 1932. She wrote of the difference between the Greece of her reading and modern Greece that was divided between an idealized past and present day economic hardship. Koulouris frames the argument by turning to Woolf's analysis of Ajax in the Greek Notebook, where Woolf rewrites in Greek Odysseus's comment, which he translates: "'For I see that we are nothing but ghosts living in darkness'" (203n.139).

Perhaps Koulouris's acknowledgement in the last chapter, that he writes "from within a Marxist theoretical viewpoint," enables the broad perspective of his argument. Although Hellenism "appears as a relentless vehicle of ideological influence, disseminated both by 'public' and 'private' state apparatuses," it was sufficiently fragmented to accommodate resistance (173). The Marxist perspective, at times theoretical, is patiently spelled out in a manner that makes the book accessible to a wide spectrum of readers. I would have welcomed an examination of Woolf's engagement with the ideology of translating Greek texts, but the book seeks less to challenge than to synthesize criticism and modify received ideas. It is wide ranging, carefully documented, rich in specific insights, and a pleasure to read.

—Emily Dalgarno, *Boston University*

The Cambridge Companion to Virginia Woolf. Ed. Susan Sellers (Cambridge: Cambridge UP, 2010) xxi + 272pp

The Cambridge Companion to Modernist Women Writers. Ed. Maren Tova Linett (Cambridge: Cambridge UP, 2010) xxiii + 224pp

---

Published in 2000, the first edition of *The Cambridge Companion to Virginia Woolf* declared that its attentions would be directed towards Woolf's "mind: the breadth of her intellectual range; her impulsive flights of creative brilliance, the long labours of composition; her conversations with the present; her arguments with history" (xiii). This second edition, directed "towards those wishing to augment their reading through an introduction to the interrogations and discoveries of Woolf scholars today" (xix) has lost none of its enthusiasm for its subject, and its scope remains impressive.

The first five chapters of the revised edition focus on establishing the intellectualism and radicalism of Woolf. Andrew McNeillie's opening essay is still a lively read, concentrating on the geographical and intellectual connections of the Bloomsbury group and tracing the early cultural influences on Woolf, while acknowledging that "[w]e need to recognise Woolf's resistance, her difference, and admit her own trajectory, beyond Bloomsbury" (14). The following three chapters turn their attention to Woolf's fiction by period. Susan Dick's examination of Woolf's use of literary realism is gone, and instead the volume appears to concentrate on the more obviously modernist innovations of Woolf's fiction. Suzanne Raitt's exploration of voice(s) in Woolf's early novels is effective in its aim to move beyond the reading of these as what she terms "apprentice work"; Jane Goldman, meanwhile, explores the "lyric experimentalism" of *Mrs. Dalloway* and *The Waves*, interrogating the distinctions between poetry and prose in Woolf's writing. Julia Briggs's analysis of Woolf's later fictions of the 1930s, however, opens up the possibility of moving beyond modernist tropes. She discusses "gender, class and historical moments" (70), but one of the most intriguing aspects is her description of the way in which *Between the Acts* "adapts a way of writing with amused affection about domestic or village life that was popular during the 1930s" (77). She goes on to invite comparisons to writers such as E. M. Delafield, Jan Struther and E. F. Benson—writers typically associated with middlebrow culture. Woolf's own views on the middlebrow are of course well known, but recent developments in the study of the middlebrow have attempted to rescue the term from its pejorative associations. Critics such as Nicola Humble, Faye Hammill and Ann Ardis have led the way for the re-evaluation of the relationship between modernism and middlebrow modes of fiction. Of course, paradigms concerning high and low cultures have also shifted considerably since the first edition, and the more highbrow elements of Woolf's fiction and her interest in the "common reader" are discussed here. Lee's chapter on Woolf's essays, for example, notes their accessibility and popularity as opposed to their credibility (citing the reception of Eliot's criticism as a point of comparison). Given the impact of rethinkings of brow boundaries in criticism today, however, it does seem a pity that a more explicit and prolonged discussion of cultural hierarchy in relation to Woolf is absent.

The study does, however, touch on the sometimes difficult and tentative relationship between Woolf and modernism. The chapter that best reflects this is Michael Whitworth's excellent analysis of Woolf, modernism and modernity. (It should be noted here that this is the only essay from the previous edition to have undergone notable revisions; the majority of the other chapters, with the exception of Raitt's, have been largely untouched.) The addition of the term "modernity" to the title of the chapter is significant. Ardis has argued that literary modernism has been privileged as "*the* aesthetic of modernity" (115), and indeed criticism has tended to treat modernism and modernity as practically synonymous. Whitworth, though, emphasizes how modernist work is "in dialogue" with modernity: "sometimes in reaction against" it, "sometimes drawing aspects of modernity into its form and texture" (107). By pointing to the anachronistic use of modernism in relation to Woolf—noting for example, that Woolf herself referred to "modern" rather than modernism (108)—and arguing that "no single definition of modernity is entirely adequate" (107) Whitworth illuminates the interplay of modernism and modernity in Woolf's fiction while contributing to what he identifies as a "subtler understanding of modernist texts, in which they emerge from a troubled negotiation with the condition of modernity" (121).

Whitworth's consideration of modernism in relation to "the social and historical phenomenon of modernity" offers a contextualization for David

Bradshaw's analysis of the wider socio-political issues informing Woolf's work, before turning to a consideration of feminism. Feminism has consistently been foregrounded in Woolf studies—both in terms of the content of her work and its role in transforming Woolf from a minor writer into a major one in the 1970s. Some of the essays from the first edition with this particular focus—namely, Susan Sellers on Woolf's diary and letters and Nicola Ward Jouve's critique of Woolf and psychoanalysis – have been removed. Still present (and wisely so) is Laura Marcus's chapter. With its considerable scope, Marcus's essay remains an impressive overview of Woolf and feminism, and is a must-read for those primarily concerned with this aspect of Woolf scholarship. In light of this, however, it is curious that the majority of the writers mentioned in relation to Woolf in this study are men. Indeed, more reflection on how an emphasis on Woolf's male influences and peers sits awkwardly against the feminist imperative often at work in Woolf scholarship might merit further investigation.

Chapters by Patricia Morgne Cramer and Helen Carr, however, do contribute a fresh perspective on Woolf and feminism. Cramer looks at the position of Woolf in lesbian literary culture, and examines the impact of Woolf's relationship with Vita Sackville-West on her fiction. Carr's discussion of Woolf and empire points out how the analysis of politics in Woolf's work led to a consideration of politics in relation to modernism more generally, arguing that this was "seen as fundamental to a critical understanding of her work, well before the politics of those male modernists began to be analysed" (200). These essays, along with Maggie Humm's work on visual culture and Cuddy-Keane's exploration of the public sphere, are dedicated to what Sellers describes as "new interests and departures in Woolf scholarship" (xx). Humm's chapter effectively capitalizes on the current interest in the everyday in modernist work and in visual culture, combining both in her discussion of Woolf. Cuddy-Keane, meanwhile, questions what we might mean when we deploy the term "public sphere" in relation to Woolf, contributing, like Whitworth, to a wider consideration of how we conceive of modernism and modernity.

The status of Woolf in relation to modernism is largely untroubled in *The Cambridge Companion to Modernist Women Writers*. Taking literary modernism as its primary interest, the study extends its analysis to consider the importance of salons, magazines, and visual culture in the development of transatlantic modernist women writers. In her examination of women modernists and the novel, Bonnie Kime Scott argues that Woolf "has become a focal figure for modernist/feminist transformation of the novel" (21). In this collection of essays, though, Woolf becomes part of a literary landscape populated by other notable figures such as Gertrude Stein, Djuna Barnes, H.D., Dorothy Richardson, and Willa Cather. This does not mean that the cultural authority ascribed to Woolf has diminished: indeed, some of the chapters open in dialogue with Woolf, citing extracts from her fiction, or crediting her with a particular innovation. There is also some more sustained discussion of Woolf's work, particularly in relation to gender and race. Scott suggests that part of Woolf's experimentalism lay in her inclusion of lesbian sexuality in her fiction (25), while Patricia Juliana Smith argues that she challenged the validity of "compulsory heterosexuality" (78). Jean Radford's assertion that Woolf's fiction "triggered questions about ethnic identity, racism, and empire" enables connections to be made with Carr's reading of politics and Woolf as outlined above, but it also opens up the opportunity to discuss "questions of race and ethnicity for all women modernists' writing" (111). But it is Laura Doyle who perhaps offers the most radical way of reading Woolf and empire. In her chapter, entitled "Geomodernism, Postcoloniality and Women's Writing," Doyle uses the term "post/coloniality" in reference to Woolf and other modernist writers, arguing that the slash "register[s] the lived divide between vision and reality, the discordance between a postcolonial situation … and an envisioned postcolonial future" (130). This allows Doyle to reimagine understandings of temporal experimentation in modernism, so that "repetitions of event … are not only a compulsive return to traumatic legacy," but also a strategy to make the reader "feel that certain events have 'already happened' insofar as they are decreed by a social logic or ideology" in which "lives are driven by the barrelling locomotive of colonial or racist and sexist world history" (141).

Elsewhere, the book investigates a selection of themes in relation to other women modernists. Suzette Henke effectively refocuses the discussion of modernism and trauma away from men's experience of shell-shock to women's experience of "severe crises associated with gender, sexuality and female reproduction" (169), while Sowon S. Park builds on the examination of women modernists and politics that Carr suggests, with an interesting account of the relationship between suffrage and modernism. Where the study excels is in its analysis of more marginal or less explored forms of modernism. Particularly fascinating are Thadious M. Davis's discussion of black women's modernist literature and Penny Farfan's work on women's modernism and performance. Maggie Humm, meanwhile, expands on her essay in *The Cambridge Companion to Virginia Woolf* by considering the role of visual culture in women's modernism more generally. This companion, then, offers more insight into potential comparisons between Woolf and other women modernists.

In a study that focuses on a selection of women's writing, the question of who is not discussed will inevitably be raised. In her introduction, Linett states that "[w]hether or not their work is evidently and formally experimental, all of the writers considered in this volume break new ground by approaching modernity from women's perspectives, as diverse as these perspectives turn out to be"

(10). There is a danger that such an observation might conflate modernism with modernity: indeed, on the basis of this description, the study might have included any number of other women writing during the same period. Certainly the relationship between modernism and modernity is not critiqued in the same way here as it is in the Woolf companion. And, again, there is the sense of a missed opportunity by not elaborating on the "boundary crashing" (23-4) by Woolf in *AROO* that Scott touches on, and how this might feed into a wider consideration of modernism in relation to cultural hierarchy. What is also conspicuously absent is the lack of comparison between these women writers and their men counterparts. In her accomplished analysis of modernist form, Miranda Hickman emphasizes the poetic innovations of women modernists, but her suggestion that they "respond" to or "adapt ... ideas and techniques connected with male modernists" (34) risks making them sound like followers rather than leaders. Clearly the remit of the study is to expand our understanding of women's modernist culture, but its reluctance to compromise its focus and to make anything more than a cursory reference to men modernists means it can never quite do justice to the complex networks involved in literary modernism. But this is a minor gripe, and the quality of scholarship here more than compensates for it.

—Emma Sterry, *University of Strathclyde*

Works Cited

Ardis, Ann. *Modernism and Cultural Conflict, 1880-1922*. Cambridge: Cambridge UP, 2002.

Hammill, Faye. *Women, Celebrity and Literary Culture Between the* Wars. Austin: U of Texas P, 2007.

Humble, Nicola. *The Feminine Middlebrow Novel, 1920s to 1950s: Class, Domesticity and Bohemianism.* Oxford: Oxford UP, 2001.

British Bohemia. The Bloomsbury Circle of Virginia Woolf. International Cultural Centre, Kraków, 14 September 2010-9 January 2011. Curated by Tony Bradshaw and Monika Rydiger.

British Bohemia. The Bloomsbury Circle of Virginia Woolf. Ed. Barbara Górska (Kraków: International Cultural Centre, 2010) 185pp.

It is not surprising that British Bohemia should have been shown at the International Cultural Centre in Kraków, for Kraków has always held an important place in the development of the Polish literary and visual avant-garde. It was, for example, home of the Young Poland modernist group, the Formists, the Polish Futurists, and the Zwrotnica circle associated with the art critic and poet Tadeusz Peiper, who was editor of a little magazine called *Zwrotnica* (Railway Switch).

The Bloomsbury artists seem to match perfectly Kraków's artistic atmosphere which during the first decades of the twentieth century was as vibrant, innovative and creative as that of its counterparts in London. This is the first time the "Bloomsberries" have made an appearance in this part of Europe so the exhibition may be regarded as a milestone in the understanding of modern British art in Poland, where it has usually been French, Italian and German art that has attracted popular and critical attention.

The exhibition emphasized the lifestyle as well as the art and literature produced by the group. Although to some viewers it may have seemed slightly modest, the selection of objects was conditioned not only by limited gallery space, but by the decision of the curator, Tony Bradshaw, not to display work from major museum collections but to bring forward works from private collections. Bloomsbury enthusiasts saw perhaps for the first time several unseen or little-shown art works. Paintings dominated but the wide-ranging activity of the Bloomsbury artists was also demonstrated, particularly in the field of design.

The most prominent members of the group were represented in the exhibition, including the writer Virginia Woolf, the painters Duncan Grant, Dora Carrington and Vanessa Bell, and Roger Fry, who was both painter and critic. Large biographical panels hung alongside their work. Grant was represented most abundantly with landscapes showing the countryside around Charleston, the house in Sussex particularly associated with the group, as well as portraits and still-lifes. Some of the most remarkable landscapes included Grant's watercolor and pencil on paper work entitled *Barns and Pond at Charleston* (c. 1934) or a Cézannesque oil, *Houses at Newhaven* (c. 1934), both showing an increasing departure from representation. Charleston played an important role in the show, since the design of the exhibition reflected the interior of the house itself. There were enlarged life-size photographs of the interior which increased the visitors' feeling of an intimate encounter with the artists and the Bloomsbury ambience. These photographs highlighted the Bloomsberries' view that their lives formed part of their art, so that when they decorated their immediate surroundings—including Charleston's walls and furniture—it seemed both necessary and valid.

Charleston also symbolized the Bloomsbury Group's anti-war stance in 1914-1918. These artistic revolutionaries carried out an aesthetic crusade against bourgeois taste and academicism, but they were not at all rebels in the political sense; avoiding military conscription, they were instead employed on the land at farms nearby, so that staying at Charleston became a convenient option.

Grant's *Dancers*, from the 1930s, exemplifies his long-lasting interest in dance and ballet which began in the early 1920s, when he designed sets and costumes with Leonid Massine and Lydia Lopokova and later continued his cooperation as a set designer with the Vic-Wells Ballet and the Camargo Society. Equally impressive are two studies for the large painting *Interior* (Ulster Museum, Belfast); one of them, *David Garnett Writing at Charleston*, 1918, depicts Garnett, who resided at Charleston between 1916-1919, who "is shown translating Dostoyevsky in the dining room at Charleston" (85). Another study for *Interior*, a watercolor *Vanessa Bell Painting at Charleston* (1918) shows the artist's figure as if merged with and belonging to the interior of the dining hall, forming an indivisible entity with Charleston.

The exhibition also showed Grant's early drawings of female nudes, *Reclining Woman with Horse* (1913), and *Reclining Nude* (1919), revealing the inspiration of Matisse. The curvilinear shape of the female body announces the bulky neoclassical nudes Grant would later develop. During the second and third decades of the twentieth century Grant was regularly drawing and painting from the model, since he could afford to hire sitters. The theme of a female nude reappears in his repertoire for the rest of his artistic career and is represented in the exhibition by his more colorful and vivid oils *Reclining Nude, Fitzroy Street* (c. 1930) and *Seated Nude*, (c. 1928-30), or by semi-nudes such as the Greek mythology inspired *Demeter* (c. 1948).

Roger Fry was represented by a number of early landscapes from Italy and the south of France such as *Florence* (c.1900), *Angles-sur-l'Anglin* (1912), *Autumnal Landscape, South of France* (1920), *Le Petit Port St Tropez*, (1922). Those from Auxerre, *Auxerre* (1925) and *Evening Sunlight, Auxerre* (1925) highlight the quiescence and reticence of the site and are executed with a charge of structural rigor and emotional stillness; his depiction of this little French town lying on the River Yonne thrives on the tension between the sturdy steadfastness of the buildings and their proximity to the flowing river which also reflects the wobbling structure of the buildings. In the catalogue Bradshaw writes that "Roger Fry's depictions of town or country are never dramatic but are the product of quiet, prolonged contemplation of space, colour and light" (125). Though Emeritus Tate Keeper Richard Morphet is quoted to have claimed that Fry's paintings have "an appealing openness" (125), it feels as if Fry saw the town from the vantage of a detached observer, so that the paintings evoke a mood of nostalgic reverie.

The early sketches by Dora Carrington, *Teddy Carrington* (1912) and *Head of a Young Woman* (1914), are characteristic of the style of drawing practiced by students of the Slade School of Art in the first decades of the twentieth century, and can be compared with the work of David Bomberg, Mark Gertler and Stanley Spencer which reflect the detailed, realistic and careful rendering taught by Professor Tonks. A later oil portrait of Annie Stiles (1925), who was a housemaid at Carrington's house at Tidmarsh Mill, where the artist lived with Lytton Strachey, departs radically from these early endeavors in its simplification of form and a more outspoken handling of pigment. A similar approach can be found in Mark Gertler's *Portrait of the Artist's Sister, Sophie* (1911). Though Gertler was never an official member of the Bloomsbury group, he was a close friend to Dora Carrington, his one-time lover, and through her he befriended other Bloomsberries and was closely aligned with their activities. Gertler, a Polish-Jewish émigré artist, who left Białystok, a city in north-eastern Poland, and emigrated to England, brought an interesting connection for most visitors to the exhibition. So did the figure of Mela Muter (1876-1967), a Polish artist, whom Fry had met in St. Tropez in 1921, and who "sat with aplomb on the jury of the Salon D'Automne and ensured for Fry that three of his works were accepted that year" as Frances Spalding puts it (110). The two often sat for each other's portraits around this time, though their relationship turned out to be only short-lived.

Vanessa Bell was represented by a variety of works, including portraits, landscapes and still-lifes. Her later cityscapes of Venice, notably *Fondamenta Nani, Venice* (1948), and *On the Steps of Santa Maria della Salute, Venice* (1948), hung alongside still-lifes such as *Wallflowers, Anenomes and Narcissi* (c. 1950), and *Summer Flowers in a Glass Vase*, (c. 1945). Her early landscapes of the South Downs countryside at or around the Woolfs' property at Rodmell, *Monk's House, Rodmell* (c. 1935), evoke impressionistically the Bloomsbury ambience of a home always open to gatherings of friends. Her pointillist-style landscape designs for Shell-Mex oil company advertisements issued in 1931 present the charming historical village of Alfriston in Sussex. Bell was one of the few British artists commissioned in the 1930s to depict the beauty of the British countryside on posters to persuade increasing numbers of automobilists to explore the countryside, driving on Shell. Bradshaw claims that "[k]nown as lorry bills, these posters were an unusual form of advertising, being framed posters of a standard size attached to the sides and back of Shell lorries delivering cans of petrol and oil" (81). The pastels used by Bell evoke an idyllic atmosphere of a village paradoxically as yet unspoiled by a car industry about to enter and transform rural areas.

Perhaps one of the most alluring works by Vanessa Bell was a lithograph entitled *The Schoolroom* (1937), commissioned in that year by Robert Wellington of the Zwemmer Gallery in London. According to Bradshaw, the idea behind the commission was to produce affordable prints for newly-established state schools, and the initiative was later widened to appeal to the general public (92). The lithograph challenges conventional composition by moving the figures to the sides of the work, making them seem hardly relevant. The governess reclining in an armchair appears to be drifting away in her thoughts while her two pupils, turning away from their teacher, are concentrated on their tasks. Part of this image is used most effectively for the catalogue cover.

The exhibition also featured thirty-four first editions of hand-printed books published by Hogarth Press from the collection of Pierre and Marie-Madeleine Coumans, Belgium. They were displayed in a framed glass vitrine as if to establish a painterly analogy for these literary productions, which were themselves illustrated by Fry, Bell and Grant. Hence books become works of visual art and the mode of display enhances such a perception. First editions of Virginia Woolf's novels are particularly appealing, if not indeed moving, for lovers of literature in this country.

Artifacts from the Omega Workshops were well represented and included chairs, mirror frames and pottery. In 1914 the Omega was commissioned to redesign the interior of the Cadena Café in Westbourne Grove, London. The project included wall paintings, carpets, painted tables, a stained-glass ceiling light, decorated pottery, tiles, lampshades, painted furnishings and even uniforms for waiters. The Kraków exhibition displayed a chair designed for the scheme. Other exhibits included dining chairs designed by Roger Fry and made by the Dryad company, which were usually "painted red to simulate Chinese lacquer" (Bradshaw 158). In Fry's words, "in designing for furniture we have considered comfort and practical needs first" (Bradshaw 158). Some of the chairs on display were designed by Fry for the dining hall of Penns-in-the-Rocks, the home of Lady Dorothy Wellesley, 1929. The room turned out to be such a substantial accomplishment that the project appeared in the pages of *The Studio* magazine for August 1930. Duncan Grant later claimed that "the room was the best thing we did" (Bradshaw 159). The chairs, from the Collection of David Herbert, are made of beech wood, and have a cane seat and back with painted decoration over a gesso ground. However, the exhibition did not include a waistcoat designed by Roger Fry in 1914, made out of fabric he called Cracow, also designed by him. The Cracow weave-patterned textile clearly evokes Polish mountaineers folk design of the Tatra Mountains region in Poland, where the city of Kraków lies.

The MCK (Miedzynarodowe Centrum Kultury/International Cultural Centre) together with Bloomsbury Workshop, London, which co-curated the exhibition, published an excellent and lavishly illustrated catalogue for the exhibition featuring specially written essays by leading scholars and experts on the Bloomsbury Group and modernism, including Frances Spalding, Tony Bradshaw, Krystyna Stamirowska and Sarah MacDougall. The essays introduce the notion of the Bloomsbury phenomenon, though they do tend to concentrate on the private spheres of its members' lives and highlight their extraordinary lifestyles. Bradshaw admitted that "there is no doubt that a grouping of some nature did exist, if only as a loose association of friends" (13), implying that it was this societal nature of the circle that made the group the most distinguished among the avant-gardes in modernist Britain. Bradshaw emphasizes the intellectual contribution that Bloomsbury made to the development of liberal thought in early twentieth-century Britain, and justifies their rejection of Victorian conventions and emphasis on private life as opposed to their predecessors. Spalding argues that "whereas the Victorians had paid a great deal of attention to public virtue, this younger generation was to focus instead on personal relations, on the grounds that unless honesty can be found close at hand, it is unlikely to be found in the larger, more public sphere" (15). This is what distinguished the group from a variety of other modernist circles and places it prominently among continental avant-garde formations. One argument proposed by Monika Rydiger, who co-curated the exhibition, is that Bloomsbury "never became a formal group, never published a manifesto or a programme of any sort. It was rather a circle of friends linked by a network of complex personal relationships, and it is these relationships that are the focus of much of the available literature on the group. Hence there tends to be more of an interest in the biographies of the group's members than in their work" (15). Even Virginia Woolf herself maintained in 1924 that "All our Bloomsbury relationships flourish, grow in lustiness. Suppose our set to survive another 20 years, I tremble to think how thickly knit & grown together it will be" (*D2* 326). Spalding argues, however, that without the understanding of the artists' biographies one cannot comprehend the group's history since personal relations "form an important structuring ingredient" (15).

The essays are rather brief and in some cases repetitive. MacDougall's contribution is highly welcome and original, since it introduces the figure of Mark Gertler, a Polish Jew, who had a brief relationship with the Bloomsbury circle, though they are thought to have influenced his art greatly. Gertler met with members of the Bloomsbury Group regularly during World War One at Lady Ottoline Morrell's salon in Gower Street and then at her house in Garsington (57). A developing friendship with Lytton Strachey failed when he found out about his intimate relationship with Dora Carrington, whom he loved for many years.

In spite of controversy concerning his painting *Fruit Stall* shown in the London Group exhibition of 1915 at the Goupil Gallery, Duncan Grant welcomed his work. In a letter to Gertler he stated: "I must write to tell you that I think your big picture [*Fruit Stall*, 1915, lost] at the London Group very remarkably good. It is much the most serious picture there and to my mind much the best work of yours I have seen" (58). Later on Gertler also befriended Roger Fry, sharing his passion for Cézanne.

In Poland so far the Bloomsbury Group has usually been associated with the literary work of Virginia Woolf, and this has no doubt influenced the title of the show, which in full is "British Bohemia. The Bloomsbury Circle of Virginia Woolf." She became more widely known following the translation of her diary into Polish, as *Chwile Wolności. Dziennik 1915-1941*, (Wydawnictwo Literackie Kraków, 2007). This exhibition situated Woolf's contribution to the literary and artistic avant-garde in the wider context of an influential côterie which contributed the more personal identity of an intimate circle of close friends in an era when close social bonds were still concealed and restricted to a private sphere. "British Bohemia" gave Polish gallery-goers the opportunity to see for the first time works by Roger Fry, Duncan Grant, Vanessa Bell, Dora Carrington, Mark Gertler and others. The city of Kraków, with its long tradition of cultivating the Central European avant-garde arts and bohemian life, came to host British bohemians and hence the encounter was more meaningful.

—Dominika Buchowska, *Adam Mickiewicz University, Poland*

Works Cited

Bradshaw, Tony. "Catalogue." Górska 67-171.

Bradshaw, Tony. "Virginia Woolf and Vanessa Bell. A Collaboration at the Hogarth Press." Górska 45-50.

MacDougall, Sarah. "Borderland to Bloomsbury: Mark Gertler, A Journey from East to West." Górska 53-63.

Rydiger, Monika, Tony Bradshaw, Frances Spalding. "British Bohemia." Górska 13-20.

Spalding, Frances. "Virginia Woolf, Bloomsbury and a Journey Through Time." Górska 35-41.

Virginia Woolf's Bloomsbury. Volume 1: Aesthetic Theory and Literary Practice. Ed. Gina Potts and Lisa Shahriari (London: Palgrave, 2010) xvii + 188pp.

The essays in *Virginia Woolf's Bloomsbury* grew out of the 14th Annual Conference on Virginia Woolf, held in London in June 2004, whose theme was "Back to Bloomsbury." Volume 1 of the two-volume set clusters papers under the heading "Aesthetic Theory and Literary Practice." (A second volume centers on "International Influence and Aesthetics.") The collection conveys the sense of a lively conversation and the excitement of the peripatetic conference's return to Woolf's hometown. An interest in situating Woolf within London marks several of the papers, though the focus on the city tends, surprisingly, more toward the insides of houses and the shelves of their libraries than street haunting. The rubric "Aesthetics and Literary Practice" is broadly defined, with essays engaging topics from painting, architecture, and photography to less expected subjects like natural history and Leonard Woolf.

Indeed, following Gina Potts's introduction, first among the essays comes Cecil Woolf's warm recollection of his uncle and aunt, an affectionate corrective to accounts of a mean, authoritarian Leonard and melancholy, dispirited, even sadistic Virginia who haunt the biographical record. The fascinating essay that follows, by Suzanne Raitt, also centers on revision and return, though of a different sort, in Woolf's composition practices and as thematized in *To the Lighthouse*. Whereas writing for Woolf could be an ecstatic experience, revision was traumatic. Even the narrator's encounter in *A Room of One's Own* with Milton's and Thackeray's drafts, as Raitt shows, proves so. Placing accounts of Woolf's practices in the context of psychoanalytic understandings of textual revision, Raitt looks at Woolf's expansion, through revision, of the section of *To the Lighthouse* devoted to Lily Briscoe's practices of artistic return and argues that, in returning to that novel, Woolf came to see revision as potentially—sometimes—curative.

Beth Rigel Daugherty examines the influence of Anne Thackeray Ritchie, Woolf's "Aunt Anny," first as a model of a writing woman to balance Leslie Stephen's man of letters, and then through the prose style and preoccupations that Ritchie shares with Woolf. The younger writer admired Ritchie and at times, according to Daugherty, seems even to have echoed her sentences. In *A Room of One's Own,* Daugherty traces the recurrence of the canon of women writers that Ritchie too championed and the method that she pioneered for writing women's lives. Daugherty credits Ritchie, too, as the likely source of Virginia Stephen's copies of *Atalanta,* a progressive girls' magazine that could have served as a stand-in for the community and instruction of a schoolroom. Anna Bogen's contribution places *Room* in relation to a body of writing that made less room for women, the popular campus novels of the period. These novels nevertheless share with Woolf's essay an investment in insider-outsider tensions and the divide between modern London and the world apart that is the university, evocative alternately of history and timelessness. Yet, Bogen notes, it is from a modern London of recognizable sites that Woolf's narrator imagines a future Cambridge of women writers. Bogen shows that *Room* can be read as appropriative, rather than merely subversive, of university literature—a genre in which, though its writer was thought until recently never to have enrolled in a university course, it is now the canonical text.

Morag Shiach's and Elisa Kay Sparks's contributions return to the city. Shiach poses the question of whether, to complement the flâneur as metaphor of modernity, we can find a "comparably historicized form of cultural analysis or literary criticism that engages with the more confined, and the more static terrain of the room"—a model that would re-imagine the city's connecting streets as a "structured network" of interior spaces (51). In pursuit of this question, Shiach's essay surveys London rooms in Woolf's biography and writing. Spaces of memory, frameworks for identity, sites of integrity and security, rooms also suggest more threatening types of enclosure. If their study does not bring to light the flâneur's stay-at-home sister, the patterns of contrast that Shiach traces between Victorian and Bloomsbury interiors do map an evolving urban geography of private spaces, whose public counterpart Woolf could have found in London guidebooks in her collection, the focus of Sparks's essay. Reading in the Woolfs' library at Washington State University, Sparks inspects its assemblage of city lore, a source of fascination for Woolf and a potential source of material for *Mrs. Dalloway, A Room of One's Own,* and her London essays. In the prehistoric city and its anonymous women and lost waterways—including a river that once ran the course of characters' walks in *Mrs. Dalloway*—Woolf found, according to Sparks, an alternative to the "petrified present of statues of great men" and a precedent for the diverse, moving crowds of the modern street (73).

Caroline Marie takes up the movement of characters and spaces in *Orlando*, linking the novel's interest in transformation to precedents in theatrical and cinematic history. Expanding on existing scholarship on the photographs by Vanessa Bell that Woolf published with *Orlando*, Marie draws on Roland Barthes to describe pantomime as another visual technology that informs the novel's model of identity. Virginia and Leonard Woolf's photographic practices in personal albums of the 1930s, a period in which Woolf was especially preoccupied with memory, frame Maggie Humm's wide-ranging essay, which also covers biographical, intellectual, and stylistic convergences between Woolf and Freud in the decade—including their parallel return trips, Woolf's in person, Freud's in writing, to the Acropolis. Two impulses, Humm suggests, characterize Woolf's memory work of the period: one, Freudian, complicates and reactivates memory; the other, photographic, stabilizes and preserves. As in the current practice of "photoanalysis," the 1930s albums create narratives of identity. Humm reads Woolf's fictional scenes and her photographic albums as "object-cathexes," meant to "defen[d] against the pain of death" in a period when the losses of old friends made this pain familiar (101, 100).

One of those friends was Roger Fry, dead in 1934. Fry is a central figure in Benjamin Harvey's essay, which argues for "solidity" as a key term in Bloomsbury writing, one that connects "aesthetic pleasures and the processes and pleasures of the human body" (110). Harvey reads Woolf's story "Solid Objects" in relation to titillated Bloomsbury exchanges about the collecting impulse as characterized by psychoanalytic theory and in relation too to Woolf's portrait of Fry as a collector of Cézanne, whose canvases he celebrated for their "solidity." Collecting practices and their discontents are a subject of Christina Alt's illuminating essay, which traces Woolf's early enterprises and later familiarity with emerging ideas in natural history. Reading *Jacob's Room,* Alt demonstrates that the novel's natural symbols and its skepticism about naming, in particular about naming as a means of knowing, coincide with a contemporary shift in science away from classification. Woolf employs an analogy to discredited theories of natural history to discredit realism and offer a critique of fixity. Her alternate literary project, Alt concludes, like contemporary sciences of ethology, ecology, and zoology, centers on "[t]he renunciation of capture" (133).

Kristin Czarnecki draws lines of comparison between Woolf and Zora Neale Hurston, Bloomsbury and the Harlem Renaissance, to show how they might "be brought closer together in our minds, our scholarship and our classrooms" (135). The areas of convergence that Czarnecki identifies—between writers, communities, and reception histories—could suggest ways to use the two writers to organize a course interested in transatlantic modernism and its individual and group identities. Makiko Minow-Pinkney travels even further, to explore intersections between Woolf and a Japanese contemporary, Sōseki Natsume. In addition to the pilgrimage—or, in Woolf's case, pilgrimages—that each writer made to Thomas Carlyle's house (a site to which this collection, too, makes repeat pilgrimages: it is also a subject of Shiach's essay), they have in common, according to Minow-Pinkney, a marginal point of view that leads each to be skeptical about the objectivity of realist literary convention. Though the writers' literary results bear comparison, Minow-Pinkney shows us that Sōseki's turn away from "the Western nineteenth century was distinct from the Western modernists' concern with repudiating the nineteenth century": what for Sōseki was a way "to retain one's past" was for Woolf, like other Western modernists, a way to move beyond it (167).

There is much to value in the essays that Potts and Shahriari have collected, though the volume has shortcomings. In a book about aesthetics, illustrations would have been welcome. I felt their absence with Humm's descriptions of photographs of the Keyneses and Harvey's citation of a photograph of Fry that Woolf reprinted in her biography. The index also has omissions: for instance, it includes Thomas Carlyle but not Jane Carlyle, who became, Minow-Pinkney argues, an object of greater and independent interest to Woolf. These limitations made me appreciate advantages of the online publication of papers from recent conferences by Clemson University Digital Press, collections that are searchable, include generous selections of images, and come at a more accessible price (free in pdf, $19.95-$24.95 in print; each Palgrave volume, in contrast, costs $80). Nevertheless, this volume is worth seeking out in its own right for a wide-ranging discussion that, in going back to Bloomsbury, also takes us somewhere new.

—Emily Setina, *Baylor University*

Museum Trouble: Edwardian Fiction and the Emergence of Modernism. Ruth Hoberman (Charlottesville and London: U of Virginia P, 2011) xi + 236pp.

Ruth Hoberman's *Museum Trouble* is an extremely convincing and far-reaching treatment of the importance of museum culture to Edwardian fiction and early modernism. Her introduction provides a deft framing of her methodology—her theoretical and critical debts, her approaches to the relationship between fiction and reality, and her highly historicized treatment of museum culture. There she highlights the anxieties that seem to drive museological conflicts, such as concern about artwork being sold abroad, or questions of national identity and ownership, or methodological disputes between professional scientists, amateur collectors, and a public in need of education. She also enumerates the kinds of issues that will predominate in her study. For instance, in many of her fictional examples, she fruitfully explores a tension between the museum as an institution tending to impose order and ideology, and as a space for individualized exploration that can offer resistance or alternatives to such institutional structures. She notes museums' importance to modernity, in their growth as state-sponsored collections that enforce notions of knowledge, valuation, and citizenship. The Edwardian period (1890-1914) is the moment when museums had developed to the point—had become adequately commonplace—that they could begin to play an important role in fiction.

Museum Trouble addresses an array of instances in Edwardian fiction where museums become a site for examining underlying social and creative tensions. Through treatment of art museums, Hoberman can raise the period's concern with protecting the value of art objects from the dirtiness of the market, whether that "dirtiness" is made manifest through advertising, at the hand of Jewish art dealers, or even thanks to the risky role of private collectors. As an alternative, museums provide a neutral "space from which desire has been expelled, a space that provides a safe haven from the collector's desires, the dealer's greed, and the marketplace's uncertainties" (42). "In fact," she notes, "the whole project of the museum could be read as an effort to resacralize displayed objects to compensate for mass commodification" (41). Nevertheless, she takes care to point out continuities between museum display and that employed by department stores, shop windows, and other commercialized spaces which have, in past treatments, been distinguished as "lower" cultural venues in opposition to museum's "high" and sacred spaces. By joining in the challenges to these old dichotomies, Hoberman points to the complexity of display, viewership, consumption, and appreciation.

Hoberman's treatment of fiction similarly ranges from well-known canonical texts to works that are less familiar but nonetheless invested in museum culture in important and revealing ways. She provides rich examination of works by such writers as May Sinclair, Henry James, E. M. Forster, Gilbert Cannon, and Vernon Lee to illuminate the ways that fictional engagement with museal space can provide opportunities to examine social mores, individual inspiration, self-presentation, the vagaries of aesthetic response, and what it might mean to gain liberation from institutional pressures. Her critical attention to the interactions in these scenes between the often sterilized space of museological display and the very bodily experience of visitors seems especially important in its ability to reveal the varieties of visitor experience, despite museums' frequent attempts to ensure conformity.

The book's final chapter, "Museum Dreams," explores the dynamic in high modernist literature designated by Hoberman's title—"imaginative responses to problems posed by the turn-of-the-century museum and depicted in Edwardian fiction" (166). Part of this dynamic involves a dialectic she draws from Adorno's "Valéry Proust Museum" between the museum as "an oppressive order" and as "an invitation to dream, to revive the objects through their own imaginative responses" (167). For instance, Hoberman reads W. B. Yeats's Byzantium poems as such museum dreams—"a vision of art simultaneously immersed in and bereft of the culture that gave it meaning, both time-transcending and time-riven, at once the object of the museumgoer's gaze, and the product of his imagination" (174). She notes that in "Byzantium," for instance, Yeats's speaker is guided by a mummy—"that quintessential museum-displayed object" (174)—and Hoberman reads such architectural details of the poem as "moonlit dome" and "marbles of the dancing floor" as evocations of museum architecture (175). However, Yeats himself in the 1925 version of *A Vision* (to which Hoberman refers) positions his thinking about Byzantium in the "the mosaics of Rome and Sicily" (he changes this to Ravenna or Sicily for the 1937 version)—in churches where the mosaic decoration continues to adorn a living space whose ornaments play a very different role than do those objects set aside for enchanted looking in museums.[1] If we read Yeats's poems with the same historical attention afforded in this volume to museum culture, then the extent to which these poems—while certainly reliant on objects for their imaginative responses—are dreams not spawned by museums but rather of a culture kept vibrant becomes apparent. Perhaps instances such as this—where a deeper examination of the circumstances surrounding poetic composition might have revealed counter-arguments to her reading—are an unfortunate by-product of the otherwise very successful breadth of her treatment of the culture and texts of the period.

This final chapter also includes an examination of Virginia Woolf's employment of the physical space of the British Museum's Round Reading Room in both her fiction and non-fiction. Hoberman positions her treatment of Woolf in a wider context of remarks about the space from the same period which combine to position that room as an embodiment of the canon of English literature. Crucial to Hoberman's analysis is the 1907 renovation of the room, featuring most prominently a repainting of the famous dome with bright white and gold paint and the inscription of the "great names of English literature" under the room's nineteen windows (182, see also 162). These names' place in the architectural and intellectual experience of the Round Reading Room, she argues, led various thinkers—including T. S. Eliot, J. C. Squire, and E. M. Forster—to imagine both the tradition of English literature and the world of contemporary letters in terms of the canon emblazoned on this dome. And this repainting, Hoberman notes, features in Woolf's diary and fiction, so that Julia Hedge laments in *Jacob's Room*, "Oh damn . . . why didn't they leave room for an Eliot or a Brontë?" (182; *JR* 106). Also crucial is Woolf's depiction in *A Room of One's Own* of the great dome of the Round Reading Room as "the huge bald forehead which is so splendidly encircled by a band of famous names" (184; *AROO* 26). This comparison reveals the implicit gender bias of the space, Hoberman notes, and Woolf uses it frequently to challenge the male-centered

[1] Yeats's reference appears in *A Vision: The Original 1925 Edition*, ed. Catherine E. Paul and Margaret Mills Harper, Collected Works 13 (New York and London: Scribner, 2008),159. See also W. B. Yeats, *A Vision* (London: Macmillan, 1937), 280. On Yeats's visits to Byzantine churches in Sicily and Rome as an influence on Yeats's thinking about Byzantium, see Russell Elliott Murphy, "'Old Rocky Face, look forth': W. B. Yeats, the Christ Pantokrator, and the Soul's History (The Photographic Record)"YAACTS 14 (1996): 69–117.

culture of such other persons and institutions as Cambridge University, St. Paul's Cathedral, Woolf's own character Orlando, and even the contents of the British Museum Library catalogue. In *To the Lighthouse*, however, and in the head of Mrs. Ramsay as imagined by Lily Briscoe, the Round Reading Room transforms from a masculinized bald dome to a dynamic beehive. This image relies, Hoberman demonstrates, on the likening, in an illustration by George Cruikshank and then a description by James Barr, of the Reading Room's shape to that of a "'mighty hive' with 'lofty dome, the busy workers, the hum and buzz'" (188). Hoberman emphasizes the networks of relationships that this embodiment of knowledge suggests, concluding, "Reconfiguring bee and dome to emphasize their underlying ties to matriarchy and domesticity, Woolf imagines an emphatically embodied space conducive to female creativity" (189).

Museum Trouble impresses with its comprehensiveness: even in sections of the book focused on a particular writer or text, Hoberman's critique encompasses historical documents, cartoons of the time, theoretical reflections, contemporary curatorial theory, concerns facing museums, and so forth. Her movement among these sources brings readers a compelling sense of the importance of museum culture both to the Edwardian and modernist moment and to the imaginative spaces of the fictions she addresses.

—Catherine E. Paul, *Clemson University*

Romantic Moderns: English Writers, Artists and the Imagination from Virginia Woolf to John Piper. Alexandra Harris (London: Thames and Hudson 2010) 320pp.

Virginia Woolf. Alexandra Harris (London: Thames and Hudson 2011) 191pp.

Alexandra Harris's *Romantic Moderns* is a study of what she calls "experimental antiquarians" (15). In her densely populated and broad-ranging book, Harris argues convincingly that in 1930s and 1940s England newness and modernity were not incompatible with tradition. Following earlier work like Jed Esty's *A Shrinking Island: Modernism and National Culture in England*, which she acknowledges as a book important to her own work, Harris shows writers, artists and musicians turning back to ancient English traditions. We see W. H. Auden collecting light verse, John Betjeman touring churches and teashops, and John Piper, a major figure in the book along with his wife Myfanwy Evans, gaining inspiration and perspective on modern art as he contemplates medieval stained glass.

Unlike Esty's more strictly scholarly book, Harris's volume is clearly meant to reach a broader audience. The fact that the book was awarded the Guardian First Book Award is testament to her success and to the appeal that this period of English history still has for today's readers. Harris's uncluttered prose makes the book read as a jaunt through the English countryside. Reflecting the kind of writing Harris is doing in *Romantic Moderns* and the breadth she was aiming at, she has listed in an interview as inspiration for her work Peter Conrad's *Modern Times, Modern Places*, and Simon Schama's *Landscape and Memory* as well as Hermione Lee's biography of Virginia Woolf and Jenny Uglow's of William Hogarth. As in Conrad's and Schama's books, there's a cultural-historical range to Harris's work that allows her to consider architecture and village life alongside food and climate, to name just a few of the topics she includes.

What is particularly appealing about this book is the fact that here we find Woolf in the company of contemporaries such as Ralph Vaughan Williams, Benjamin Britten, Adolf Loos, Evelyn Waugh and Flora Thompson—names that are not typically seen alongside Woolf's. A discussion of *Orlando* sits in a chapter about Georgian revival in which Harris discusses Edith Sitwell's wardrobe and Piper, Evans, Betjeman and Geoffrey Grigson's "church crawls" (66); *Between the Acts* is read in terms of the turn away from Fry's formalist ideas about art; and Woolf's "Reading at Random" appears in a chapter about the weather beside analysis of work by Stevie Smith, Paul Nash, Fry and Herbert Read. Central to Harris's book is the discussion of magazines such as Myfanwy Evans's *Axis*; this serves as a good reminder of some of the debates that were going on in the art world as Woolf wrote. Harris also shows how series such as Hilda Matheson's "Britain in Pictures," involvement with which Woolf declined, saw writers and artists generating nationalist propaganda on the eve of and during World War II.

Appropriate to its subject matter, *Romantic Moderns* is beautifully illustrated with color reproductions and attractively packaged by Thames and Hudson. Piper's work figures prominently alongside paintings and photographs of houses and artwork by Edward Bawden and Eric Ravilious among many others.

One finds a similarly paced prose, but less density in Harris's biography of Woolf. Short chapters are interspersed with captioned photographs, book illustrations and paintings, some that will be very familiar to Woolfians, others less so. Harris mixes some of the best-known photographs of Woolf and family and friends with paintings and illustrations by Vanessa Bell, Mark Gertler, Dora Carrington and Roger Fry and Hogarth Press covers and announcements. It makes Harris's *Virginia Woolf* a fast and enjoyable read, less daunting than Hermione Lee's hefty biography. Despite the book's brevity it does have the feel of a complete life.

Perhaps even more so than *Romantic Moderns* (which addresses trends in literary criticism with a discussion of F. R. Leavis, for example) this is a book for the common reader. One feels like one is chatting about Woolf with Harris. The voice of this biography is fresh and reassuring: "If the characters of *The Waves* are at some level 'all one', it doesn't matter that we sometimes lose track of who is speaking. It is part of the point of the novel that the voices elide; though they are speaking about different things, they share the same plot" (114). The book is dedicated to Harris's students at Liverpool University, suggesting the ideal audience for this work, one she affirms: students and those new to Woolf. Even as an experienced reader of Woolf, however, I found new ideas and interpretations as well as an extremely useful survey of her life.

Harris weaves Woolf's fiction with her life effectively. Early mentions of *Between the Acts* and *The Waves*, for example, are used to illustrate aspects of Woolf's childhood. Extracts from letters and diaries provide Woolf's voice. Harris successfully emphasizes the "tremendous variety" of an author readings of whose work, she suggests, are too often "dominated" by "the abstract idea of Woolf" (99). While Julia Briggs chose to subtitle her biography of Woolf "an inner life," and to build her life of Woolf around the works, Harris might have called hers "an outer life" in the sense that her Woolf is someone one could imagine passing in the street. The Woolf that emerges from Harris's book, foreshadowed by Lee's Woolf, is an approachable Woolf, a Woolf "half laughing, half serious" (122). Thus, in terms of *Orlando*, Harris asserts that "Woolf's sensuality … is not in the strip but rather in the tease" (106) and she describes *Flush* as "pushing at the limits of life-writing, arguing for a telling change of perspective, looking up at Elizabeth Barrett Browning from a point of view close to the floor" (122). Harris makes the case that *Orlando* and *Flush* belong on the same shelf as Woolf's other more serious work, arguing that "[t]here is plenty of holiday spirit in Woolf's most intensely lyric novels" (100).

Readers will find a more modern Woolf, a Woolf for the twenty-first century in Harris's *Virginia Woolf*. One gets an excellent sense from Harris of Woolf's push for independence, in terms of travel, and especially her love of the English countryside: highlighted, for example, is Woolf's romance with the Sussex Downs. Chapter 3, which covers the period 1904-1915, shows Virginia Stephen in her twenties, in the uncertain days before her marriage, escaping on trains to out of the way hotels and taking off on solitary walks in search of herself. A reflection of the book's interest in place and the author's contention that Woolf is "one of the great writers of place" (46), Harris includes a list of excursions for Woolf devotees at the back of the book.

In the closing chapter, "Afterwards," Harris offers a useful summary of the scholarship and publication, of diaries, letters and posthumously published work, that succeeded Woolf's death. My only quibble with the book is that this chapter and the further reading section in the appendix might have reflected some of the more recent critical and biographical work on Woolf. Both books represent important contributions to Woolf studies.

—Helen Southworth, *Clark Honors College, University of Oregon*

Fascism and Anti-Fascism in Twentieth-Century British Fiction. Judy Suh (New York: Palgrave Macmillan, 2009) ix + 211pp.

Judy Suh's *Fascism and Anti-Fascism in Twentieth-Century British Fiction* is part of what promises to be a new wave of studies in modernist women's literature. The title of the book is misleading, for there is no mention of gender or sex or even the "middlebrow novel" which are its real subjects. Suh's study begins with Wyndham Lewis, the lone male in the study, then moves through a range of little discussed 1930s female writers—Olive Hawks, Phyllis Bottome, Nancy Mitford, Elizabeth Bowen—and ends with Muriel Spark's *The Prime of Miss Jean Brodie* (1961). Virginia Woolf is placed in this context as well and the study begs the question of Woolf's conscious participation in and appropriation of cultural currents and genres beyond the "high modernism" of her earlier novels.

Fascism and Anti-Fascism interprets the political significance of British middlebrow fiction during the rise and fall of fascism from the 1930s to the 1960s. It analyzes the way spy narratives, domestic novels, family sagas, country house fiction, and adolescent *bildungsromane* not only attempt fascist consensus-building but also defy the assumption that middlebrow novels lack political implications. Suh extends the line of inquiry initiated by such critics as Gill Plain, Phyllis Lassner, Maroula Joannou, and Laura Frost, whose work has provided insight into under-discussed women's writing of the 1930s and 1940s. Suh argues that many women's novels during these decades draw on familiar narrative elements, elements that help to "maintain or dismantle British fascism's self-representation as a national-popular movement" (2). Suh's detailed argument points to the ways "middlebrow literature comfortably dwells in familiar narratives, characters, and settings to plant within them fascist and anti-fascist cultural strains" (2). The novels she discusses are complicated by the emphasis on their political and polemic nature.

Suh opens her study with a recalibration of Wyndham Lewis's fascist sympathies and reformed anti-fascism. Though she could have developed her reasons and the implications of using Lewis's novel as a starting point, she does point to how his work presents a unique opportunity to explore facets of the "British fascist imagination" (16) in the domestic novel. Lewis's *The Revenge for Love* (1937) pays "attention to the home as an active site of political significance in the mid-1930s," and this "is painstakingly distinct from what we associate with 'masculine' fascism" (17). *The Revenge for Love* creates active sympathy with "a distinctly fascist sexual politics" through an "unexpected domestic focus that makes the choice to support fascism in Britain appear both objectively reasonable and personally motivated" (18). Suh gives a fascinating analysis of Lewis's allusion to Woolf's *A Room of One's Own* and his high disdain for Bloomsbury aesthetics. In *The Revenge for Love* Lewis identifies "Bloomsbury and feminism as catastrophic cultural elements" for Britain. Margot, the domestic heroine of the novel, is initially inspired by her reading of *A Room*, but the narrative eventually delegitimates Margot's move into political agency. Margot's choices ruin her domestic stability; her attempt to move beyond the domestic sphere creates chaos. With this turn in his narrative, Lewis "illuminates his sympathy for fascism" because fascism "appears to forge peace and benefit women who only pose a threat to society and themselves when they demand political agency" (43). Suh convincingly demonstrates how Lewis's masculine, virile fascism transforms and propagates itself in the domestic fiction of the time.

The use of the domestic novel and its relationship to fascism continues in the chapters that follow. Suh begins the thread of her argument that both distinguishes it from previous critical work and takes a much more pragmatic and surprising approach to women writers of the1930s and 1940s. The subject of her second chapter is Olive Hawks's *What Hope for Green Street?* Hawks was a fascist supporter and BUF journalist, and her narrative defends fascism as a politics that prioritizes the interests of modern British women. Suh illustrates how Hawks employs a middlebrow lexicon in her representations of urban working-class and suburban middle-class domestic scenes. Hawks's radical, political satire "represents the family as a site for racial fortification and proof of national health, and calls for domestic women's authority over family, health, medicine, and sexuality as proxies of the racist imperial nation" (47). Ultimately, we see that Hawks adeptly used middlebrow satire to make a female argument for the biopolitics of fascism.

In stark contrast to Hawks, Phyllis Bottome, the subject of the third chapter, is anti-fascist and uses the same kind of satire in order to criticize fascism's views of women. Bottome's work is conspicuously realist and reflects some of the commonplaces of Victorian fiction. Friend of Rebecca West and Ezra Pound, Bottome was a consummate middlebrow, in between the popular and the modernist. Suh argues that Bottome's "anti-fascist strategies—the revalorization of private patriarchal families, companionate marriage, and educational reform—are drawn by the parameters of middlebrow fiction" (72). Suh's chapter traces the evolution of Bottome's *The Mortal Storm* (1937), *Survival* (1943), and *The Lifeline* (1946) as they articulate the women's stakes in anti-fascism. Bottome's novels imagine for England "the continuation of its imperial superiority in the postwar period, a superiority presumably won by humaneness rather than the bare fact of domination" (98).

Virginia Woolf's *The Years* (1937) is then discussed within the anti-fascist context of Bottome's work, and Woolf's use of the domestic novel to critique fascism and mass politics is investigated. Unlike the previous authors, Woolf is highly skeptical of mass politics; Suh gives a fresh and engaging reading of *The Years* by illustrating how Woolf's novel reveals "typical middle-class fantasies and fears surrounding modern extra-parliamentary mass movements over the course of six decades" (100). The anti-fascist strategies of *The Years* are placed within the context of interwar-middlebrow dispositions, and Suh fleshes out Woolf's comic skepticism toward romantic heroism and depictions of middle-class anxiety.

The Years begins with Delia Pargiter's fantasy of "passive revolution" at the start of the novel and then traces how "Victorian bourgeois hegemony's inauguration of women into modern mass politics had prefigured a reactionary desire that combines conservatism and radicalism" (106). It investigates "the nexus of individual pleasure, attraction, and mass politics across party lines" (113). Though not a satire like Lewis's, Hawks's, and Bottome's novels, *The Years* employs comedy as a political weapon. Suh focuses on how Woolf presents humor in relation to oratory and public speaking, and their place in the increasing militarization of civilian life. Finally, Suh addresses Woolf's rejection of "biopolitical intolerance and anti-Semitism as key features of fascist ideology" (122).

Fascism and Anti-Fascism then moves to an analysis of the "Country House Ethos" in the work of Nancy Mitford and Elizabeth Bowen. Suh explores how Mitford's *Wigs on the Green* (1935) and Bowen's *The Heat of the Day* (1949) give direct attention to the domestic sources of fascism in the 1930s and 1940s. Mitford's country house novel, Suh argues, is written from a different perspective than Hawks, Bottome, and Woolf because it "indicts the failure of the moribund aristocracy for leaving open the way for fascists to define alternatives to bourgeois hegemony" (139). In stark contrast to Woolf, Mitford's work "disavows the metropolitan avant-garde and suggests that it has been eclipsed as a literary and artistic form for debating national politics" (142). Through the post-World War II period, the relevance of the country house setting for anti-fascist literature survived and thrived. Bowen's *The Heat of the Day* reinvigorates the genre by locating in it the domestic sources of fascism, and even more strongly than Mitford, Bowen emphasizes the country house's anti-fascist potential. Bowen's novel "rescinds the nostalgia for aristocratic hegemony to install democratic narrative and organization" (149).

Suh concludes her study with a chapter on Muriel Spark's 1961 novel, *The Prime of Miss Jean Brodie.* The discussion clearly calls our attention to the aftermath of British fascism and provides a strong connection between the interwar anti-fascist middlebrow strategies and more contemporary theoretical challenges to fascism in poststructuralist and feminist critique. Spark too critiques fascism's modes of consensus building rather than its authoritarian qualities. She questions why female subjects attributed to fascism the capacity to break from patriarchal conceptions of womanhood, and she implicates various forms of "feminism" that resonate with British fascism's approach to women's roles.

The chapters of *Fascism and Anti-Fascism* are sometimes broken down into too many small subsections, causing the reader to desire a more sustained argument about each author. Still, this well researched and convincingly argued study reveals a range and depth of women writers and domestic novels that are inflected with the political realities of the 1930s and 1940s. Suh has created a dense context for understanding the domestic novel and elevates middlebrow women writers by reevaluating their roles in the creation of the political aesthetics of late modernism.

—Beth C. Rosenberg, *University of Nevada, Las Vegas*

Virginia Woolf, Fashion and Literary Modernity. R. S. Koppen (Edinburgh: Edinburgh UP, 2009) ix + 182.

Clothing was deeply implicated in the fashioning and refashioning of what it meant to be modern in the nineteenth and twentieth centuries. For Virginia Woolf, as for contemporary historians, psychologists and sociologists, sartorial fashion served as a privileged metonym for modern metropolitan life, while the dressed body was the primary site at which competing versions of modernity were proposed and contested. While the fashion system was taken as an apt model of social and economic organization in the modern metropolis, the fact that clothing operated on the boundary between the body and the external world enabled fashion to serve as the dominant mode of negotiation between subjective and objective culture, between the individual and society. The liminality of clothing imbued the sartorial register with dialectical as well as symbolic power, with the capacity to make connections between and to trace the shifting relations of subject and object, organic and inorganic, masculine and feminine, in constituting the modern.

R. S. Koppen's *Virginia Woolf, Fashion and Literary Modernity* maps the traffic between literary, visual and material cultures from the Victorian period to the 1930s, revealing the ways in which Virginia Woolf employed the language of clothing and cloth to articulate the conditions of modernity, to formulate a critical historiography and to conduct her analyses of culture. Woolf draws on both the alienating and the exhilarating aspects of the fashion system, with its capacity to regulate and standardize as much as to liberate and transform. Clothes are included as both material fact and metaphorical construction in Woolf's meditations on the economies of class, gender and power. Koppen presents a comprehensive study of Woolf's work as cultural analyst and writer of fiction; of clothes as things, commodities and symbols; and of fashion as theory and practice.

Striding through the cultural landscape of the Victorian period and into the 1930s, we meet the sartorial figures and clothed fantasies of the age; contested modernities dressed up in different outfits, from the Pre-Raphaelite swathed in flowing robes to the suited and booted lesbian dandy. The dressed body is shown as the star performer in a range of political and cultural movements, and Koppen's extensive frame of reference spans Surrealism, suffrage and sexology to popular physics, psychoanalysis and social reform. A sure-footed grounding in theory, taking in both the usual suspects and the lesser known, complements historiographical breadth.

Drawing on the work of period thinkers such as Walter Benjamin, George Simmel, and J. C. Flugel, as well as contemporary theorists of material culture and exponents of "Thing-Theory" such as Bill Brown, Koppen's skilful handling of complex issues is one of the great successes of the book. Yet, at times, the level of involvement with theory tends to crowd out what's distinctive about this period in general, and about Virginia Woolf in particular. The result is a kind of heaviness at odds with Woolf's own lightness of touch. A sense of lack arises, I think, from a certain dismissal of the personal and the idiosyncratic. While Woolf, in Koppen's own words, is concerned with both the "seemingly trivial and the ostensibly serious," Woolf's engagement with fashion on a personal level, the trials and tribulations, however "trivial," of her embodied experience, is only briefly touched upon in the opening chapter, before vanishing without so much as a dangling thread.

Despite an emphasis on the principle of the embodied mind, of the (dressed) body itself as cultural and political agent, I found the voice of Virginia Woolf becoming more disembodied as the book progressed. Koppen cites Woolf's assertion in *Three Guineas* that "Since marriage until the year 1919 … was the only profession open to us," and since clothing has a function of attracting a male, "the enormous importance of dress to a woman cannot be exaggerated." Yet the importance of dress to Woolf, as a woman, in a female body, tends to be overlooked. Where comparisons and connections might be made between Woolf's embodied experience of fashion and the ways in which the sartorial is woven into her writing, these tend to go unremarked.

For example, Koppen highlights the way in which Rhoda's existential fear of being exposed to another's gaze, in *The Waves*, is consistently expressed in terms of dress and nudity. The fact that this is also a consistent feature of Virginia Woolf's diaries is overlooked. In fact, Woolf expresses the same fear of exposure in strikingly similar terms when reviews of her writing are due to appear in the press: she anticipates being flagellated and pointed and stared at. Likewise, Rhoda's experience of both the revitalizing and alienating effects of the fashion system reflects Woolf's own ambivalence, her experience of both the joy—the "lovely stuff and shapes" (*D*3 86)—and the agony—"I can never look like other people" (*D*3 132)—of sartorial fashion.

The most successful chapters, to my mind, are those that bring out the rich historical detail of the period, as well as drawing on the personal. "From Symbolism in Loose Robes to the Figure of the Androgyne" also deals with the generational, something with particular relevance to a study of Woolf and fashion, because so much of her rebellion against, and release from, the Victorian modes of the previous generation, she figured through clothes. Tracing the experiments in self-fashioning of the avant-garde, from the high-minded aesthetes of the late Victorian period to the sexually ambiguous figures and playful sartorial games of the 1920s and 30s, Koppen focuses on Julia Margaret Cameron's aesthetic idealism, the earnest disciples of symbolism sent up by Woolf in *Freshwater*, and the alluringly exotic, cross-dressing aristocrat Vita Sackville-West, whose sartorial idiom of ambiguity Woolf celebrated in *Orlando*. While retaining an abiding interest in the visual vocabulary of the Cameron circle and sharing her great-aunt's understanding of the transformative, allegorical and theatrical potential of clothing, Woolf satirized the wholesale aestheticization of everyday life to the point where the quotidian became tangled in a web of compulsive, symbolic referral. In *Orlando*, while poking fun at a similar compulsion, the "English disease" of appropriation, whereby one becomes "oriental" simply by donning a pair of Turkish trousers, Woolf nevertheless revels in the power of such clothes to "disguise the sex": the transformative potential of sartorial self-fashioning. The celebration of gender ambiguity in *Orlando* continues in Woolf's meditations on the "man-womanly mind" in *A Room of One's Own*, a holistic and humane androgynous ideal, to which, as Koppen explains, the liminality of clothing shows the way: "in its transformative, transvestite, hybrid modality, [clothing] figures modes of being and writing which give women, as individuals and writers, what Woolf has been looking for: room of their own."

Threading its way through the book, hybridity is an enduring theme, defining the character of modernity as much as Woolf's writing. If, as Koppen suggests, the sartorial constitutes much of the character of Woolf's work, it's precisely because the hybrid character of clothing offered the most fitting mode in which to figure her arguments for a subtler, more hybrid approach to both reading and writing culture.

Thinking through clothes enabled Woolf to figure her analyses differently, to reveal the subtle in-betweens, as Koppen's fruitful comparison of Leonard and Virginia Woolf's contrary conclusions in *Quack, Quack* and *Three Guineas* reveals. Both are concerned with the fascist appropriation of the performative power of dressed bodies. Yet, while Leonard trusts in the rational mind and civilized discourse to counteract the irrationality of performative culture, Virginia, by focusing on gender and thinking through clothes, reveals that ritualized and ceremonial, so-called primitive, modes of sartorial performance and display are still very much in operation. This unveiling of the irrational in the midst of the ostensibly civilized undermines any conclusive differentiation between rational and irrational, civilized and primitive. Virginia insists that gender is the fundamental question to be resolved; as long as the irrationality of male vanity and female subjection continue to exist at the heart of civilization, any appeal to reason is redundant.

Virginia Woolf, Fashion and Literary Modernity is a rigorously researched, persuasively written study, and a compelling read. Its breadth of scope adds to its value as a resource for scholars of Woolf, theorists of dress and historians of modernity alike. R. S. Koppen has crafted a seamlessly interwoven and richly rewarding tapestry of myriad theoretical, historiographical and socio-cultural sources; it's just a shame that, on occasion, Virginia Woolf tends to get lost in the folds.

—Catherine Gregg, *Independent Scholar*

Notes on Contributors

Evelyn T. Chan finished her PhD at the University of Cambridge on "Virginia Woolf and the Professions" in 2010, and is now Assistant Professor at the Chinese University of Hong Kong, where she continues to teach and study Woolf.

Kimberly Engdahl Coates is Assistant Professor of English at Bowling Green State University in Bowling Green, Ohio. Her work has appeared in *Literature and Medicine*, *Journal of Narrative Theory*, and *PsyArt* as well as in *Virginia Woolf: Art, Education, Internationalism* edited by Diana Royer and Madelyn Detloff, *Woolf and the City* edited by Elizabeth F. Evans and Sarah E. Cornish, and *The Theme of Peace and War in Virginia Woolf's War Writings: Essays on Her Political Philosophy* edited by Jane Wood. She is currently working on a project entitled *'Come See My War': Feminism, Politics, and the Performance of Affect in British and American Women's Literature, 1900-1945*. Tracing a historical aesthetics of the female body, the project situates both canonical and non-canonical literature by British and American women writers alongside the lives and work of modern dancers and argues for the significance of their performances and written work to an early feminism originally articulated through the bodies of suffragettes agitating for the vote and culminating in women's political activism during and between the two World Wars.

Amanda Golden is a Visiting Scholar at Emory University's Fox Center for Humanistic Inquiry and an Instructor of English at Agnes Scott College. She is completing the book manuscript, *Annotating Modernism: The Reading and Teaching Strategies of Sylvia Plath, John Berryman, and Anne Sexton*. She is the Book Review Editor of *Woolf Studies Annual* and has a forthcoming essay entitled, "'A Brief Note in the Margin': Virginia Woolf and Annotating" in *Contradictory Woolf: Selected Papers from the Twenty-First Annual Conference on Virginia Woolf*, edited by Derek Ryan and Stella Bolaki (Clemson UP, 2012). She also co-edited *Virginia Woolf Miscellany*'s special issue on Woolf and Sylvia Plath (2007).

Helen Southworth is Associate Professor of Literature at the Robert D. Clark Honors College at the University of Oregon. Her recent publications include the edited collection *Leonard and Virginia Woolf, The Hogarth Press and the Networks of Modernism* (Edinburgh UP, 2010), "'Perfect Strangers': Francesca Allinson and Virginia Woolf'" in the *Virginia Woolf Bulletin* (Jan 2012), and "Virginia Woolf et Colette: Deux visions de la sexualité féminine" in Editions de l'herne's *Cahiers Colette* (2011).

Diana L. Swanson holds a joint appointment in Women's Studies and English at Northern Illinois University and also serves as a faculty associate in Lesbian, Gay, Bisexual, Transgender Studies and in Environmental Studies. Her keynote address, "'The Real World': Virginia Woolf and Ecofeminism," was recently published in *Virginia Woolf and the Natural World: Selected Papers from the Twentieth Annual International Conference on Virginia Woolf*, edited by Kristin Czarnecki.

Policy

Woolf
Studies
Annual invites articles on the work and life of Virginia Woolf and her milieu. The *Annual* intends to represent the breadth and eclecticism of critical approaches to Woolf, and particularly welcomes new perspectives and contexts of inquiry. Articles discussing relations between Woolf and other writers and artists are also welcome.

Articles are sent for review anonymously to a member of the Editorial Board and at least one other reader. Manuscripts should not be under consideration elsewhere or have been previously published. It is strongly advised that those submitting work to *WSA* be familiar with the journal's content. Among criteria on which evaluation of submissions depends are whether an article demonstrates familiarity with scholarship already published in the field, whether the article is written clearly and effectively, and whether it makes a genuine contribution to Woolf studies.

Preparation of Copy

1. Articles are typically between 25 and 30 pages, and do not exceed 8000 words. Inquiries about significantly shorter or longer submissions should be sent to the Editor at woolfstudiesannual@gmail.com.

2. A separate page should include the article's title, author's name, address, telephone & fax numbers, and e-mail address. The author's name and identifying references should not appear on the manuscript to preserve anonymity for our readers.

3. All submissions must include an abstract of no more than 250 words.

4. Manuscripts should be prepared according to most recent MLA style.

5. Submissions may be sent *either* by email to woolfstudiesannual@gmail.com *or* by mail to Mark Hussey, English Dept., Pace University, One Pace Plaza, New York NY 10038. For mailed submissions, please send **three** copies of the article and abstract.

6. Authors of accepted manuscripts are responsible for any necessary permissions fees and for securing any necessary permissions.

All editorial, review, and advertising inquiries should be addressed to woolfstudiesannual@gmail.com.

Inquiries concerning orders should be addressed to PaceUP@pace.edu.

Other Woolf titles available:

"The Hours": The British Museum Manuscript of Mrs. Dalloway, transcribed and edited by Helen M. Wussow (paper 2010).

Virginia Woolf, Jacob's Room: *The Holograph Draft.* Transcribed and edited by Edward L. Bishop (paper 2010)

Women in the Milieu of Leonard and Virginia Woolf: Peace, Politics and Education Ed. Wayne K. Chapman and Janet M. Manson (1998)

Virginia Woolf and Trauma: Embodied Texts Ed. Suzette Henke & David Eberly (2007)

Woolf Across Cultures Ed. Natalya Reinhold (2004)

Woolf Studies Annual 5 (1999)

Woolf Studies Annual 6 (2000): The *Three Guineas* Correspondence, edited by Anna Snaith

Woolf Studies Annual 7 (2001)

Woolf Studies Annual 8 (2002): The Fawcett Library Correspondence, edited by Merry Pawlowski

Woolf Studies Annual 9 (2003): *Virginia Woolf and Literary History Part 1*, edited by Jane Lilienfeld, Jeffrey Oxford, and Lisa Low

Woolf Studies Annual 10 (2004): *Virginia Woolf and Literary History Part 2,* edited by Jane Lilienfeld, Jeffrey Oxford, and Lisa Low

Woolf Studies Annual 11 (2005) - *Woolf Studies Annual 16* (2010)

Virginia Woolf and Communities: Selected Papers from the Eighth Annual Conference on Virginia Woolf edited by Jeanette McVicker and Laura Davis

Virginia Woolf Turning the Centuries: Selected Papers from the Ninth

Annual Conference on Virginia Woolf edited by Ann Ardis and Bonnie Kime Scott

Virginia Woolf Out of Bounds: Selected Papers from the Tenth Annual Conference on Virginia Woolf edited by Jessica Berman and Jane Goldman

www.ingramcontent.com/pod-product-compliance
Lightning Source LLC
Chambersburg PA
CBHW070522100726
47907CB00004B/947
9781935625087